SMASHING

the

DC MONOPOLY

SMASHING

the
DC MONOPOLY

USING ARTICLE V *to* RESTORE FREEDOM
and STOP RUNAWAY GOVERNMENT

TOM A. COBURN, M.D.

FORMER U.S. SENATOR

 WND Books

Published by WND Books, Washington, D.C. WND Books is a registered trademark of WorldNetDaily.com, Inc. ("WND")

Book designed by Mark Karis

ALL ROYALTIES FOR SMASHING THE DC MONOPOLY WILL BE DONATED TO THE CONVENTION OF STATES.

WND Books are available at special discounts for bulk purchases. WND Books also publishes books in electronic formats. For more information call (541) 474-1776, e-mail orders@wndbooks.com or visit www.wndbooks.com.

Hardcover ISBN: 978-1-944229-75-7
eBook ISBN: 978-1-944229-76-4

Library of Congress Cataloging-in-Publication Data
Names: Coburn, Tom A., author.
Title: Smashing the DC monopoly : using Article V to restore freedom and stop
   America's runaway government / Dr. Tom Coburn.
Other titles: Smashing the District of Columbia monopoly
Description: Washington, DC : WND books, [2017] | Includes bibliographical
   references and index. |
Identifiers: LCCN 2017002279 (print) | LCCN 2017012685 (ebook) | ISBN
   9781944229764 (e-book) | ISBN 9781944229757 (hardcover)
Subjects: LCSH: Constitutional conventions--United States. | Constitutional
   amendments--United States. | Federal government--United States. | United
   States. Constitution. Article V.
Classification: LCC KF4555 (ebook) | LCC KF4555 .C63 2017 (print) | DDC
   342.7303/2--dc23
LC record available at https://lccn.loc.gov/2017002279

Printed in the United States of America
17 18 19 20 21 22 LBM 9 8 7 6 5 4 3 2 1

CONTENTS

Foreword   ix

Preface   xii

Introduction   1

1   A Capitol Education   5

2   The Failure of Big Government   29

3   Constitutional Amendment by *We the People*   57

4   The Current Quest for an Article V Convention   83

5   Article V: The Founders' Gift to the People   107

6   Limited Government for a Self-Ruling People   137

7   A Judicial Foundation for Big Government   155

8   Lessons from Past Conventions and Applications   173

Appendix 1: Complete Text for Article V of the U.S. Constitution   201

Appendix 2: Most Successful Article V Convention Advocacy Groups   202

Appendix 3: Information Sources about an Article V Convention   204

Appendix 4: Article V Convention Legislative Progress Report   206

Appendix 5: Legislature Groups   208

Notes   210

Index   222

FOREWORD

CAMPAIGNING FOR THE OKLAHOMA SENATE more than six years ago, I realized that the majority of my fellow Oklahomans shared my concerns with the direction of our nation. Many believed that without better controls on our federal government, our nation was doomed. I vowed to find a way to regain the limited government that our nation's founders first established.

During my first year in office as a state senator, I studied the uses of nullification and interposition to limit federal power, two concepts credited (inaccurately regarding nullification) to James Madison and Thomas Jefferson. I found these concepts unsuited for the dilemma facing the states.

Since late 2013, I have become committed to studying and championing the use of Article V in the Constitution, which provides for amendment proposals initiated by both Congress and the states. Our founders provided this right to the states to give the people a more direct means to correct any imbalance of power between the states and the federal government, and to attempt to solve problems that Congress could not or would not address.

I have been honored to help with an effort began by Oklahoma senator Josh Brecheen to secure Oklahoma's application for an Article

V convention of states to propose a balanced budget amendment. In spring 2014, I came upon the work of Michael Farris, founder of the Home School Legal Defense Association and Patrick Henry College, who had begun the Convention of States (COS) Project along with Mark Meckler, president of Citizens for Self-Governance.

The purpose of COS is to limit the federal government by way of an Article V convention of states. In my subsequent discussions with Farris, I realized we both shared a deep Christian faith and a sincere desire for solutions to a country on a pathway to destruction. The two of us debated opponents of an Article V amendments convention, and I believe our efforts helped persuade the Oklahoma Legislature to approve this application in spring 2016.

I have studied the origins of the Article V amendments convention and the states' attempts to use this measure since our nation's birth. I have also read the opinions of many Americans both for and against this action over the years. The founder of the John Birch Society, Robert Welch, strongly supported the use of an amendments convention, although the group is now opposed. Eagle Forum founder Phyllis Schlafly, an ardent conservative, argued against an amendments convention.

That two staunch conservatives like Welch and Schlafly could hold opposite views on an Article V convention underscores the lack of understanding of this inherently safe constitutional provision. To succeed in getting the necessary thirty-four states to apply for an amendments convention, I realized that an educational effort was needed to better inform concerned citizens on the origins, procedures, safety, and importance of this action. Authored by former U.S. senator from Oklahoma Dr. Tom Coburn, this book is meant to provide this information.

Having worked with Dr. Coburn to convince Oklahoma legislators and citizens that an amendments convention could solve some of our nation's most critical problems, I asked the former senator if he might consider telling the nation how he lost faith in Washington and came to place his hopes in an Article V convention. I knew that most citizens could greatly benefit from hearing how he came to this conclusion following his years in the inner workings of our federal government.

Fortunately for the nation, Dr. Coburn agreed to put his thoughts on paper. In fall 2015, I asked my good friend Larry Floyd, an Oklahoma City journalist and college history teacher, to join us in the task of getting this important book written. After nearly a year in the making, this narrative provides not only the insight of one of America's most respected leaders, but also a thoroughly researched and considered history of how we came to our current national crisis—and how Article V can be an effective, constitutional solution.

Much of this book also concerns removing the mystery of an amendments convention and illustrating the safety of this constitutional process. Although baseless, fears of a convention of states have permeated many past writings on this subject—opinions usually provided by proponents of big government. This narrative dispels myths about an Article V convention (it is *not* a constitutional convention) and illuminates the Founders' intention that this constitutional provision provide a means for *We the People* to act through our state representatives to effect needed structural changes to the national government.

The nation owes its gratitude to Dr. Coburn both for his service in Washington and for putting his experiences and conclusions in written form. We all need to know more about how a former U.S. representative and senator came to the realization that we must look to our founders and ourselves for a solution big enough for our nation's considerable problems. It may be a narrative some of us in the battle for limited government largely know, but one that will benefit all Americans who truly cherish our Great Experiment in self-governance.

Of course, the true value of this book will be measured in the number of citizens and state legislators who are persuaded to join this fight to preserve the American dream for their children and grandchildren.

—OKLAHOMA SENATOR ROB STANDRIDGE
NORMAN, OKLAHOMA (JUNE 2016)

PREFACE

THE 2016 ELECTION YEAR PROVED the most chaotic and divisive in living memory, highlighting the distrust and anger shown by much of the electorate toward the ruling elite in Washington. The nominees of both parties had high unfavorable ratings.

I heard the pent-up frustration of many Americans that presaged this bitter election year when I visited twenty-one states in 2015, the year after I left the Senate. I listened to everyday citizens express their fears and concerns about their lives and their families' future. Americans could readily see that their government in Washington was broken and that Congress and the president could not or would not address the nation's problems.

The vast administrative state established by Congress, the courts, and the executive branch works largely to the benefit of the bureaucrats, career politicians, and special interests. The less-connected "normal Americans"—working diligently, living within their means, and funding the federal bureaucracy—are witnessing and suffering the aftermath of the bloated state: the decline of America's great economic engine and a related loss of liberty and security.

The election process was intended by the Founders to be the primary means for the people to express their will in government. Yet repeated elections have failed to provide leadership to restore and unite the nation. It saddens me to say that the 2016 election of Donald Trump will by itself do little for weary and worried Americans.

The "purchasing power" of incumbency has made an entrenched Congress—the seat of power and policy in our constitutional republic— almost impervious to the ballot box and to presidential persuasion. Washington, DC, is broken and will not be fixed by the constitutionally limited powers of a newly elected Republican *or* Democratic president. During his campaign Donald Trump called for term limits on Congress. We should all hope he meant it.

Deeply troubling to me, I fear that the new president will handle an implacable Congress by "making a deal" on popular entitlement spending. This has been the modus operandi in Washington back to the 1970s and the driver of our $20 trillion in national debt—not to mention the obscene mountain of unfunded liabilities. Trump was frighteningly unspecific about what he would do about America's domestic spending addiction.

I also fear a public complacency arising from the election of Trump and the change of party leadership in the White House. I fear that the energy and emotion that drove the anticipated changes in Washington will dissipate as mainstream America awaits policies from the new administration to "fix" the nation. Americans will face further disappointment if they continue to wait for solutions from Washington.

I am heartened by the words of Jeb Bush, the former Florida governor and early contender for the Republican presidential nomination who was rejected in the antiestablishment tide of 2016. Magnanimous in defeat, Bush calls for Republican leaders to build on their electoral success in 2016 by supporting an amendments convention. "Americans, by wide majorities, agree that Washington is broken," Bush said two weeks after Trump secured the presidency, "so let's send power back to the people and back to the states. Republicans should support convening a constitutional convention to pass term limits, a balanced budget amendment and restraints on the Commerce Clause, which has given the federal government far more regulatory power than the Founders intended."[1]

I would quibble with Governor Bush over his use of the term "constitutional convention" (this gathering is more correctly an "amendments convention"), but his reasoning is sound. America needs stronger medicine than what Donald Trump or any president can administer. We need the structural changes from an amendments convention of state delegates because our constitutional system of governance has been thrown too far out of balance by ambitious politicians and overreaching courts. The incremental changes from political elections barely affect the entrenched bureaucrats and pandering politicians in our nation's capital. The Constitution—originally designed to limit and contain political ambition and federal overreach—has been distorted and bypassed, leaving a polarized nation with an onrushing fiscal crisis.

Article V in the Constitution gives the nation hope even after the inevitable disappointment of another new administration in Washington. Our founders codified two means to rebalance governmental institutions through amendment of our foundational laws—either by Congress or by a convention of states. The widespread corruption in our political system, however, has paralyzed Congress. Some mistakenly believe that the election of Donald Trump will spur congressional leaders to rebalance the federal government. These officials took no action before; they will not with a new president.

Anticipating this kind of recalcitrance at the federal level, our founders provided the second mode of amendment. The Article V–convention provision in the Constitution enables the people to act through their state representatives when Congress is unwilling or unable to address dysfunction in government. (The complete text of Article V can be found in appendix 1 on page 202.)

A convention of states allows for amendment proposals through the state legislatures—proposals to limit the ruling elites' power and to address problems avoided by a feckless Congress. Convention-of-states amendments evolve closer to the will of *We the People* and embody the constitutional pillar of federalism—the division of power between the state governments and the aloof central government in Washington. Acting at an amendments convention, state delegates stand for the people and can propose solutions to an intrusive, failing national government.

As the following chapters will show, *constitutional amendment by state delegates in convention is neither dangerous nor extreme*. Indeed, the Article V convention of states was the constitutional safety feature that the Framers included as an endowment to the people—an orderly means to protect the citizens' interests from an inevitably self-interested and overreaching federal government. I believe the Founders would view as unusual and extreme the fact that the country has gone nearly 230 years without resorting to the constitutional protection of an Article V amendments convention.

Washington, Madison, and Jefferson would consider it irresponsible for Americans not to use their constitutional tools to counter a self-serving, leviathan federal government. The current centralized national authority is a reactionary reversion the Founders would scarcely recognize as descending from their revolutionary concept of limited national government by the people and for the people. The Founders' united voices cry out for us to use our republican tools of self-governance to rebalance the institutions of national government, to save the world's greatest experiment in self-rule.

The American people's right to determine their future is analogous to the owners of a company having the right to determine the direction of their business and the duties of their employees. We have gotten away from this republican principle, much to our detriment as a people and a nation. Our inattention and complacency have enabled a hostile take-over of our national enterprise by our public servants—elected officials and bureaucrats. *Our workers have been running our business for the past five decades mostly for themselves, their rent-seeking constituents, and their identity-group supporters.*

Even with an outsider like Trump in the White House, looking for federal solutions to fix our broken economy after the 2016 elections will bring only more frustration and stagnancy. The Washington establishment can provide no legislation to revive the economy and restore jobs other than to get out of the way of the economy—to quit overregulating, to quit overtaxing, to quit pandering to constituents and cronies. You will not hear that from federal officials because they draw their lifeblood from the concentration of wealth and power in the centralized bureaucracies of Washington. They will continue to tell you that they and their plans hold the key to prosperity and growth—if you will only place or keep them in power.

It is well past time for *We the People*—the shareholders of this nation—to take charge of our own affairs. Americans outside Washington must do the job of restoring the nation's economic engine by limiting the federal government through constitutional amendment. ***Americans must constitutionally resist the liberty-leeching federal bureaucracies.*** Limited government promotes individual and economic freedom; expansive government diminishes both the people and the economy. Americans must always remember: the larger the government, the smaller the people. Looking at this another way in his book *The Conservative Heart*, American Enterprise Institute president Arthur Brooks contends that learned dependency is tyranny and only earned success leads to happiness.[2]

The people have the constitutional right and the means to determine their future. As Americans, we should appreciate the opportunity to act in the nation's best interest at an amendments convention of the states. What we truly *should fear* is the failure to act in the face of growing dysfunction and impending fiscal disaster. If we fail to act, history and future generations will judge us harshly for the calamity to follow.

The sound and the fury of the 2016 elections are subsiding, and the newly elected Republican administration will unavoidably disappoint. It can only disappoint because clumsy, centralized government by either political party cannot deliver economic progress or truly promote the common good—except by getting out of the way, by relinquishing the power and authority that national officials covet, by returning government control to state and local officials closer and more answerable to the people. And these limitations on the federal government will only be brought about by a convention of states. ***Only limited government, free markets, and broad individual liberties can deliver a prosperous, united nation—and "make American great again."*** That is a lesson that history teaches and that most Americans have forgotten.

Donald Trump and distant politicians in Washington will never save America through more government programs and policies. The best the new administration can do is to encourage the American people to take control of their affairs in the nation's capital. And Americans can best do so by supporting their nearest representatives in our state legislatures—public officials closer and more responsive to their needs and desires—who are working for a convention of states to propose limits on the concentration of wealth and power in the nation's capital.

An Article V amendments convention is the endowment from our founders that can return control of the national government to *We the People*. This is the gift from our founders that can save the world's greatest constitutional republic from the managed decline now exhibited by the collectivist European countries.

Are we truly an exceptional nation—or are we destined to fail like all past self-governing nations? Only *We the People* can make America exceptional—and great again. This book explains how.

—DR. TOM COBURN

INTRODUCTION

LATE ON A THURSDAY MORNING IN DECEMBER 2014, I gave a formal farewell to my colleagues from the Senate floor. My address lasted just under thirty minutes. It was an emotional time for me. Some of the words came hard.

I apologized for offending some of my fellow legislators over the years in some of our contentious debates. No offense was intended, I explained, and our disagreements often stemmed from my core belief that our nation's founders were smarter than those of us in the Senate. I expressed my conviction that the constitutional limits on the federal government really meant something, and that adherence to this principle protected us as a nation.

The ultimate purpose of those limits, I stated, was to help prevent what history says always happens to a republican form of government like ours. "They have all died," I said. "They have all died."

The year leading up to my retirement from the Senate had been difficult. In September 2013 I learned that the cancer I had been treated for several years earlier was recurring. Physically draining medical treatment soon began.

More dispiriting, my last years in the Senate had been hampered by Senate Majority Leader Harry Reid's clamping down on members' ability to offer amendments and force debate on important issues. I could not let that pass without note in my farewell address. "No single Senator should be allowed to decide what the rights of another Senator should be," I protested to the forty or so Republican and Democratic senators seated that morning. "That is tyranny."[1]

With two years left in my Senate term, most of the news reports at the time attributed my early departure to my battle with cancer. Yet nearly two years earlier I had told Senate Minority Leader Mitch McConnell that I planned to retire from the Senate before the end of my term. None of the media would accept that my leaving resulted from my frustration with the political dysfunction in both the Senate and Washington.

I am a medical doctor by training, which taught me to fix problems, not just to treat symptoms. A doctor who only treats symptoms gets sued; a doctor who successfully treats disease cures patients. All that Washington politicians generally do when confronting problems—bitter years of experience both in the House and Senate taught me—is treat symptoms. I was actually happy to be leaving the Senate and relieved to stop banging my head against a wall.

I still had a fight with cancer ahead of me. But my thoughts at that time were already filled with another battle that lay ahead. This new struggle could do far more good for the country than I could accomplish in two remaining years of frustration on the Senate floor. This repurposing of my efforts seemed to me the logical culmination of what hard experience had taught me in six years in the House and ten years in the Senate. I wanted no more of just treating symptoms in Washington. My new efforts would be directed at treating the disease.

After my farewell address, I had a few days of work at the end of the session. I began thinking of how much I owed to the hard work of so many of my staff and tried to express to each my appreciation. The sights and sounds of the holiday season in Washington brought a flood of memories from the sixteen years I had spent in Congress. Those years left me with good memories as well as bad. Amid the pomp and history of our nation's capital, I had witnessed and battled, with sadness and frustration, the careerism and partisanship that ruled Washington.

As I packed my personal belongings over my last days in the capital, my thoughts turned to a whole new approach to reverse the damage to our nation from careerism and unlimited government. This solution had been available to Americans since the country's founding. It put the power to solve national problems squarely in the hands of the people— the everyday Americans who work, budget, and live within their means.

For many years I had known about the right of state legislatures to petition Congress for a convention of states to propose amendments to the Constitution. I had never considered it necessary or practicable. I saw it only as a final option, and that is what the Founders intended it to be. They hoped a republic led by "virtuous" national leaders might not need it. *The Founders defined virtue as the willingness to sacrifice personal interest to that of the public good.* Yet, showing their knowledge of human nature and man's imperfection, they put the safety feature of an amendments convention in Article V of the Constitution. It could be used by the people if necessary.

Toward the end of 2013, attorney Mark Meckler, a former Tea Party activist and founder of the Citizens for Self-Governance, had asked me to support a convention of states to propose constitutional amendments. I liked his work promoting citizens' involvement in government, but I still had reservations about the feasibility of a convention of states. At the time I offered no help to Meckler, who had teamed with attorney and educator Michael Farris to promote public awareness and support for an amendments convention. Their project to help organize a convention of states would be under the umbrella of the Citizens for Self-Governance organization.

As my last year in the Senate drew to a close, I explored this idea further. I wanted to know why the Founders had given in Article V of the Constitution a right to the people to petition Congress through their state legislatures for a convention to propose amendments to the Constitution. *Hamilton argued in the final installment of the* **Federalist** *essays that this right ensured that Americans could "safely* *rely on the disposition of the state legislatures to erect barriers against the encroachments of the national authority."* Furthermore, this right would ensure the possibility of amendments by the people even if opposed by "the persons delegated to the administration of the national government" who might be "disinclined to yield up any portion of the authority of which they were once possessed."[2]

I had witnessed how "national authority" encroached on the liberties of Americans with the suffocating power of big government, threatening the freedoms and financial security of generations to come. And I had all too often seen members of Congress "disinclined" to stop squandering the taxpayer dollars used to ensure their grip on the power and perquisites of their office. Most of the career-oriented members of both parties in Congress I had served with displayed few, if any, of the virtuous ideals of the Founders. The system had become corrupted, and no one inside it could provide a solution.

After sixteen years in Congress, it became chillingly clear to me that the constitutional safety feature in Article V had become necessary. Only the people could restore American ideals. Washington politicians could not and would not save us. Our steady delegation of power to and unhealthy dependence on our national government had lowered us to this condition. The Founders, who had incorporated the "experience of all ages" in the Constitution, understood how the American people might someday have to save the republic from their central government. We the People would have to assert our rightful sovereignty under the Constitution and rebalance our badly unbalanced federal government. Washington had grown too self-interested, politically correct, and feckless to meet the challenge. *As a republic "of the people, by the people, and for the people," we alone must save ourselves.*

I cast my final vote as the Senate concluded its business for the year on Tuesday, December 16. My thoughts were already turning to what I could do to help the people save the American dream. By Wednesday afternoon I was back in Oklahoma among family, friends—and the people of America. I already felt closer to a solution for the nation.

1

A CAPITOL EDUCATION

The inquiry constantly is what will please, not what will benefit the people. In such a government there can be nothing but temporary expedient, fickleness, and folly.

— ALEXANDER HAMILTON

I HAD BEEN ONE OF SEVENTY-THREE freshmen Republicans who stormed into the U.S. House of Representatives in January 1995. The historic congressional elections of 1994, dubbed the Republican Revolution, delivered a fifty-four-seat swing in the House. The Republican Party controlled the lower house of Congress for the first time since 1952.

My decision to enter politics had been impulsively made just seven months before my swearing in as a member of the 104th Congress. With no political experience and practicing as a family physician in Muskogee, Oklahoma, I woke up one morning in June 1994 and told my incredulous wife, Carolyn, that I wanted to run for Congress. I hoped to replace Oklahoma's Second District congressman, eight-term Democratic representative Mike Synar. Just a few days before my decision, I had read an alarming comment by Synar about nationalizing health care, a position opposite my values and most of those in the district. This proposed expansion of the federal government added to my growing unease over the increasing power and reach of Washington.

Those were heady days in the nation's capital in 1995. Inspiring with his "Contract with America," Georgia representative Newt Gingrich led Republicans in a number of reforms to try to correct the chronic abuse of power and unbridled growth in government. As one of the zealous outsiders in the House class of '94, I relished the challenges ahead as we deployed Gingrich's action plan.

As Washington reformers, many of us focused on what we saw as uncontrolled spending on wasteful and often duplicative federal programs. Indeed, most of my future career in Congress would be spent fighting unnecessary government spending and red ink. But before I left the House after three terms—my term-limit pledge before election—I began to see firsthand how this destructive spending was actually a symptom of an age-old political disease: *the basic human desire to acquire and hold power.*

Our nation's constitutional framers had a better understanding of this natural human craving for power than do many modern political theorists. We know this from careful study of our national rulebook for limiting the power of the federal government—the U.S. Constitution. Unfortunately for the nation, many of the elite in society view this foundational document as perhaps quaint and outmoded.

The current U.S. intelligentsia in particular appears to question how these mostly Eurocentric, eighteenth-century provincials could have imparted guidance still relevant to us more than two centuries later. A closer look at these uncommon founders of the "last best hope of earth," as Abraham Lincoln later described their revolutionary republic, reveals that many of them were actually the fruit of the Enlightenment. Some of the founders were scholars, some were self-educated, and almost all were steeped in the political theories of classically liberal philosophers such as John Locke and Baron de Montesquieu.

Gaining independence from a distant and oppressive British monarchy, the Founders had a well-earned fear of power concentrated in a strong central authority. So they focused on limiting the power of the new federal government and containing the natural drive for power in the country's leaders. Underscoring these concerns, one of these founders, Alexander Hamilton, famously wrote, "A fondness for power is implanted in most men, and it is natural to abuse it when acquired. This maxim, drawn from the *experience of all ages*, makes it the height of folly to entrust any set of men with power which is not under every possible control."[1] Attendant to this power, I observed in Washington, is the personal flattery of being an insider—a key player who shares the inner circle of knowledge and control with other power brokers.

The legal framework the Framers crafted for the new United States in 1789 established a system of checks and balances to diffuse the power of the various branches of the government. This system would serve as a safeguard to the personal ambitions of the country's leaders. To protect individual liberties, a Bill of Rights was added to these foundational laws. Many of these individual rights derived from the natural rights theories and laws of those European philosophers so popular among the educated founders.

I thought of these founders as I took my oath of office in January 1995. The pledge taken by all members of Congress includes the words: "I do solemnly swear that I will support and defend the Constitution of the United States against all enemies, foreign and domestic; that I will bear true faith and allegiance to the same." Some of the wording in the oath has been modified since 1789, but not the part about the pledge "to support the Constitution of the United States."

Unfortunately, even disastrously, many members of Congress take this pledge perfunctorily. This vow to support the Constitution should serve as a hard check on our national leaders' love for power and the resultant oppressive, overreaching federal government. If our country's sworn representatives honored their vows to support our Constitution and maintain its founding principles, I believe the federal government could be limited to its enumerated powers.

It became obvious to me after my first years in the House that the uncontrolled spending and unconstitutional growth of our national

government provide the means for all-too-human Washington politicians to gain and keep the power that humankind naturally desires and
often abuses. Our national leaders' failure to hold principle higher than
power lies at the center of our federal government's crises of uncontrolled spending and unconstitutional growth.

If power is the motivating principle of many politicians in
Washington, I soon saw how "careerism" is both a means and a by-
product of gaining and clinging to that power. And career politicians in
Washington operate in a manner both destructive to the health of the
nation and totally foreign to the average citizen. To gain and hold power
in a lengthy congressional career, politicians of both parties appropriate
and approve the spending of rivers of taxpayer dollars, often on wasteful,
duplicative, even fraud-ridden programs. The pressure on members of
Congress to go along with this spending is relentless. The more career-
oriented these representatives are, the more likely they will succumb.

In a book released just the year before I was elected to Congress,
conservative commentator George Will warned of what I would soon
experience in our nation's capital. He attributed the "Leviathan-like
federal government" to "the nexus between legislative careerists and the
capacity of the modern state to be bent to the service of their careerism."
And he warned that a "permanent class of career legislators is inherently
inimical to limited government—government that is discriminating in
its ends and modest in its methods."[2]

The federal behemoth created by uncontrolled spending naturally
attracts an army of lobbyists, campaign financiers, and assorted hangers-
on, who are there to protect their own or their employers' interests in
the federal pork barrel.[3] Their tools include dollars, publicity, flattery,
and more. These Washington camp followers owe their very existence
to the oversized, intrusive federal government, so their focus generally
is to expand an already bloated government, certainly not to limit it.
This army of influence brokers (federal bureaucrats included) exerts
nonstop pressure on members of Congress, and especially vulnerable
to this coercion are the congressional careerists.

"Career politicians do not have the courage to prioritize spending and say no to demanding special interests groups who do not reflect the best interests of the country,"[4] I wrote in *Breach of Trust* after leaving the House at the end of 2000. This earlier book of mine provides more examples of the corrosive effects of power and careerism described in this chapter.

So here was the political world I entered in 1995, and my education in the power-driven, career politics of Washington began quickly that first year. Initially, most of us in the class of '94 felt like bold soldiers in Gingrich's army as we rallied around the Contract with America to change the culture of Washington. Many of us wore "Cut Spending First" buttons to underscore one of our prime objectives. Our Republican leaders ably and faithfully led us the first couple of months.

Yet our march first stalled in 1995 when it came to proposing term limits, which I believed fundamental to the Contract with America. To me, the replacement of career politicians with citizen legislators represented the ultimate cultural shift in Washington. A handful of us in the class of '94 had already taken a vow of term limits and looked forward to passing the Citizen Legislature Act, a proposal to limit federal politicians to six terms in the House and two terms in the Senate. House Majority Leader Dick Armey, however, gave a troubling signal in March. "Now that we have elected a Republican House," he told Republican representatives, "maybe there is no more need for term limits."[5]

A debate over the number of allowable terms began to divide us, and Republican leadership was ambivalent and deceptive when it came to this important legislation to amend the Constitution. To disunite our efforts, bills with varying term-length limitations were offered. House conservatives were allowed to vote for term limits, but splitting the votes between different proposals prevented us from mustering the two-thirds required. This was cynical and disgusting "leadership," and many of us foot soldiers in the class of '94 were outraged.

The failed term-limits proposal stalled our efforts, but I believe our short revolution completely unraveled over the shutdown of the federal government later in the year. Gingrich and President Bill Clinton came to loggerheads in November over the House plan to balance the budget in seven years, and Clinton refused to sign appropriations bills that reduced the increase in spending and even refused to sign continuing resolutions with flat spending levels. The subsequent government shutdown scared career Republicans to death. They feared our party would be blamed for the dysfunction and lose the majority. I believed this fear was born more of the Washington mentality, and a group of us urged party leaders to stay the course.

Gingrich got wobbly during negotiations with the White House, however, and Senate Majority Leader Bob Dole grew disdainful toward us "conservatives" who wanted to sustain the shutdown. In retrospect this was a fight for government austerity that could have been won. In his book *All Too Human*, former Clinton adviser George Stephanopoulos later wrote that the president was privately wavering during the shutdown and that the Republican leaders may have stolen defeat from the jaws of victory when they capitulated in late November.[6] But the narrative became set in stone. In the future, Republican representatives who tried to use their constitutional power of the purse would be portrayed in the media as "unable to govern" if any president allowed the government to shut down by refusing to sign a budget deal.

Those of us who had come to Washington to change the extraconstitutional culture of ever-expanding government, spending, and debt felt betrayed by our own party leaders. To my thinking this ended the short-lived Republican Revolution. And it seared in my mind the fatal flaw in Washington that I would see again and again in coming years: *to cling to power, career politicians of both parties put their own and their party's self-interest ahead of the public good and long-term interest of the nation.*

Our party leadership grew even more timid during the election year of 1996. The fiscal year 1997 budget cobbled together by leadership included a fat increase in spending and national debt. Even worse, plans to reduce spending and the deficit would be postponed until 1999. By then I had learned that "postponed" actually means "canceled" in

Washington-speak. So the fear of losing control of our majority in the House was overriding any of our plans to change the spending addiction in Congress.

Republican senator Trent Lott had already declared the "revolution" over when he became majority leader earlier that year. "In 1995, we were new, we were exuberant, we were excited, maybe a little out of control," Lott explained to a *Washington Post* reporter. "Now everything is different, the world is different. We're different, first of all, because we learned a lot."[7] What Lott really meant was that he and other party leaders were teaching the new House members how "to go along to get along."

Our formerly "revolutionary" Republican leaders had become defenders of the system that many of us had vowed to change in Washington. They were teaching us the merits of partisanship. Partisanship, I learned, is just another way that career politicians of both parties cling to power. Rigid partisanship, Republican or Democratic, paves a pathway for success for members of Congress, whose party leaders tell them how to vote and take care of them in upcoming elections.

I was not surprised when the Republicans lost eight House seats in fall 1996. Republican voters were doubtless as dismayed with party leadership as were many of us from the class of '94. Those long-suffering, conservative taxpayers had hoped for bold change, but all they got was a pale pastel of the conservative party colors. They expressed their disappointment at the polls, some not bothering to vote at all.

Many of us Republican foot soldiers trudged into 1997 dispirited by our leadership but cautiously hopeful over party plans to pass the Balanced Budget Act of 1997. Passage could end years of deficit spending by 2002. Yet when I saw the actual numbers in the bill, I groaned. The budget for 1998 and 1999 would continue the spending binge; then somehow historic fiscal restraint was to be discovered in 2000 and thereafter. This was the same old "postpone the hard choices" game played in Washington.

The hard-pressed chairman of the House Budget Committee, John Kasich, was somewhat defensive when I confronted him to express my concern late in 1997. Meeting with me informally in the National Statuary Hall chamber in the Capitol, he told me it was the best bill we could get. As we talked, Kasich appeared weary and resigned. Both of us understood that the plan for a balanced budget by 2002 was a sham.

Just how much of a sham became obvious as we began working on the 1998 Highway Bill. This was a key bill, and at a cost of $217 billion, an astounding 42 percent more than the previous bill some six years earlier. This was a pork-laden, undisguised admission that the Balanced Budget Act of 1997 meant nothing. Kasich privately called it an "abomination." An attempt was made to buy the votes of some of us who adamantly opposed this bill by offering each of us $15 million in pork to spend in our districts as we wished. I went public with this shameful offer, fearing little with my term limit only three years out. Kasich led us in this fight against the bill, appearing on *Fox News Sunday* just before the vote with a telling statement: "I just hope we don't get comfortable with governing in this way, because if we do, we wouldn't be any better than the way the Democrats ran the place."[8]

The day of the vote on the Highway Bill, several amendments were attempted, including one by South Carolina representative Lindsey Graham to cut the $9 billion in "demonstration projects" from the bill. The amendments failed, but the bill itself, of course, passed easily in the House with more than three hundred votes. Those of who had openly fought this "abomination" at least had the consolation of providing the public with some insight on how Congress works. The passing of this wasteful piece of legislation also served as another stellar illustration of the old warning about democratic governments: *When the people learn they can vote themselves money from the public treasury, democracies inevitably begin to crumble.*

The year 1998, my fourth full year in the House, was filled with the tiresome Clinton White House scandal and more budget-busting spending. Speaker Gingrich, who had long since lost support from those of us still battling to plug the spending geyser, failed to confront the embattled president over fiscal issues in the run-up to the 1998 elections. Gingrich's strategy was to make no waves and hope that Clinton's self-inflicted wounds would help Republicans at the polls. He badly miscalculated public sentiment, and our fifty-four-seat majority in 1995 was now a slim five seats going into 1999.

A small group of us instigated a leadership change following the 1998 election debacle, and Gingrich was forced to resign. He disparaged the "cannibals" in the party whom he blamed for his demise. Notably, a number of us dissidents who pushed for a new House speaker were term-limited. Certainly for me and probably several others, the knowledge that our tenure in Washington was already limited freed us to do what we hoped would best serve the country. We could act without fear of damaging our limited political futures.

Although I had seriously considered returning to my medical practice after my second term in the House ended in 1998, I ultimately decided on a third and final term. Interestingly, I won my final term with a larger margin than in my two previous wins. This larger margin of victory came despite my refusing pork spending in my district and generally becoming a pain in the derriere to Republican Party bigwigs. I say this not as a boast, but as an encouragement to other politicians to act on their convictions.

As I started my final term in the House, the Balanced Budget Act of 1997 was already shredded. Still, a few of us fiscal hawks hoped new Speaker of the House Denny Hastert would salvage something from this legislation. Encouraging to some of us, the Republican budget resolution that passed *did* stay within the budget caps. Yet the allocation process soon followed with the Agricultural Appropriations Bill more than $250 million over the previous year. The charade was obvious. The difficult cuts were being postponed for the final appropriations bills, which meant they were never going to happen. I determined to fight hard and at least go down swinging.

I sent a notice to the Agriculture Committee that if the rule were adopted I planned to "filibuster" the bill with 115 amendments. Even if House members did not stay within the budget caps, I could at least draw attention to the charade. And part of the deception included the so-called budget surplus that year that came from borrowed Social Security funds. During consideration of the rules for debate on the agriculture bill, I took to the floor to explain my de facto filibuster:

> Mr. Speaker, I come to the floor today to talk about where we are going in this country. This rule is symptomatic of the problem that we face. . . .
>
> If in fact this body intends to protect Social Security, if it intends to do that, if we are true with our votes about what we meant on the various budgets, then there is no way if this rule passes that this bill should pass. . . .
>
> Do we really mean it when we say we are going to protect Social Security, or do we not? I believe we do not mean it.[9]

Obviously, many in the House did not mean it. What they meant to do was raid the Social Security surplus to pay for new spending. Their voting record would prove it.

My first amendment failed by a wide margin. Undeterred, I proposed other amendments. My delaying actions were contentious—and embarrassing to Speaker Hastert. Also making the Speaker uncomfortable were a few of the big Republican Party names that supported some of my amendments. Yet why were Hastert and every single representative present not more discomfited by the public scene of the U.S. House voting to spend Social Security trust money on a wasteful bill?

I later ended my de facto filibuster after the Speaker offered a sizable cut in the agriculture bill and reductions in upcoming appropriations bills. Some savings to taxpayers were realized from my efforts, but ultimately Congress again failed the nation as it exceeded the budget caps by $39 billion that year.

A year later, the budget process for fiscal year 2001 was at least more honest than the previous. It made no pretense of staying within the budget caps from the 1997 agreement. I had promised Speaker Hastert that I would temper my disruptions in the allocation process as the various spending bills were proposed. He in turn pledged to hold spending down significantly. Unfortunately for the taxpayers, Hastert was unable to keep his promise. The pressure from spendthrifts in the Speaker's own party eventually broke his resolve. Looking back, I should not have promised to be less disruptive. I forgot that the only language career politicians understand is power and leverage.

As I prepared to leave Washington to resume my medical practice in Oklahoma, I felt disheartened over how little the Republican revolutionaries in the class of '94 had actually accomplished. In addition to more than two hundred wasteful government programs targeted for extinction, we hoped to eliminate three cabinet-level departments: education, energy, and commerce. Just like Republican Party icon Ronald Reagan the decade before, we failed to shrink the overreaching, bloated government bureaucracy. The three targeted departments remained firmly rooted upon my leaving in December 2000, and the Department of Commerce budget had actually grown by 45 percent since 1994.

A message at this time to my constituents in the Second District of Oklahoma succinctly summarized my thoughts on the previous six years in Washington:

> Congress continues to be an elite ruling class that represents not the people but itself and special interests. The fault, however, does not rest solely with Republican leadership. I have never shied away from criticizing my own party when I thought we were abandoning our core principles for a temporary political gain, but what happened in Washington the past six years reveals more about human nature and the addictive quality of power than the failings of either party.[10]

Looking back at that message, I realize today what a strong argument it makes for a convention of states to propose amendments to address these ills. The Framers provided us with this constitutional means for the people to bypass our elected officials when they are derelict in their duties to preserve and protect the Constitution and the people. The wording in the message to my constituents about "human nature and the addictive quality of power" that lay at the core of Congress's failings closely followed the reasoning behind the Framers' addition of the Article V provision. Although I had struggled through six years of the very governmental dysfunction that the founders foresaw and prepared for in the Constitution, I was not yet sold on an amendments convention as the solution. My "Capitol education" would continue in the years ahead.

The return to my medical practice in Muskogee felt like a return to sanity. My days filled with the familiar rhythm of illness and treatment, newborns and elderly. From the comforts of my practice and home in Oklahoma, I watched the transition of power to the Bush administration in 2001. The election process had been tumultuous, but I felt some relief that a Republican president was now in the White House. I had spent my three terms in Congress as a Republican in a Democratic administration. With a Republican president now in office, maybe the Republican House and Senate could whittle away at the waste and overreach in government.

Soon embroiled in the War on Terror, the Bush administration actually increased the size and scope of the federal government, and deficit spending quickly reached new heights. Some of these expenditures were necessary to fight the new threat from global terrorism, but much of it continued to be wasted taxpayer dollars on the same swollen, inefficient programs. I watched this with concern but for the time was glad to leave these problems to others.

In fall 2003, Oklahoma Republican senator Don Nickles announced plans to retire at the end of his term in 2004. My successor in the House had been a bright, young Oklahoma Democrat named Brad Carson, and he began eyeing this open Senate seat. Although quite happy with my return to medicine, I considered running for a couple of reasons. First, I had learned a lot about the wasteful spending in Washington and felt a certain civic duty to continue fighting it. Also, as a senator I might have more influence to effect change than I had as a representative.

But mulling over this Senate race, I felt nagging pangs of doubt. My six years in the House had mostly brought frustration, though I had been honored to serve. Also, Republican leaders in my own state were not supportive of my return to Washington. I decided not to run.

After writing a press release announcing my decision, I awoke in the middle of the night concerned that I was making a mistake. Perhaps the doctor in me could not live with the decision to ignore a sick federal government. I had seen the disease in Washington—the career politicians whose love of power subjugated the nation's interests to their party's and their own. The symptoms of that disease included an expansive, extraconstitutional federal government and attendant deficit spending and national debt. Washington was a political sick ward in need of extensive treatment.

To resolve what I thought I should do versus what I wanted to do (keep practicing medicine in Muskogee), I wrote out a list of reasons why I should run for the Senate seat. Included in these were the following:

> I believe we have a deficit of moral courage in the United States Congress. . . .
>
> I believe we have lost sight of the moorings of the Constitution in that it was founded upon the principles of a creator and that we have inalienable rights given by that creator. . . .
>
> I believe that we must address squarely the problems that face us with Medicare and Social Security and discuss openly how we honor commitments to our seniors and protect the future of our children and grandchildren. . . .
>
> I believe the U.S. Congress lacks effective leadership to control spending and point out the process by which self-serving politicians sell our children down the river with deficit spending. . . . [11]

These were the first four of a list of reasons I finally decided to run. I later had all the reasons printed as a one-page campaign flyer.

Winning the Senate seat in November, I was well aware of the daunting challenges ahead in Washington. The toughest of all, spending cuts, I would later compare to pushing boulders up ice floes. And upon my return to the capital, I knew I might be a little short of friends. *Breach of Trust* had been out only a short time, and a *New York*

Times article said I had burned some bridges in Congress by naming Republican leaders who "were more concerned with being re-elected than with spending tax dollars wisely."[12]

The night I won the Senate race, I received a call from President Bush congratulating me and welcoming me to the Republican team in Washington. I was already serving as cochairman of the president's advisory council on HIV/AIDS. "Mr. President," I said, "I'm looking forward to helping you cut spending." The silence on the other end of the phone was deafening. *Welcome back to Washington,* I thought.

My return to the capital as a U.S. senator in January 2005 coincided with growing concern by conservative Republicans over President Bush's excessive spending. The Medicare Part D prescription drug legislation signed into law by Bush late in 2003 had added a $13 trillion unfunded liability to the federal balance sheet. More disheartening, many saw this prescription-drug entitlement program as a crude political maneuver to garner votes in the 2004 election. I understood it as another classic example of politicians recklessly indebting future generations to buy votes from current constituents—a big crack in the wall of the republic.

I had campaigned for the Senate on a promise to go after wasteful spending in general and earmarks in particular. Ending earmarks, a gateway drug to congressional profligacy, could give members of Congress the moral authority and credibility to confront even greater spending abuses. Going after earmarks would be the first objective in the larger goal of controlling spending and downsizing government. My staff readied for the battle ahead by studying the Senate rules, which we intended to use to our every advantage.

Following the Hurricane Katrina disaster in late summer 2005, I gave a speech on the Senate floor with ideas to more cost-effectively manage the disbursement of recovery funds to the Gulf Coast. This led to some bipartisan work with new Illinois Democratic senator Barack Obama to produce legislation on Katrina-related oversight. Obama and I had connected during Senate orientation sessions. We often sat together during these meetings and shared thoughts on our upcoming work. I started teasing my younger, more liberal colleague a bit, and we enjoyed bantering with each other.

The aftermath of Katrina triggered some healthy debate about spending priorities in Congress. It also gave me an opening sally against individual earmarks, including the construction of two bridges in Alaska for $452 million. The media had already begun calling one of these bridges—the link from Ketchikan to Gravina Island (population fifty)—the "Bridge to Nowhere." I would frame my argument as pork spending versus disaster relief, and I would be up against Alaskan Republican Ted Stevens, a thirty-seven-year Senate don and old-time porker.

I proposed an amendment to the transportation appropriations bill that would shift $223 million from the Gravina Bridge construction to a critical span over Lake Pontchartrain damaged by Hurricane Katrina. I explained this on the floor in what was later called by some the "rumble speech":

> All change starts with a distant rumble, a rumble at the grassroots level, and if you stop and listen today, you will hear such a rumble right now. That rumble is the sound of hard-working Americans who are getting increasingly angry with out-of-control Government spending, waste, fraud, and abuse. It is the sound of growing disillusionment and frustration of the American people. It is the sense of increasing disgust about blatant overspending and our ability to make the tough choices people on budgets have to make each and every day, our inability to make priorities the No. 1 priority rather than spending our children and grandchildren's future.[13]

Senator Stevens was shocked and angry that anyone, let alone a freshman senator, would challenge his earmark. He warned the Senate not to cross him over this amendment and promised that if it passed he would "be taken out of here on a stretcher."[14] A number of other senators came to the floor to defend the right to earmarks. These speeches revealed just how parochial and unjustifiable these kinds of individual earmarks really were. Yet unsurprisingly my amendment went down by a 15 to 82 vote.[15]

Although I lost the fight, I believe this was a strategic win. More earmark battles would follow, and each time the public became better informed and angrier over this shameful practice. A Harvard Business School study in 2010 helped our cause with findings on the bad economics of these earmarked expenditures.[16] With the Tea Party mobilized by 2010, Congress finally succumbed to the pressure. A former supporter of earmarks, Senate Republican Minority Leader Mitch McConnell took to the floor in November 2010 and spoke in support of an earmark moratorium. With this gateway drug at least temporarily halted, Congress could now talk about cutting billions instead of millions. Wins like this for the American taxpayer, present and future generation, would be hard to come by in my Senate years.

Another revealing fight soon began over my resistance to the Senate's passing bills by "hotline"—approving legislation without recorded voting if no one dissents. The hotline process was originally intended to pass noncontroversial motions, like the naming of federal buildings. Over time this had expanded to an abusive system that often rubber-stamped costly, duplicative legislation with no debate. For example, in the 110th Congress (2007–2008), of the more than twelve hundred bills approved, only fifty-nine received a roll-call vote. The hotline process amounted to a perfect scheme to grow government and debt by the "Party of Yes"—the dominant party in Washington and loaded with Democrats and Republicans.

At the beginning of each Congress, I began sending a letter to my Senate colleagues, announcing that I would not grant unanimous consent to bills that I considered extraconstitutional or that were not offset by spending cuts. This soon led to another confrontation with Republican senator Ted Stevens, who asked to meet with me in December 2007 to discuss four of his bills on hold because none were offset.

"Tom, I need these bills," Stevens forcefully argued in the expansive Strom Thurmond Room in the Capitol. "I have an election!" He had five Commerce Committee staff members present to support him. I offered to work with his office to find offset spending. Following a fruitless discussion and an expletive-laced tirade, Stevens promised that he would never let another of my bills pass, "Not one, Tom. Not one," he vowed. At an impasse with my Senate colleague, I left the meeting room with my accompanying staff member. As we walked down the long corridor, the senator's voice boomed behind us: "Not one! Not one of your bills, Tom!"[17]

Another powerful but softer voice, this one from the Democratic Party, also rose against my holding up other legislation that was not offset and often just wasteful. In summer 2008 Senate Majority Leader Harry Reid rolled thirty-five of the more than one hundred bills I was holding into the Advancing America's Priorities Act, derisively called the "Coburn Omnibus" by Reid's staff. The majority leader included several pieces of legislation to portray my opposition as mean-spirited. Actually, I would have supported some of this legislation if it had been offset. Reid also larded his package with a number of measures—like the Senator Paul Simon Study Abroad Foundation Act—that were hard to stomach even by some of the jaded members of the Senate.

The majority leader failed to muster enough support for a motion to proceed to vote on his package, and he took to the floor to vent his spleen: "The only effort that my friend, the distinguished junior Senator from Oklahoma, wants is to throw a monkey wrench into proceedings around here. That is what this is all about. . . . Next time you see someone in a wheelchair at home, explain to them how you voted against moving forward on something that may get them out of that wheelchair."[18] Over-the-top rhetoric even for Harry Reid.

During the Senate debate over this, some in the media began calling me "Dr. No." The new title was probably meant sarcastically, but I was actually okay with it. As I later wrote about this episode in my second book, *The Debt Bomb*, released in 2012: "No is a word we need to hear more often from politicians in Washington. No is also a word the founders would have associated with the Senate. . . . Again, the problem is not that we have said no. The problem is we have said yes and agreed to run up a $15 trillion debt."[19] Of course, with "no" so seldom heard in Congress, this debt had increased to $20 trillion just four years later.

Entering the White House in January 2009, President Barack Obama quickly moved to stimulate America's stricken economy with a massive $840 billion spending program. This stimulus spending has been a great exposition of the failings of Keynesian economic theory, a plague on America since the 1930s. With its key tenet of advocating government spending to prime the economic pump during sluggish periods, Keynesianism also provides politicians the justification to do what they love to do best—spend taxpayer money (someone else's money, not theirs) to secure their political careers.[20]

In lieu of Obama's spending binge, conservatives argued for tax cuts, tax reform, spending cuts, and serious deficit reduction. I also pushed the 2008–2009 economic crisis as the ideal time to eliminate the more than $300 billion in wasteful expenditures my office had identified. Democrats instead pushed through the stimulus package, which was loaded with earmarks whose existence they denied. Another major flaw in the stimulus were the bailouts for several states that had been financially irresponsible, including California, Illinois, Michigan, and Nevada. Some $54 billion was sent to states under the heading of State Fiscal Stabilization Fund, with the monies to be used to avoid cuts and layoffs of state and local government workers.[21]

Several years after the stimulus expenditure, the entire program was proven wrong. By the administration's own estimates, the economy was worse off by the end of 2010 than if these expenditures had never been made. The Congressional Budget Office released a report late in 2011 that estimated as few as six hundred thousand jobs were saved, and at a staggering cost of $1.4 million per job. Even in the CBO's best-case scenario of total jobs created, the government spent $233,000 per job. The report also estimated that the additional debt from the deficit spending for the stimulus would slow annual economic growth by as much as 0.2 percent after 2016.[22]

I later reflected on the lessons to be learned from the costly, wasteful expenditures in the stimulus effort:

The central challenge of our time is not to remember what government can do, but what it cannot do very well. We are on the edge of an abyss not because we had too little faith in government but because we had too much faith.

In the debate between the founders [who envisioned a limited government] and today's career politicians and progressives, the stimulus rendered a resounding verdict in favor of our founders. . . .

A government that works is a government that is limited.[23]

With the stimulus plan coughing and wheezing its way to failure, Washington turned its brief attention span to the serious issue of fiscal sustainability. In 2010 several commissions would be formed to address this issue—never mind that a debt commission already existed in the form of Congress. Commissions give political cover to Washington careerists. They can appear to deal with an issue without the responsibility of actual decision making. This would mark the beginning of what I later called the Year of the Commission in the capital.

The first of the commissions that year was the president's bipartisan, deficit-reduction panel of eighteen members, commonly known as the Simpson-Bowles Commission. Senator McConnell asked me to serve with this group, which drew its name from its two chairmen—former Republican senator Alan Simpson and former Clinton White House adviser Erskine Bowles. The commission began meeting in April.

Before these meetings started, my staff assembled a four-hundred-page-plus report detailing how $150 billion could be saved annually by eliminating waste and duplication in the federal government. These findings received mixed reviews when I presented them to the commission. Going a step further in May, I presented the group another report that showed how $100 billion more could be saved annually through spending and management reforms in the Department of Defense. I hoped to show the commission how even some of my own party's sacred cows would be on the table to address this fiscal crisis.

As the commission's work proceeded through the year, I grew concerned at the lack of real-world experience of many of the participants.

Mostly political and government careerists, they did not approach this task as bottom line–oriented business leaders. By late in the year, the group had bumped and ground its way to a proposal that would reduce the deficit by $4 trillion over ten years. Three-fourths of this would come from spending cuts and the rest in revenue increases. Perhaps the proposal's deepest flaw was that it made no recommendation to save or even address Medicare, the nation's biggest driver of long-term deficits.

In December eleven of the members voted to support the plan, four votes short of the required tally to officially report the commission's findings. Pleased that we had reached at least some show of bipartisanship, we reported the proposal anyway. Unfortunately, President Obama basically ignored his own commission's work, which I believe will be remembered as one of the greatest failures of presidential leadership in American history.

As the Simpson-Bowles Commission chugged along in the summer and fall of 2010, another bipartisan group of senators was meeting to address deficit reduction. Republican Saxby Chambliss and Democrat Mark Warner led this group, which was later joined by several senators from Simpson-Bowles after it disbanded. By early 2011, I had joined this group, soon dubbed the Gang of Six.

Our purpose was to put the Simpson-Bowles findings into legislation. This would entail a $500 billion down payment in spending cuts, later spending reductions and reforms, and finally Social Security reform. By summer 2011, I temporarily convinced the group to address real entitlement reform, including a breakthrough on Medicare and Medicaid. This soon fell apart, however, when Democrats in our band grew concerned over the political effects of this bold step.

As the Gang of Six discussions continued, a debt-ceiling deadline loomed in August. President Obama reacted angrily to Tea Party freshmen resistance to an automatic increase in the debt ceiling. To provide some spending reductions to ease this gathering storm, my office released a 624-page report detailing $9 trillion in savings from federal waste over ten years. This *Back in Black* report demonstrated how easy it was to find savings if a real will for it existed. Even a part of these recommended savings could have greased the political wheels during this debt-ceiling impasse, but of course few in Congress seriously considered any of these reforms.

The debt-ceiling crisis loomed as the Gang of Six finalized its plans for long-term deficit reduction in July. In mid-July President Obama essentially embraced our work in a public address. Our inchoate plan could have been attached to a bargain on the debt ceiling. Efforts by the Gang of Six soon disintegrated when it appeared that the president had feigned adoption of our work as a ploy in his public dispute with Speaker John Boehner.

As the Year of the Commission ended, the compromise that emerged to get through the debt-ceiling crisis was an alleged $917 billion in cuts and the appointment of a "super committee" to make recommendations for deficit reduction. Automatic, widespread cuts in spending, called "sequestration," would begin if Congress failed to approve the new committee's plans. The ceiling was raised by another $1.5 trillion. Days later the United States received a humiliating credit downgrade from Standard & Poor's.

As predicted by many, the super committee failed to reach a consensus on recommended deficit reduction late in 2011, and sequestration began. Even this craven process was to have actually *increased* overall spending by $1.65 trillion in the next ten years. But, of course, even slowing the increase in spending would be too much for our politicians in the nation's capital. The hard caps of sequestration would soon be lifted, just as they had been with the Gramm–Rudman–Hollings Deficit Reduction Act enacted by Congress in 1985.

During my ongoing battle to reduce deficit spending in Washington, I hoped for as much success ending waste and duplication in federal spending as I had with eliminating earmarks. I forced through legislation requiring the Government Accounting Office to investigate duplication in government programs. This report, released early in 2011 and titled *Opportunities to Reduce Potential Duplication in Government Programs,*

Save Tax Dollars, and Enhance Revenues, covered only a third of all government programs but showed potential savings of $1 trillion over ten years. These findings echoed similar results from the Reagan-era Grace Report, which estimated as much as one-third of federal spending is lost to waste, inefficiency, and duplication.

Initially, both parties touted the GAO report as a simple way to reduce deficit spending. Even Democratic representative Nancy Pelosi applauded the potential savings: "Again, we all agree to get rid of waste, fraud, abuse, duplication, obsolescence, and the rest. The GAO has given us a blueprint for that, and we subscribe to that."[24] A few months after the report, the Senate voted to eliminate $5 billion in duplicative waste highlighted in the report, and Democratic senator Mark Warner and I offered an amendment to get this done.

Unfortunately, Majority Leader Reid pulled the legislation to which we had attached our amendment, ending the brief, bipartisan "era of good feelings" and efforts to end this deplorable squandering of taxpayer money. For bringing to light the potential savings for taxpayers, the GAO suffered a budget cut by the Senate Appropriations Committee in September.

As a backdrop for much of the deficit-reduction efforts that pervaded President Obama's first term, the constitutionality of the Affordable Health Care Act's individual mandate made its way through the courts. Some of us in Congress warned of Obamacare's enormous potential to add to the deficit, and I hoped an adverse ruling by the Supreme Court would eliminate this threat. The Supreme Court, however, upheld the individual mandate as within Congress's constitutional power to tax. Additional rulings have further strengthened Obamacare, which will add backbreaking federal debt in coming years if this legislation is not repealed or replaced.

Further efforts in 2012 and 2013 to get Congress to act on the waste, duplication, and fraud revealed by the GAO and my office amounted to little. I did finally get some legislation out of the House to eliminate a small part of the massive duplication uncovered in the federal jobs training programs, a small drop in the ocean of waste. Career politicians refused to do the work to eliminate similar wasteful, ineffective programs because they were worried about upsetting some interest group.

An additional roadblock to my efforts was the tight control on the Senate's business by Majority Leader Reid. Looking back, I think Reid never got over the fact that he lost his sixty-vote lock after the 2010 elections. He had been spoiled by his ability to thwart a filibuster in 2009 and 2010. Reid's frustration led to his working to change Senate rules early in 2013. This greatly handicapped my efforts to stop some of the wasteful legislation coming to the floor.

Epitomizing my frustration with government inaction was an attempt by my office in 2014 to stop some of the egregious fraud in the Social Security Disability Insurance Program. A truly heroic worker in an Oklahoma City Social Security office had called my staff to report the disability scams she saw on a daily basis. In a subsequent study by my office, two hundred randomly selected disability cases in three different states were scrutinized. We found that 40 percent of those receiving benefits were not disabled. More sickening, we found widespread corruption by lawyers, doctors, and administrative judges, all getting fat from their seamy roles in this taxpayer swindle. To address this outrage, I filed the Protecting Social Security Disability Act late in my final Senate year. The Committee on Finance never took it up. The dysfunction in Washington had never been higher.

The 2014 elections returned the Senate to the Republican Party, but by late 2013, I had already announced plans to retire from Congress after these elections. My frustration in the Senate had peaked, and I lost all confidence in the ability of capital politicians to truly address problems. There had been plenty of proposed solutions in Washington to fix the mammoth bureaucracy and uncontrolled spending, but the critical courage to act was always in short supply. Too many of the elected problem solvers had become the problem.

I left Washington to work with those who might have some answers for our broken federal government. The Founders had never quit while fighting for the nation's independence and while continuing the struggle to establish a republic by and for the people. Those of us dedicated to preserving this Great Experiment in self-governance will not quit either. A convention of states to propose solutions to our national dysfunction is a continuation of the struggle inherited from our founders. Our nation's early leaders had warned us that the price of freedom would be eternal vigilance. Even with all my frustration as I left Washington, I still wanted to help find solutions.

2

THE FAILURE OF BIG GOVERNMENT

Such a power does not destroy, but it prevents existence; it does not tyrannize, but it compresses, enervates, extinguishes, and stupefies a people, till each nation is reduced to nothing better than a flock of timid and industrious animals, of which the government is the shepherd.

— ALEXIS DE TOCQUEVILLE

I'VE SEEN THIS MOVIE A THOUSAND TIMES," University of Maryland economist Carmen Reinhart told me as we walked back to my office at the Russell Senate Office Building in late March 2011. "I know how it ends." This "movie" featured the complacent attitude of policy makers toward mounting debt and fiscal chaos throughout history.

Reinhart and Harvard economist Kenneth Rogoff (coauthors of best seller *This Time Is Different: Eight Centuries of Financial Folly*) earlier that day had warned a gathering of Democratic and Republican senators of the danger from our nation's uncontrolled spending and high ratio of debt to annual gross domestic product (GDP). Around forty of us attended this closed-door briefing in the Capitol Visitor Center. In response to those who offered a remedy of tax cuts and stimulus spending to promote economic growth, Reinhart responded in blunt terms: "Debt is the problem. You have a debt crisis because of debt."

The two economics professors met in my office for an informal debriefing after their presentation. They were widely celebrated for their book's thesis: Disaster follows the hubris of policy makers throughout history who believe "this time is different" and somehow the laws of economics do not apply to their mounting debt or financial misman-agement. They spoke with authority and frightening clarity when they told me that countries rarely pass the 90 percent debt-to-GDP tipping point. "If it was not risky to hit the 90 percent threshold, we would expect a higher incidence," Reinhart said.

Once a nation's debt nears or exceeds its GDP, lenders grow averse to further financing. At that point the crisis can turn into catastrophe. The creditors dictate the terms of a country's financial restructuring. "You get killed when people don't buy your debt," Rogoff pithily summarized.

At the time of Reinhart and Rogoff's presentation in 2011, our gross national debt was about $14.5 trillion (near 96 percent of GDP). This was about the time of the Year of the Commission covered in chapter 1 and supposedly a period of great concern about our nation's fiscal health. So what did our dysfunctional federal government do in the subsequent years to address this national crisis? By the end of fiscal year 2015, our national debt had climbed to $18.2 trillion and 102 percent of GDP, according to the Congressional Budget Office. By the end of fiscal year 2016, our national debt stood at $18.6 trillion. Another $4.1 trillion had accrued to the national debt over those five years, a 28.3 percent increase to the previously staggering burden. Despite eight centuries of evidence to the contrary, our national leaders have convinced themselves that "this time is different."[1]

In the last chapter I chronicled the careerism and partisanship that overrules common sense in Washington and accounts for much of why our leaders continue to grow government and fail to deal with its fiscal fallout. These public officials—contrary to the original constitutional framework for limited government—have led us into an expansive federal authority with an insatiable appetite for spending. Stated in more Madisonian terms: *An unbalanced system of governance has led to the political corruption that renders our leaders incapable of addressing the nation's pressing fiscal problems.* Bear in mind our definition of corruption in this book—leaders acting more in their own and their party's interest than in the long-term interest of the public.

Unfortunately, our nation's problems extend further than spiraling debt and dysfunctional leadership. Divisions in politics and society stymie the consensus needed to address these national problems. The corrupted politics in Washington has factionalized both Congress and American society. The quest for both individual and party power in the capital has pitted the people against each other, encouraging them to identify by interest group—race, class, gender, or party—rather than as Americans. Related to the desire of our leaders in Washington to maintain power, the people are considered by politicians foremost for their vote and treated more as dependents in need of government largesse and close regulation. So our expansive, overreaching government and subsequent political corruption has led to where it has throughout history—a debt-ridden nation of dependent, divided people *with reduced liberties.*

This is a tragic state of affairs for America just a little more than two centuries after the start of the Great Experiment in self-governance. American exceptionalism has inspired real "hope and change" in the world for two centuries, but now we are struggling to find our own way. Victims of our own success, we became complacent. We were warned by our founders about the need for eternal vigilance. Now we must confront our dereliction. Directly addressing our current plight is the first step toward righting our ship of state. The nation needs to regain the ideals at its founding—and the world needs us to achieve this.

Only the people can restore American ideals. Washington politicians have failed us and will continue to do so. As a republic, we were always warned about trading our liberties for security. Now, *We the People* must assert our rightful sovereignty under the Constitution and rebalance our badly unbalanced federal government. No one can save us but ourselves.

After this chapter most of this book will be about the political process and actions by the people to rebalance our constitutional system of governance and restore our self-governing republic. To strengthen our resolve to restore order in our nation's capital, let us first review the sad results of our acquiescence to decades of nearly unlimited government.

BIG GOVERNMENT GROWS, THE NATION DIVIDES

Polarization in the country may be at an all-time high, and this disunity is found more in the people than in Washington. While Congress may sometimes divide over its service to special interest and support groups, the media's lament over the perils of gridlock is overwrought. Elected officials in Washington are almost universally united by their desire to extend their careers in government and to spend taxpayer dollars to purchase support. During my years in Washington, I saw presidents and members of Congress from both parties enact massive entitlement programs, tax breaks, and projects for special interest groups. Rather than as adversaries, the two political parties have acted more as a unified force generating trillions in national debt.

Although every dollar should be spent for the execution of Congress's constitutional duties, taxpayer money is routinely dispensed otherwise. During my years in the House, I saw firsthand how the process of the Appropriations Committee was used to aid the reelection of representatives from both parties. Appropriators judge a representative's request for funding of a district project by individual and party election needs more than the merits of the proposal. Bipartisan careerism trumps actual benefits to the people. Reacting to pressure from individuals and party leaders, the appropriators serve as guardians of the political spoils system in Washington.

This bipartisan system transcends national interests and works primarily for reelection purposes and to further the careers of congressional elitists. I saw a perfect illustration of this elitism in my final term in the House when Democratic senator Tom Harkin and Republican senator

Arlen Specter attempted to use an appropriations bill to rename two federal institutions after themselves. Harkin aspired to see the Tom Harkin Center for Disease Control, and Specter pined for the Arlen Specter National Library of Medicine. Fortunately, their plans foundered.

Further undermining theories on Washington gridlock, the so-called extremists in Congress are often the very politicians to cooperate and compromise to pass difficult legislation. Although from different parties and ideology, Senator Barack Obama and I worked together on several issues, including oversight legislation for Hurricane Katrina disaster relief. I also worked with Democratic progressives Henry Waxman of California and Russ Feingold of Wisconsin. Democratic Party icon Ted Kennedy had a reputation for working across the aisle on difficult legislation. My experience taught me that congressional leaders with clear ideas and a desire for sound legislation have little trouble working with their ideological opposites.

The periodic budget tiffs in Washington are largely between those who want a whole lot of spending and those who want unlimited spending. These congressional budget squabbles would be more manageable if the federal government had not so outlandishly exceeded its constitutional framework and become a conduit for special-interest spending. The beneficiaries of services and special treatment—many in the bureaucracies overseeing these programs—put tremendous pressure on Washington politicians to continue the benefits and government rents. With taxes and debt spiraling, Congress finds it increasingly difficult to keep funding its demanding constituencies.

The rare gridlock seen in Washington reflects the divide in the nation from the continued profligacy and reach of government. A large part of the public and legions of bureaucrats want the spending and federal intervention to continue; another part of the public is exhausted from paying for big government, frightened by the debt, and furious at government overreach—let alone abandonment of limited government that was envisioned and intended by our founders.

Thus Washington's extravagance and overreach has bred a

factionalized, highly partisan public. This divide in the nation's politics plays out in the media, on the streets, and on college campuses across the country. The shrillness on talk shows and the chaotic demonstrations in large cities and on college campuses reached a fever pitch in 2016 not seen since the Vietnam War years. The rancor in the late 1960s was largely about American sacrifices in a foreign war; *the disagreements today are rooted in who gets what from government and how we pay for it.*

Predictably, government overreach and meddling in all aspects of society have created a kind of culture war. Interest groups are pitted against their ideological opposites. Using a "divide and rule" mentality, the two parties in Washington promote and ally with this or that faction to gain support and leverage.

The Founders designed a limited federal government to minimize and control the factions and partisanship that inherently stir the people. These early leaders had suffered social and political turbulence throughout the 1780s from the divided, ineffective government under the Articles of Confederation. With his keen insight into human nature, Madison in particular promoted limited government to enhance social harmony and avoid the dangers of factionalism. "A zeal for different opinions concerning religion, concerning government, and many other points," Madison wrote, often divided society into interested groups and "inflamed them with mutual animosity, and rendered them much more disposed to vex and oppress each other, than to co-operate for their common good." By providing few opportunities to corrupt federal officials, Madison's limited government and balanced system under the Constitution would minimize partisanship and its tendency to "vex and oppress."[2]

We no longer have anything close to a limited, balanced government, so the vexation runs rampant on the airways and in other public discourse. The public faces of this discord are factions and interest groups. A later chapter in this book describes author Jay Cost's concept of how the federal government's unconstitutional growth promotes political corruption in Washington and unbalances the system of governance. Cost elaborates on the role of factions and interest groups:

The carrier of this disease [political corruption] is the organized faction. Responding to some new governmental beneficence or imposition, a faction organizes itself to apply pressure to the government. Through campaign contributions and lobbying, it induces the government to tilt public policy to its favor, at the expense of the public good. This, in turn, creates a vicious cycle. The success of a given faction induces another to organize, then another, then another, so that the original effect is multiplied.[3]

Following his contention that unchecked corruption in government always spreads, Cost similarly argues that factions and interest groups promote more of the same. Each interest group that pressures the government for special status or some kind of rent instigates another interest group to counter these efforts, and this continues ad infinitum. *So we begin with a government that exceeds its constitutional limits and evolve into a fractious nation of grasping special interests, including grievance groups that identify by party, race, class, gender, age—and any other way to curry government recognition and support.* This is factionalism doing its worst.

The pretensions of victimhood by these interest groups sometimes produce a politically correct theater of the absurd. The inanity of students at elite universities bemoaning their contrived misery can only be understood in terms of how this furthers some special interest with a response from government. Public officials pander on cue to these bizarre affectations of victimhood from their cry-bully constituencies.

Note the special-interest groveling by political candidates on the national stage. Some 2016 presidential aspirants refused to acknowledge publicly that all human lives have equal value to those of one of their constituent factions, who feign grievance and rage at the acknowledgement that "all lives matter" as much as their own. This speaks volumes about how brazen the grievance industry has become in its demands for special treatment from government. It also says much about how low public officials have sunk in their debasement of our government for the support necessary to cling to their positions of power and authority.

This is the bizarre world of political correctness and feigned grievance spawned by big government and its pandering politicians. This is how we became a disunited land of factions and interest groups, each pitted against another. The *E pluribus unum* (out of many, one) on our nation's Great Seal has been turned inside out by constituent-hungry politicians. With this kind of factional lunacy, how can Washington ever muster the sober-minded leadership to face real problems, like our $20 trillion-plus in national debt and $143 trillion in unfunded liabilities?

Nebraska senator Ben Sasse indirectly spoke to this factional pandering when he addressed the Senate in November 2015 and said that the "people despise us all." The freshman Republican gave a reason for this contempt: "The Senate isn't tackling the great national problems that worry those we work for." He poignantly added, "But we all know deep down that the political class is unpopular not because of our relentless truth-telling, but because of politicians' habit of regularized pandering to those who already agree with us."[4]

Where will we find the "virtuous" public leaders willing to talk straight with the voters and tell them of big government's failures? The leadership and solutions are not to be found in Washington. The American people—even with the divisions created by ambitious, pandering politicians—must come together and look to themselves, and we should hope this might change with the presidency of Donald Trump. And the most urgent problem the people must face is the unsustainable growth of public debt, courtesy of their bloated federal government.

OUR BIG FAT GREEK GOVERNMENT

The Founders were keenly aware of the miseries that could befall the people from public debt. They could readily see the plight of their British cousins who labored in a reduced standard of living to support their monarchy's spending and debt. Thomas Jefferson wrote that governments move inexorably toward increased spending and debt. He warned how private wealth could be lost to a profligate government and how the people could be reduced to a state of poverty and chaos.

"Then begins, indeed, the *bellum omnium in omnia* [war of all against all]," Jefferson wrote, "which some philosophers observing to be so general in this world, have mistaken it for the natural, instead of the abusive state of man. And the fore horse of this frightful team is public debt. Taxation follows that, and in its train wretchedness and oppression."[5]

The limited federal government and enumerated powers of Congress expressed in the Constitution were of course intended to control federal spending and debt. Yet we have seen ambitious leaders and strained court rulings lead the nation away from limited federal government. David Walker, who served as comptroller general of the United States from 1998 to 2008, asserted that only 40 percent of spending between fiscal years 2008 and 2011 was devoted to functions expressly delegated to the government by the Constitution. Sadly, that describes much of the federal spending back to the 1930s.[6]

Our estimated $19.57 trillion and growing national debt at the end of fiscal year 2016 stood at 106.7 percent of our gross domestic product.[7] Although outside the full faith and credit of the government, the approximately $143 trillion in long-term obligations from federal entitlement programs are part of this grim story. The cost of these programs exceeds the net worth of the economy, so technically the country is already bankrupt. The prior standing of the United States in the world economy and the U.S. dollar's role as the dominant reserve currency has allowed us to continue borrowing funds to maintain spending levels.[8]

How much longer can our national debt grow? At what point do our foreign creditors get nervous and stop buying U.S. Treasury bills? Remember what Rogoff warned: "You get killed when people don't buy your debt."

In my 2012 book *The Debt Bomb*, I describe a future scenario that depicts where the United States is headed, despite the prevailing attitude in Washington of "this time is different." My account picks up with a fictitious Japanese company, Entrust, that determines that U.S. debt is no longer a safe investment. With a sluggish economy, the American government has kept the interest rate historically low for some time and continues to print money. It appears the United States is trying to inflate and devalue their way out of a financial crisis. Entrust leaders decide to sell their holdings in U.S. Treasury bills because they believe America's political leaders are leading the country into financial ruin.

Others soon follow the Japanese company's lead. With the value of the dollar dropping in relation to other currencies, the international community fears that holding U.S. debt could bring staggering losses. The dollar continues to drop precipitously, and Americans soon lose a third of the value of their retirement plans, savings, and houses. In less than a month, the U.S. stock market loses 40 percent of its value.

Not wanting to see the United States default on its loan payments and face bankruptcy, members of the G-20 (a forum of twenty major national economies) make an offer and give an ultimatum to the struggling United States. These countries will continue to loan money to America, but they dictate Greece-style reforms in return for these funds: The retirement age for Social Security is immediately raised to age seventy-two, and U.S. tax rates are doubled.

With the American economy stable but sputtering two years later, an international crisis arises when the People's Republic of China begins an invasion of Taiwan. The United States threatens military action. The Chinese, who have strategically kept their large investments in U.S. Treasury bills, warn that they will dump these holdings if the United States intervenes. Fearing another financial meltdown, America abandons Taiwan.

Although fictitious, this scenario could become a humbling and sad reality for a country that has led the free world since the end of World War II. It is not improbable; it is predictable. Democrat Erskine Bowles, with whom I served on the Simpson-Bowles debt commission in 2010, famously called a system failure or something similar to that outlined above "the most predictable crisis in American history." Even as far back as 2010, Joint Chiefs of Staff Chairman Admiral Michael Mullen said, "The most significant threat to our national security is our debt."[9]

Besides the potential financial meltdown described above, large national debt inhibits growth in our economy. Reinhart and Rogoff argue that longitudinal research indicates that a debt-to-GDP ratio of 90 percent creates a 1-point drag on a country's economic growth. That may not sound like much, but that is 25 percent of a 4 percent economic growth rate.[10] Each point of GDP missed represents around 1 million lost jobs in the U.S. economy.[11] Thus, hopes of "growing" our way out of debt with a robust economy are diminished by the very debt we hope to reduce.

Confirming the economy-killing debt-to-GDP theory of Reinhart and Rogoff, at the end of 2015 the country concluded its tenth con-secutive year in which economic growth failed to reach 3 percent. Even without the recession years of 2008 and 2009, the average of economic growth since 2005 barely cracked 2 percent. The once-great economic engine of America has no parallel for this in living memory, perhaps in U.S. history. Again, growing our way out of this appears more and more remote with current government policies.[12]

Economic metrics aside, the issue of slow economic growth is more clearly expressed in human terms. A stagnant economy like ours thwarts the aspirations of American families and of our largest demographic cohort, the millennials. And this aspiration includes the American legacy of economic improvement from one generation to the next. Growth in the U.S. economy provides a corresponding improvement in the standard of living, but only if clumsy big government gets out of the way of the free market.

As I wrote in *The Debt Bomb*, America's financial crisis is really a spending and entitlement-program crisis. More than 25 percent of federal spending is on health care, so much of our long-term debt comes from health care spending in the Medicare and Medicaid pro-grams. With the aging of America, spending on these health-related programs is set to escalate dramatically in the years ahead, as it will on Social Security. The interest on the additional debt load from these programs will increase exponentially, especially once interest rates rise to free-market levels.[13]

Others besides Reinhart and Rogoff warn that this level of spending cannot continue. Former head of the Federal Reserve Ben Bernanke said back in 2011, "By definition, the unsustainable trajectories of deficit and debt the [Congressional Budget Office] outlines cannot actually happen, because creditors would never be willing to lend to a government whose debt, relative to national income, is rising without limit." Punctuating his remarks, Bernanke invoked a now-familiar quote by economist Ben Stein: "If something can't go on forever, it will stop." *The question remains whether Americans will stop their rising national debt on their own or foreign creditors will stop it with Greece-style reforms.* Americans show great alarm over short-term government shutdowns during congressional budget tiffs; they should worry more about foreign creditors imposing longer-term, targeted shutdowns of entire federal programs.[14]

Avoiding a government shutdown in December 2015, Congress responded to all the dire predictions in their usual "this time is different" manner. Our nation's leaders voted to fund the government through September 2016 with a $1.15 trillion spending bill, predicted by Goldman Sachs political economists to boost the federal budget deficit to a three-year high and called by President Obama "a good win." This funding excluded entitlement spending, which is outside the appropriations process. Although the allegedly more fiscally conservative Republicans in Congress controlled the House and Senate after the 2014 elections, they failed to staunch the flow of red ink. "Republicans started the year [2015] by passing a budget resolution that promised to end deficits over the next decade by cutting $5 trillion in spending," the *Wall Street Journal* reported. "But the revenue and spending measures enacted this year did little to curb the biggest long-term driver of deficits—entitlement spending that isn't subject to the annual appropriations process."[15]

In more personal terms, each U.S. taxpayer's share of the federal debt in 2015 was more than $154,000. Worse, this has been growing at an annual rate of more than 7 percent since 2004, far more than earnings have increased in this same period. Worse still, this doesn't take into account the nation's unfunded liability per taxpayer, which is mind-boggling to even contemplate.[16]

As much of this book has shown, Washington is now inherently incapable of providing solutions to America's spending and debt problems. In fact, political officials in our nation's capital *are* the problem. As the following chapters will demonstrate, *Americans have been given a constitutional right to look to themselves for improved national governance, and this provides their only solution to this fiscal nightmare.*

Answers outside Washington have already begun, with a few state governments rolling back spending and breaking the demoralizing debt spiral. Led from 2005 to 2013 by Governor Mitch Daniels, Indiana has shown how spending addiction in government can be dramatically reversed without "rolling Granny over the cliff." When Daniels took office in 2005, Indiana was already $700 million in debt and facing a nearly $1 billion shortfall in its fiscal year 2005 budget. The state was in its seventh consecutive year of unbalanced budgets. Just four years later, it had paid all its debts and accrued $1.3 billion in "rainy day" reserves. The state received its first AAA credit rating, one of few states to achieve this. When asked how Indiana made this rapid turnaround, Daniels had a simple answer: "We spent less money than we took in."[17]

There is, of course, more to the state's success story. Indiana was in deep trouble by 2005 because state leaders had deliberately spent more money than they had—just as Washington has been doing for decades. While making private-sector job growth a priority, Daniels clamped down on the flouting of spending restrictions by state agencies. He also rescinded a 1989 executive order that had swept state workers into employee unions without their consent. This action gave the governor more flexibility to shift workers into areas of need and to make other cost-saving moves. Another big factor was Daniels's use of his power of "reversion," which allowed him the option not to spend every dollar budgeted by the Indiana General Assembly.

Perhaps the best measure of Indiana's success was its ability to provide better services to its citizens at lower cost. Carefully evaluating its service to the public, the state improved at almost every level even with a whopping 20 percent fewer workers in 2011 than in 2005. By 2011 Indiana was the lowest in the nation in public employees per capita and had fewer state workers on the rolls than in 1978. Daniels, who is now the president of Purdue University, says he has a stock answer when he hears citizens voice fears of cutbacks in public spending: "You'd be amazed how much government you'd never miss."[18]

The Indiana turnaround proves that real determination to reduce government spending and debt can succeed without a decline in public services. Moreover—and certainly instructive in the context of this book—this fiscal success occurred outside Washington and closer to the people. Daniels tell this story of his years as governor in his national best seller *Keeping the Republic: Saving America by Trusting Americans*, where he also wrote, "I am desperately alarmed about the condition and direction of the American Republic." The director of the U.S. Office of Management and Budget from 2001 to 2003, Daniels abhors the federal government's spending addiction and America's growing dependence on public funds: "As a people, we have discovered the ability to vote ourselves largesse from the federal treasury in such vast sums that we are destroying our own chances at prosperity."[19]

The Hoosier leader's comments strike at the essence of our federal spending addiction and debt problem. Despite a long history of failure from social programs and big government, many in our country still take a wrong-headed, reactionary stance for more government dependence. The trajectory of official poverty in the United States in the forty-five-year period from 1967 (three years into the federal War on Poverty) through 2012 remained flat or increased slightly upward. Welfare spending soared during this period, but the results were abysmal.[20] These decades of federal social programs have contributed to our destructive, unsustainable national debt, but the miseries of unlimited government extend well beyond factional divisions and economic woes.

FROM MAKERS TO TAKERS

Reduced spending on entitlement programs—Medicare, Social Security,

Medicaid, and income maintenance (financial assistance to the needy)—through means testing and eligibility may provide limited solutions to our entitlement trap. Yet a more meaningful change needs to come in the hearts and minds of Americans. Big government's false promise of easy living and smug security has wreaked havoc not only in the nation's finances, but also in the American ideals of self-reliance and human dignity. In what would be heartbreaking to our nation's founders, we have become a government-dependent "nation of takers."

The benefits from America's entitlement programs comprise the big drivers of long-term U.S. debt. These expenses (government transfers) have been growing at an unsustainable rate for some time. Medicare and Medicaid already cost more than $1 trillion per year, and their current growth rate makes them the country's "single greatest threat to budget stability."[21] Despite Washington's refusal to address the nation's entitlement problem, change will come. "We can't save Medicare as we know it," Connecticut senator Joe Lieberman said in 2011. "We can only save Medicare if we change it."[22]

The groundwork for the federal government's extraconstitutional role as the provider of social welfare may have been laid by the progressives in the 1930s, but the big spending truly soared with Lyndon Johnson's Great Society programs of the 1960s. Between 1960 and 2010, federal entitlement spending escalated from 19 percent to 43 percent of annual federal spending. The total outlay of government transfers in 1960 was a paltry $24 billion, or about $134 per citizen. In just fifty years, this expense increased by an inflation-adjusted 1,248 percent, a real growth rate of 5.2 percent annually for fifty straight years. *Adjusting both for inflation and population growth, these annual entitlement expenses increased 727 percent, an average of 4 percent every year. In 2010, this translated into an entitlement expense of $7,200 in 2010 dollars ($974 in 1960 dollars) for every man, woman, and child in the country.*[23]

Government transfers for income-related entitlements (welfare programs) totaled $650 billion in 2010—an inflation-adjusted thirty-fold increase (7 percent annual growth rate) since 1960. Government transfers for age-related entitlements for older Americans (Medicare and Social Security) rose to $1.2 trillion in 2010, an inflation-adjusted twelvefold increase (5 percent annual growth rate) since 1960. Although the poverty- or income-related transfers have grown at a far greater rate, the dollar outlay for age-related entitlements doubled the former in 2010.[24] But with the Affordable Care Act in high gear, spikes in Medicaid expenditures may cause income-related entitlements to close the gap on age-related transfers in future years.

Age-related entitlements aside, what has America gained since the Great Society's War on Poverty programs of the mid-'60s? These efforts were not just to alleviate the ills of poverty but to eliminate the root causes altogether. In 1966 when the massive means-tested entitlements to address the poor began, the overall poverty rate in the United States was 14.7 percent. In 2013, and more than *$15 trillion later*, the poverty rate was measured at 14.5 percent. That could be a statistical error, rather than even this miniscule 0.2 percent decline. By any standard the War on Poverty has been a government-administered fiasco, and any private-business executive would have been sacked well before the numbers were this far out of control. Zombielike, this failed beast of big government staggers on.[25]

The percentage of "takers" of government entitlements has increased over the last five decades to where a majority of American voters live in a household with at least one member either applying for or receiving benefits from a government program. This increase in entitlement recipients has seen a corresponding decline in labor force participation by American males. From 1948 to 2008 work participation by men declined by 13 percent. Just another disillusioning by-product of America's entitlement society, stated Nicholas Eberstadt in his 2012 book *A Nation of Takers: America's Entitlement Epidemic.* "Transfers for retirement, income maintenance, unemployment insurance, and all the rest have made it possible for a lower fraction of adult men to be engaged in work today than at any time since the Great Depression—and, quite possibly, at any previous point in our national history."[26]

Although Americans have paid into the Social Security and Medicare trust funds over many decades, both are woefully underfunded by actuarial standards. Social Security has an underfunded liability of about $8.6 trillion in 2012 U.S. dollars for the seventy-five years beginning in 2012. The Medicare program's trustee's report, which some officials call optimistic, has an even greater underfunded liability, estimated at $27 trillion for this same time period. By comparison, the U.S. GDP for 2012 was a little over $15 trillion.[27]

The poster children for "takers" in America may be the abusers of the Disability Insurance program, which is under the aegis of the Social Security Administration. Although many cases were undoubtedly legitimate, I know from past experience as a doctor and a U.S. senator that frauds and abusers were rampant among the nine million Americans who received disability payments in 2014. These payouts totaled $142 billion that year. The rampant waste and fraud in the disability program also underscores the abysmal lack of program oversight by our federal government. A 2015 study revealed that the disability program overpaid nearly half the beneficiaries by a total of almost $17 billion over the previous decade.[28] This occurred while the program teetered on insolvency, and it actually ran dry early in 2016. The disability program only continues because it borrows from Social Security retirement funds. And this of course means Social Security monies for retirees will deplete even sooner.

None of these entitlement programs can be sustained over the long term, and their budget competition with military readiness makes our nation less safe in the short term. President Eisenhower's warning in 1961 about the "military-industrial complex" taking a growing share of the national budget for defense readiness has been mooted by the nation's ravenous appetite for entitlements. Reflecting the nation's new priorities, the two-to-one defense dollars to domestic entitlements in 1961 had been more than reversed by 2010 with a three-to-one ratio of transfer payments to national defense spending.[29] It should be noted that the Constitution specifically empowers the federal government to provide for the nation's defense but nowhere cites spending taxpayer dollars on entitlement programs.

One of the saddest and most shameful aspects of America's entitlement addiction is its unfairness to future generations, who have no say in this money grab by the present generation. While America's tenuous credit holds, future taxpayers are being obligated to repay the trillions for entitlement spending borrowed from private sources to keep the gravy train rolling for the present generation. This is a grotesque twist to the Founders' lament over "no taxation without representation." The disenfranchised children and grandchildren of today's generation will likely not forget this plundering of their futures. Somewhere . . . Jefferson weeps.

Attempts by constitutional conservatives to limit the federal government's role in the modern welfare state and to bring fiscal responsibility to America's failed giveaway programs are generally criticized as heartless. Unquestioned support of the poor with endless financing, food, and shelter is largely championed by progressives (many in the media and academia) as a tenet of social justice. Yet author Marvin Olasky persuasively argues in his groundbreaking book *The Tragedy of American Compassion* that America had a much more compassionate and successful system of charity before the modern welfare state. With voluminous research Olasky clearly demonstrates that the problems of America's underclass are not rooted in poverty, and the governmental approach widely accepted in the twentieth century has only harmed society's most needy over the long run.

Olasky chronicles how before the twentieth century America's economically distressed were provided only basic relief, with private charities playing the key role. Importantly, aid to the poor without requiring returned effort was considered "as much a threat to true compassion as those who turned their backs on neighbors and brothers." This sort of "tough love" approach was considered an act of kindness and required more effort from the charitable than the mere provision of a handout. Real progress was made in the inner cities with a "challenge to change" accompanying material support.[30]

This earlier approach to aiding the underclass stands in direct contrast to the irresponsible, intergenerational failure of current government programs. The crisis of the modern welfare state has been brought on by its failure to look beyond the material needs of the poor, Olasky argues, resulting in the unintended but quite real treatment of the needy as less than noble creatures and incapable of self-improvement.[31] Again, as Arthur Brooks warns: Learned dependency is tyranny. Increasing people's dependence on government decreases their freedom.

Olasky's heart-wrenching book is a must-read for those truly interested in fighting poverty and helping the underprivileged succeed in America. Progressives, however, balk at the author's criticism of government's role in these efforts. Olasky's clear evidence and sound reasoning responds: "Governmental welfare programs need to be fought not because they are too expensive—although, clearly much money is wasted—but because they are inevitably too stingy in what is really important, treating people as people and not animals."[32]

In his acclaimed best seller *Free to Choose*, Nobel Prize laureate Milton Friedman further explains the failure of centrally planned economies and the welfare state in the post–World War II era in Europe and the United States. By 1970, the economist wrote, most Western leaders saw the dismal economic results of the collectivist mentality and began to reverse the trend of nationalizing large industries. Still, the allure of collectivism dies hard, and big government efforts in the closing decades of the twentieth century were redirected to welfare programs and regulatory activities. "The objectives have been noble, the results, disappointing," Friedman contends. "The failure is deeply rooted in the use of bad means to achieve good objectives."[33]

While Olasky explains the failure of the welfare state in terms of its ignoring the dignity of individuals, Friedman also describes its shortcomings in economic terms. The acclaimed theorist argues that the inherent lack of individual freedom in welfare spending results in unsatisfactory efforts to alleviate poverty. Both Olasky's and Friedman's explanations have merit.

In his exposition of the failure of the welfare state, Friedman uses a classification of spending to show the undesirable results of government entitlements. My own service in Congress attests to the usefulness of this approach in analyzing almost all other government spending. As illustrated in the following table, four categories of spending exist: *Category I*, your money spent on yourself; *Category II*, your money spent on someone else; *Category III*, someone else's money spent on yourself; and *Category IV*, someone else's money spent on someone else.[34]

Category I spending is the most efficient because you as the spender are spending money on yourself. An example would be your shopping for groceries. Out of your own self-interest, you will search for the lowest price to get the foods you most desire.

Category II is less efficient. You will look for a good value, as it is your money, but you have less concern over the kind of food and its quality.

Category III is still less efficient from a cost standpoint. Someone is spending someone else's money on something they want. An example would be the government food stamp program. Purchasers will buy something they want, but the value is not of prime importance.

ON WHOM MONEY IS SPENT

		YOURSELF	SOMEONE ELSE
WHOSE MONEY IS SPENT	**YOURS**	THE FREE MARKET AT MAXIMUM EFFICIENCY FREE INDIVIDUALS SHOP FOR THEMSELVES AND EXERCISE CHOICE **I**	THE FREE MARKET BUT LESS EFFICIENT FREE INDIVIDUALS BUY GIFTS FOR SOMEONE ELSE STILL EFFICIENT BUT THE BEST PRICE IS NOT THE HIGHEST VALUE **II**
	SOMEONE ELSE	THE GOVERNMENT ECONOMY AT ITS BEST THE FEDERAL FOOD STAMP PROGRAM **III**	THE GOVERNMENT ECONOMY AT ITS WORST FEDERALLY FUNDED PUBLIC SCHOOL FOOD BACKPACKS **IV**

Category IV is the least efficient of all. Someone is spending someone else's money on someone else. An example would be government workers purchasing food to place in public schoolchildren's weekend backpack. (Yes, our nanny-state government provides backpacks of food for qualified schoolchildren to take home on weekends.) Little thought is given to the cost or value of this spending, or to its spirit-killing stigma.

Public welfare programs—and most other government spending—fall into either Category III or IV. Little wonder so much of government spending returns such meager results to hardworking taxpayers. "The bureaucrats spend someone else's money on someone else," Friedman summarizes. "Only human kindness, not the much stronger and more dependable spur of self-interest, assures that they will spend the money in the way most beneficial to the recipients. Hence the wastefulness and ineffectiveness of the spending."[35]

Friedman wrote that inefficiency in spending decisions is compounded by its corrupting effects on government spenders. Bureaucrats and politicians often use their spending power for their own benefits. I covered this corruption extensively in chapter 1. The eminent economist writes about waste and corruption from a theoretical standpoint; I saw it firsthand in Washington and testify that it is worse than Friedman imagined.

"The waste is distressing," Friedman concludes, "but it is the least of the evils of the paternalistic programs that have grown to such massive size. Their major evil is their effect on the fabric of society. They weaken the family, reduce the incentive to work, save and innovate; reduce the accumulation of capital; and limit freedom."[36]

In his best seller *The Conservative Heart: How to Build a Fairer, Happier, More Prosperous America*, American Enterprise Institute president Arthur Brooks echoes criticisms of big government's failed War on Poverty because of its "materialistic, mechanistic view of human development." Following the economic approaches of Friedman, Brooks calls for an end to the failed redistributionist policies of the past and offers a vision of hope through personal responsibility and free enterprise.[37]

The author's upbeat approach to America's big government–induced enervation also serves as a wakeup call for the nation to "stop taking and start making" again: "The world needs us to stop losing. There are too many people in America who are being left behind. There are too many people overseas who don't enjoy the benefits of democratic capitalism and free enterprise. There are too many people everywhere who have been denied the happiness that comes with earned success. Those people need us."[38]

AMERICA'S ROAD TO SERFDOM

As covered earlier, America's turn to big government and the mushrooming growth and power in Washington is rooted in the progressive New Deal ideas of the Roosevelt administration. The Great Depression was mistakenly viewed as a failure of capitalism, and big government was alleged to be the remedy to prevent future economic calamities. Thus the New Deal policies ushered in a new philosophy regarding government. As did other world elites in the first half of the twentieth century, many American leaders in the 1930s and afterward traded their belief in individual responsibility, free markets and limited government for a trust in the social responsibility of a large federal bureaucracy.

Some of the New Deal programs no doubt relieved immediate distress, but the legacy of dependence on big government has been destructive. Moreover, the legacy is about more than the spiraling debt from entitlement spending: Perhaps more frightening is the loss of liberty experienced by Americans over the past seventy years, and especially so in the last several decades.

In a startling reversal of its economic freedoms, the United States has plunged from the number two position in the world in 2000 to sixteenth in 2015. These freedoms include the ability to start a business without onerous bureaucratic red tape and expense, and extend to the ability to get financing without several rounds of government approval.

Once envied for its economic opportunities, America now ranks behind Canada and the United Kingdom in the degree to which individuals, families, and businesses are free to determine their well being without government interference, according to the 2015 edition of Canadian-based Economic Freedom Network's annual publication, *Economic Freedom of the World.*[39] This is another sad legacy foisted on America from big government–enthralled leaders in Washington. Stumbling away from the system that made the country great, these officials have truly led many Americans down the road to serfdom—a state of subsistence living and limited freedoms.

Much of this lost liberty results from the growth of the federal government's modern administrative state, which has become a kind of fourth branch of government. Chillingly, this progressive army of bureaucrats, technocrats, and meddlers is unelected and operates with little and sometimes no oversight. Wielding awesome power, this vast bureaucracy of federal agencies operates almost entirely outside our constitutional structure. Without changing a jot or tittle in the Constitution, the bloated federal administrative state has vastly expanded the power of the executive branch at the expense of the duly elected officials of the legislative branch and those of state and local government. Infuriating to those tormented by these bureaucrats, these overpaid minions of big government have no worries about the voters turning them out.

These agencies churned out a staggering 82,036 pages of new and proposed rules and instruction in the *Federal Register* in 2015. This number eclipsed the previous record of 81,405 in 2010, giving the Obama administration the dubious distinction of six of the seven most prolific years of regulating in U.S. history. President Obama's bureaucratic legacy was noted early in 2016 by the *Wall Street Journal:* "He's a champion when it comes to limiting economic freedom, and American workers have the slow growth in jobs and wages to prove it."[40] But first and foremost he is a champion of big government. His and other U.S. leaders' responsibility for limited economic freedoms stems from their stubborn and misguided reliance on big government.

Economist and Nobel laureate F. A. Hayek, born in 1899 in Austria-Hungary, wrote a book in the 1940s that was ahead of its time in warning of the dangers of state-controlled economies and the threat this poses to economic prosperity and to individual liberties. Hayek's experiences with European collectivist governments informed his revered classic, *The Road to Serfdom*, a caution to Western societies that had become enthralled with big government in the first half of the twentieth century. His central insight was that governments that turned away from individual voluntary cooperation from its citizens and installed centralized government to coordinate and regulate society almost always brought economic decline and, importantly, reduced the freedom of its peoples. Hayek enraged many big-government advocates at the time with his argument that collectivist-type governments inevitably led their citizens down "the road to serfdom."

The rest of the twentieth century, however, proved Hayek's thesis. One after another, the socialist states of eastern Europe enslaved and impoverished their citizens. The "social democracies" of western Europe, collectivist if not outright socialist, fared better, but by the beginning of the twenty-first century, many of them were mired in stagnant economies, spiraling debt, and restricted opportunities. These countries' failures are epitomized by the meltdown in Greece, but other European states are not far behind.

What is this connection between centralized government and reduced liberties that Hayek warned about some seventy years ago? At the heart of it is the quest for power, the economist contended. Echoing James Madison, he argued that the desire of a few to organize society springs from this all-too-human yearning for control. Moreover, Hayek argued, "in order to achieve their end, collectivists must create power—power over men wielded by other men—of a magnitude never before known," and "their success will depend on the extent to which they achieve this power."[41] While Hayek directed most of his thesis at truly totalitarian, socialist governments like the Soviet Union and its future satellite countries of eastern Europe, his argument holds for less severe forms of collectivist governments—not unlike the United States of the last decade or so. Who can argue with a straight face that freedom and liberties are not threatened in this big-government era of America?

For evidence, look no further than the federal government's symbiotic relationship with politically correct power groups, a textbook example of which was provided by the trampling of the legal rights of the Duke University lacrosse team in 2006 over false allegations of sexual abuse. A power faction alleging "war on women" perpetrated this scam, and on cue the pandering, progressive politicians in Washington responded to this and other overwrought cries of sexual abuse. Despite the brute facts of the case, the Obama administration followed up the travesty of justice at Duke University with Title IX directives to universities across the country, establishing kangaroo courts and reeducation classes to address this false—but politically correct—narrative of rampant sexual abuse of women in America.

The "war on women" is just one example of how political correctness and big-government pandering combine to limit the liberties of Americans with official directives and programs. "Policies like that don't emerge from the marketplace of ideas, much less political debate," journalist Daniel Henninger opined of this politically correct form of governance. "They come from a kind of Americanized Maoism. The left goes nuts when anyone suggests political correctness has totalitarian roots. But the PC game has always been: We win, you lose, get over it, comply."[42]

Indeed, even in the 1940s Hayek worried that the great, classically liberal traditions and freedoms in Great Britain and America were threatened by the collectivist mentality of progressive big government and the warped polity it begets. "Almost all the traditions and institutions in which democratic moral genius has found its most characteristic expression, and which in turn have molded the national character and the whole moral climate of England and America, are those which the progress of collectivism and its inherently centralistic tendencies are progressively destroying."[43]

The preceding examples of big government's inherent inefficiency and soft tyranny justify Hayek's concerns for America's future as far back as the 1940s. *Unnerving to contemplate, Hayek's warning of our future is the reality of our present.* The reactionary progressive movement and its collectivist-socialist mentality have never been completely discarded despite the ultimate and utter failure of socialism whenever and wherever it has been tried. The great thinker Hayek ended his book with a statement that should resonate with all liberty-loving Americans who cherish self-government and their independence: "The guiding principle that a policy of freedom for the individual is the only *truly progressive policy* remains as true today as it was in the nineteenth century."[44]

BREAKING THE CYCLE OF REACTIONARY BIG GOVERNMENT

While the above review of the failings from our oversized, extraconstitutional government should be instructive and motivating, for at least a generation many Americans have already felt at a visceral level that something dangerous is afoot in America. With incomes stagnating, the middle class shrinking, and government oppression growing, ordinary citizens—those best suited to judge the efficacy of our government—have for some time been uneasy about their own and their children's future. Moreover, they are losing faith in the time-honored approach of electing better officials to change the direction of their failed government.

Count me among these ordinary citizens. I never went to Washington to become a part of the political class. And I did not, as some of my exasperated former colleagues will attest. As a practicing physician, I felt the same uneasiness two decades ago that more and more Americans feel today. I was given the honor to represent my compatriots, not just those in Oklahoma but across the nation. Chapter 1 is my account of what I found and where it led me.

I have come to the inescapable conclusion that Americans must act to save themselves from a federal government that has grown inherently incapable of governing in the best interest of the people and the country. As factionalized as we have become under our divisive, feckless government, we must come together as a people and take action. I certainly did not come to this understanding after a brief stint in Washington.

I spent six years in the U.S. House of Representatives and another ten years in the U.S. Senate. I never served a day in our nation's capital where I was not self-term-limited, so my "career" in government was never influenced by any desire to stay in power. My original calling was to medicine, not politics.

We should all be grateful that our forefathers, in their providential wisdom and experience, provided the people with a constitutional remedy to act in their own and their country's interest. At our core we are a self-governing republic with written, foundational laws. We should never be a nation of exalted political leaders and entrenched bureaucrats. Article V was an endowment to the people to propose amendments to these foundational laws if their elected representatives proved unable or unwilling to act in the people's and the nation's best interest. Of course, this is the main thrust of this book, and the remaining chapters will explain and explore this gift from these extraordinary men from our nation's beginning.

Some of the previous narrative in this book has been dark, and not without an element of sadness. Much of the remainder should be more upbeat and hopeful. Although we should never propose amendments to our foundational laws without somber consideration, we as Americans *should* feel a certain relief and joy at this right. As the aging Revolutionary War veteran Levi Preston once said, "We always had governed ourselves, and we always meant to."

An Article V amendments convention provides us as Americans with an opportunity to govern ourselves. Let us proceed with the coming chapters on how an Article V amendments convention can be applied to this noble experiment in self-governance known as the United States of America.

3

CONSTITUTIONAL AMENDMENT BY *WE THE PEOPLE*

As there is a constitutional door open for it, the People (for it is with them to Judge) can as they will have the advantage of experience on their Side, decide with as much propriety on the alterations and amendments which are necessary [as] ourselves. I do not think we are more inspired, have more wisdom, or possess more virtue, than those who will come after us.

—GEORGE WASHINGTON

AT A MEETING OF THE MULTISTATE LEAGUE of the Southwest in August 1920 in Denver, a New Mexico official offered a resolution. State engineer L. A. Gillette's resolution included a request for a convention of seven Southwestern states to recommend a plan for the equitable distribution of waters of the Colorado River and its tributaries. The seven states that surrounded the upper and lower basins of the river acted on this resolution, appointing delegates to what became known as the Colorado River Commission.

This commission, in all respects a convention of states, convened twenty-seven times in 1922 to negotiate the Colorado River Compact. "Measured by the vastness of the region and the magnitude of the interests regulated," future Supreme Court associate justice Felix Frankfurter wrote at the time, "The Colorado Compact represents, thus far, the most ambitious illustration of interstate agreements." Moreover, it represented a constitutional and successful effort by a number of states to prevent the federal government from asserting control of this vital water resource.[1]

Authorized in the U.S. Constitution, these seven states met as equal semi-sovereigns to draw up this treaty to regulate an interstate river. The opening sessions of this convention were held January 26–30 in Washington, D.C. Afterward the delegates moved westward, reconvening once in March in Phoenix and once in April in Denver. The final eighteen sessions were held November 9–24 at the storied Bishop's Lodge resort in Santa Fe, New Mexico.[2]

What should rightfully be called the "Santa Fe Convention" began its first meeting at the Commerce Department in Washington with opening words by the temporary presiding officer, Secretary of Commerce Herbert Hoover. The noted engineer and future president had been selected by President Warren G. Harding to represent the federal government at this conclave. Unlike at an Article V amendments convention, a federal representative at this compact convention was appropriate. The meeting's purpose was to establish an interstate compact, and as such this treaty between the semi-sovereign states would need the approval of Congress.[3]

After Hoover's opening remarks, Colorado commissioner Delph E. Carpenter immediately nominated the commerce secretary as the "permanent chairman of this Commission." After a unanimous yea vote, Hoover suggested a formal recording of "the credentials of the various Commissioners," whereupon followed a review of the state documents authorizing the various commissioners to deliberate on the subject matter of the convention—"the use and disposition of the waters" of the Colorado River.[4]

The commissioners followed the established rules for a convention of states, just as this legal tradition had been handed down since the English colonies' gatherings in the late 1600s and throughout the 1700s.

Each state had one vote; the convention decided its own procedures; the commissioners stayed within their prescribed subject matter; and their proposal was ultimately ratified by the seven participating states.[5]

This Santa Fe Convention of 1922 may be the most significant of any relatively recent U.S. convention of states. These states met to recommend solutions to a regional problem—the equitable distribution and management of the waters of the Colorado River—and to preclude federal control of this vital water resource. This convention is a remarkable and noteworthy example of semi-sovereign American states meeting as equals to address a common problem. The delegates understood and followed the venerable American tradition for this kind of ad hoc gathering. Moreover, the states demonstrated the American principal of federalism, the constitutional pillar so vital to maintaining a balance between state and federal power in our constitutional republic.

It is past time for another convention of states to address a common problem. This problem is not regional, like that of the distribution and conservation of the Colorado River; it is national in scope and greater in importance. The urgency of this convention can hardly be overstated.

The nation is at $20 trillion in debt, with an unfunded liability of more than $140 trillion. Burdened by taxes, regulations, and a bureaucracy often hostile to free markets, the U.S. economy struggled from 2005 to 2015 with the lowest growth rate in living memory. After six decades of steadily increasing earnings, median household income (adjusted for inflation) peaked at $57,909 in 1999 and had declined to $56,516 by 2015.[6]

Overpaid government workers plan their lucrative retirements as the American middle class shrinks. Private-sector U.S. workers who once made automobiles and high-tech equipment now struggle to support their families with jobs in call centers and fast-food restaurants. These economic issues could be solved through a united effort and responsible leadership, but our self-interested officials in Washington instead pander to constituencies and divide us into factions. Instead of conducting the nation's business, cynical politicians shut down the House of Representatives with staged "sit-ins" while singing fifty-year-old civil rights anthems.

The Great Experiment in self-governance could fail in our lifetimes. Our elected leaders in Washington have lost sight of their duties to safeguard and manage the republic. With the public's opinion of politicians in Washington at historical lows, the 2016 elections reflected the anger and frustration of the American people.

A bright spot in this otherwise bleak picture is the numerous states since 2010 that have applied to Congress for an amendments convention. This is a good start and a hopeful sign that the states and the people have not lost sight of federalism and the power of the people to effect change. It is also a confirmation that *We the People* still have faith in the Constitution, which provides the safety valve of an Article V convention to protect the people and the republic from a self-interested, dysfunctional federal government.

Although it has been nearly a century since the Santa Fe Convention demonstrated the usefulness of a convention of states, a profound assertion of this power now appears imminent. Later in this book we will review the various advocacy and legislative groups that are preparing for an amendments convention, and the significant number of active applications for an amendments convention. The nation may soon see the additional states needed for Congress to call this convention. Exercising its ministerial duties under Article V of the Constitution, Congress will issue the convention call and name the time and place.

Congress's call will set in motion a series of events. Let us now look ahead to these proceedings as the state legislatures—the most direct representatives of *We the People* in our federal system—exercise their constitutional powers endowed by the Founders. Understanding the process of an Article V convention of states in advance of this gathering will better enable us to make the best use of this action.

THE PROCESS OF AN ARTICLE V CONVENTION
The wording of Article V is explicit and preemptory. Congress has a legal obligation to call an amendments convention upon the thirty-fourth state application to deliberate in convention on a defined subject

or subjects. Failure to issue the call would be unconstitutional. This mandatory duty is not a legislative function of Congress; it is an executive one exercised by the national legislature on behalf and as an agent of the applying state legislatures. As this is a ministerial role, failure to issue the call could be enforced judicially with a court order, a declaratory judgment, or an injunction.[7]

By historical precedent from the founding era, the prerogative of the call includes prescribing the time, place, and purpose for the convention. Of course, the prescribed purpose of the conclave will have been predefined in the subject matter of the thirty-four aggregated applications. Congress has no authority to specify any purpose other than that in the state applications, and any attempt to exceed this authority could result in refusal by the states to participate in the convention—not to mention legal action.[8]

Any attempt by Congress to locate the convention in an area where federal officials might have informal influence or control (Washington, D.C.) would likely prove futile. After its initial meeting, a convention can relocate anywhere it chooses. The Santa Fe Convention began in Washington but relocated three times, finishing the bulk of its work in Santa Fe.

DELEGATE SELECTION FOR THE CONVENTION OF STATES

After Congress makes the general call, the various state legislatures have complete control over delegate selection and instruction. States that did not apply for the convention can still send voting delegations. These delegations, or "committees of commissioners," have traditionally been selected by the state legislatures. A legislature may choose the state's commissioners by joint vote of both chambers or separately. Other selection methods have also been used, including selection by the governor or by legislative committee. In theory, the state legislatures could empower the people of the state to select these delegates in a direct election.[9]

With the long-standing convention precedent of "one state, one vote," the size of a delegation has little or no bearing on an individual state's influence at the assembly. As the delegations vote among themselves to determine a state's vote, an odd number of commissioners in a delegation guards against deadlock. Historically, states have usually chosen anywhere from three to seven delegates, but the number at a few conclaves has varied wildly. For the Washington Peace Convention of 1861, the largest convention of states in U.S. history, twenty-one states sent 131 delegates—an average of about six per state. Seven delegates per state at a modern-era convention would result in an assembly of 350, a manageable size for deliberations.

Traditionally, delegates are "commissioned" with formal documents (credentials, essentially) to present at the convention. The document includes the delegate's name, the commissioning authority (usually the state legislature), and how the delegate was selected. More important, these credentials define the all-important scope of authority granted to the delegate. Founding-era leaders clearly understood the connection between the commissioned authority of delegates and the validity of their actions. "There is no position which depends on clearer principles," Alexander Hamilton wrote, "than that every act of a delegated authority, contrary to the tenor of the commission under which it is exercised, is void."[10]

At the convention's opening, delegates are expected to present their credentials, usually to a committee selected by the assembly. Delegates may be given other, undisclosed instructions by their commissioning authorities. These may define the delegate's authority to a greater extent than their presented credentials. Criminal or civil penalties may be imposed by the states on "rogue" delegates who abuse their commission. Indiana, which passed the Convention of States Project resolution early in 2016, enacted a law making it a Class D felony for a delegate to vote outside the scope of his or her instructions from the state legislature.[11]

CONVENTION RULES AND PROCEDURES

Before the adoption of rules, a temporary, informally selected official presides over the opening of the convention. A permanent presiding officer, who is also a delegate, is promptly elected by the delegations. A secretary or clerk is then elected to preserve the records of the convention. Traditionally, this official is not a delegate. After election of officers, conventions choose a rules committee. Committee staffing is the prerogative of the presiding officer, but most of the major conventions of states have elected the rules committee. The committee later presents the proposed rules to the convention for debate, adoption, or rejection.[12]

The courts have relied on tradition when interpreting the wording of Article V, and conventions of states have customarily adopted their own procedural rules. Opinions and statements that Congress has a right to determine or influence these rules are not supported by history or law. As former law professor Robert Natelson has explained, "The overriding purpose of the state application and convention procedure is to bypass Congress. If Congress could structure the convention, this would largely defeat its overriding purpose."[13]

But conventions do not start with a blank slate in regard to rules. As would be expected, historical precedent has largely determined the rules of past conventions of states. The Washington Peace Convention of 1861 closely adhered to the rules of the Federal Convention of 1787. Even with a less lofty purpose than these two conventions, the Santa Fe Convention of 1922 still deferred to these historical precedents for its procedural rules. Moreover, these past rules have largely reflected parliamentary law, a branch of Anglo-American common law. At conventions, parliamentary law controls proceedings both before a convention adopts its own rules and in situations not addressed by the adopted rules.[14]

Past conventions have not adopted comprehensive rules for deliberation, so parliamentary law has decided most matters. Used by most of the state legislative chambers, *Mason's Manual of Legislative Procedure* provides a comprehensive reference source for these parliamentary laws. In his written compendium to assist legislators with the legal issues of an Article V amendments convention, Robert Natelson recommends *Mason's Manual* as a source for default rules. (Much of this section on convention procedure uses Natelson's compendium as a source, as cited in endnotes.)

As reviewed in the next chapter, the Assembly of State Legislatures began work in 2015 on proposed rules for an amendments convention. ASL planned to complete these rules in 2016. Natelson has also proposed a set of convention rules under the aegis of the Convention of States Project. These two sets of rules are posted respectively at the ASL and COS websites, whose URL website addresses can be found in appendix 5 on page 208.

When voting on motions or on proposed amendments, each state has equal weight with one vote. This time-honored "one state, one vote" rule draws on the principle of federalism, a pillar of the U.S. Constitution. Indeed, the entire process of an Article V amendments convention exemplifies this principle, with the semi-sovereign states exercising their right to bypass Congress in the amendment of foundational law. Thus the "one state, one vote" practice upholds federalist principles.[15]

Prior conventions and parliamentary law have allowed approval of motions and proposals by simple-majority vote, and a voting quorum has traditionally been a majority of eligible voters. Thus, the Federal Convention of 1787 adopted a quorum of seven states (of the twelve in attendance). Following this precedent, an Article V convention would have a voting quorum with the presence of twenty-six state delegations.[16]

An amendments convention can create any committees necessary for efficient functioning of the assembly. Some might be routine, like that for checking commissioner credentials. Others might be more significant, like that of developing the wording for a proposed amendment. The presiding officer has the authority to staff committees, but the assembly may also opt to elect committee members.[17]

Past conventions of states have generally practiced a rule of secrecy for the proceedings, to allow more open discussion without concern over public criticism or embarrassment. This tradition may be outmoded in the modern era of extensive media and communication, and open disclosure of proceeding has some advantages. First, it could reduce public concerns over a convention exceeding its authority, as unwarranted as these concerns may be. It also would allow a state to ensure that its delegation stayed within their commissions and followed instructions.[18]

The amendments convention may conclude with one, several, or no proposed amendments. Only proposals related to the subject matter of the convention call are valid. At the conclusion of its deliberations, a convention of states permanently dissolves. The presiding officer sends written notice and the wording of any proposed amendment to Congress. It remains unbinding, of course, until ratified by three-fourths of the states.

CONGRESS INITIATES THE STATE RATIFICATION PROCESS

Although an amendments-convention proposal does not technically pass through Congress, Congress will likely decide if the proposal is "*intra vires*" (within the powers) of the convention and thus valid, or "*ultra vires*" (beyond the powers) and thus invalid. Congress is under no expressed requirement to determine the validity of proposals, but would almost certainly make this a de facto prerequisite before further action. Proposals that do not align with the subject or subjects of the original call by Congress are considered *ultra vires* and invalid. They require no action by Congress. Proposals that are determined valid require Congress to select "one or the other Mode of Ratification," either by state legislatures or by special state ratifying conventions.[19]

Congress has no authority to materially alter the wording of a convention proposal. Changing the wording of a proposal would transform it into a Congress-proposed amendment requiring a two-thirds vote of each house. Congress also has no authority to set a time frame for ratification of a convention-proposed amendment. Since Article V is silent on time frames, this authority rests with the amendments convention.[20]

Once Congress has initiated the ratification process, few procedural questions remain. The approval process for a convention proposal and a congressional proposal are the same. Thirty-three proposed amendments have been sent to the states for ratification since 1789, and more than two dozen were approved after receiving the support of the required three-fourths of the states. Thus, the procedures are well established. Although it took 203 years, the most recent ratification became final with approval of the Twenty-Seventh Amendment by three-fourths of the states in 1992. The amendment places a restriction on congressional pay raises.[21]

The archivist of the United States, who heads the National Archives and Records Administration, submits proposed amendments to the state governors in a letter of notification. Depending on the mode of ratification selected by Congress, the governors either submit the proposal to their state legislatures or call for a convention.[22]

RATIFICATION BY LEGISLATURE OR STATE CONVENTION

If Congress chooses the state legislatures as the mode of ratification, a majority vote in both chambers (or the one chamber in Nebraska) is required for ratification. This has been the selected mode in thirty-two of thirty-three Congress-proposed amendments. The one exception was the ratification of the Twenty-First Amendment, for which Congress chose the state-convention mode. The Twenty-First was ratified to repeal the Eighteenth, which had prohibited alcoholic beverages in the United States beginning in 1920. The history behind approval of the Twenty-First Amendment might prove instructive to the ratification process for an Article V amendment proposal.

The national argument for and against a ban on alcohol was especially bitter. By 1933 Congress had mustered the required two-thirds votes in both houses to propose a repeal of the amendment that had brought Prohibition. Some national legislators argued that the state-convention mode to repeal the thirteen-year-old ban would lessen the influence of lobbyists, as delegates would be chosen on their position either for or against repeal. A delegate's decision would largely be made before deliberations. Also supporting the state-convention mode were congressmen who believed a referendum in the states would be the most democratic way to settle the contentious alcohol issue. With ratification by referendum unavailable under Article V, a convention was thought the best means to approximate it.[23]

As consensus grew for the state-convention mode for ratification, dispute began over whether Congress should dictate the states' delegate-selection procedure. Many in the House of Representatives agreed with New York representative Emmanuel Caller's argument that the states should establish their own methods for organizing their conventions. "I may be wrong," Caller told his colleagues, "but I incline to the belief that by reasonable interpretation the word 'convention' as used in Article V of the Constitution precludes and repels the idea that the convention shall be called, elected, organized, or governed by congressional fiat. I incline to the belief that that must and shall be a State matter exclusively. . . . Each state shall set up its own procedure. There may be 48 different types of machinery."[24]

The matter was settled. The states would establish their ratification conventions as each saw fit. A follow-up speech by New York representative John O'Connor celebrated and affirmed the state-convention mode of ratification for what would become the Twenty-First Amendment. Representative O'Connor's praise for the significance of this democratic process was also a ringing endorsement of the republican principle that the people are the ultimate source of all authority in the federal government:

> Mr. Speaker, to my mind this day is not only an historical day in this country and throughout the world, but to those who are interested in a democratic form of government it points a new way and inaugurates a new era in the conduct of our democratic form of government, because for the first time the Congress of the United States is recognizing that we are made up of, not of States, not of State legislatures, but that all Federal powers come from the people of the States, and we are sending this resolution back to conventions in the States for the nearest thing to a direct referendum that was ever had in this entire country.[25]

As no Article V amendments convention has ever been held, of course, Congress has never chosen a mode of ratification for a convention-of-states proposal. With an amendments convention and its proposal largely a creature of the state legislatures, one could speculate that Congress might very well choose a mode of ratification as distinct as possible from the origins of the proposal. The state-convention mode would be the only alternative to the legislature itself. If so chosen, the convention mode would also better affirm the constitutional principle of federal power originating with the people, as Representative O'Connor stated so well.

AN AMENDMENT BECOMES PART OF THE CONSTITUTION

After a state ratifies a proposed amendment, it sends notice to the archivist of the United States in the form of an original or certified copy of the state's action. The archivist forwards these documents to the director of the Federal Register. The Office of the Federal Register (OFR) examines the documents for authenticity and maintains custody until the proposal is ratified or expires (if a deadline had been set). After ratification, the OFR transfers the documents back to the National Archives for preservation.[26]

A proposed amendment becomes a part of the Constitution immediately upon approval of three-fourths of the states, presently the thirty-eighth state's ratification. The signing of the certification recognizing the new amendment is ceremonial. As witnesses, Lyndon Johnson and Richard Nixon signed the certifications for three amendments, but no signature is required by the president for an amendment to become law. Indeed, the president has no official role in the entire process of an Article V amendment. The archivist signed the certification for the Twenty-Seventh Amendment.[27]

Much of the text in this book serves to define, justify, promote, and demystify a convention of states to propose amendments to restore limited government and fiscal sanity to the nation. Political pundits, constitutional scholars, and various advocacy groups have promulgated numerous amendment ideas over the last decade. Almost all have two common themes: reining in our runaway federal government or addressing national problems that Congress has proved too dysfunctional or craven to confront.

As an adviser to the Convention of States Project, I admit my partiality to this advocacy group's primary goal: a convention of states to address the subject matter of "limiting the power and jurisdiction of the federal government," rather than convening for only a particular amendment. The problem in Washington has metastasized to where a single amendment will not control the disease. Certainly we need spending restraints, but we need ceilings on taxes as well. We also need a tool to curb unrealistic federal regulations and to stop unfunded mandates. Thus, to properly address the problems in Washington, the people need a package of restraints to counter the misuses of power by all branches of the federal government.

The last section of this chapter explores a number of amendment proposals aimed at rolling back the growth, power, and jurisdiction of the federal government. Two of these, a balanced budget amendment and term limits on Congress, have their own advocacy groups apart from Convention of States. These two proposals have been widely supported by the public for a number of decades. Several other amendment proposals are examined on the following pages.

It is outside the scope of this book to describe and justify numerous ideas that could restrain the federal government and address important national issues. It is useful, however, to briefly discuss some of the more popular amendment proposals promoted by a number of advocacy groups. The national conversation must continue on how the state legislatures can effect key constitutional change to save the American dream from an imbalance of power in the institutions of the federal government. This discourse must be expanded beyond its current scope, and the discussion that follows is only a starting point.

In 2007, an important book by a University of Virginia professor of political science did much to promote the current discussion on constitutional amendment. Larry Sabato's *A More Perfect Constitution* is a nonpartisan, objective work that explains why constitutional amendments are needed to stay apace with a nation that has changed dramatically from the founding era. It takes an in-depth look at a number of recommended amendments to address the national government's current dysfunction. We need more contributions like this from scholars like Professor Sabato.[28]

Although a strong advocate for an amendments convention, Sabato by no means advocates the undermining of the "ageless values" contained in the Constitution. Following the thesis of his book, Sabato argues for change by an amendments convention rather than hoping for reform by a resistant Congress. The Framers included Article V in the Constitution largely premised on Sabato's same argument:

> Many of our nation's most prominent elites will resist such an approach. These beneficiaries of the current system in government— officeholders, bureaucrats, and supplicants of all sorts—are concentrated in the District of Columbia "Beltway," where the status quo has delivered a comfortable life of privilege and power. Some sincerely and others conveniently believe that a Constitutional Convention would become "runaway" and enact destructive changes from the far right or left. I believe these dangers are greatly exaggerated, and a convention may be precisely the device needed to open up a closed system, to seize back for the people the ability to define their destiny.[29]

Notice that Professor Sabato stated that many only "conveniently believe" that a convention of states could become "runaway." This belief must be based solely on convenience because the brute facts completely undermine it. First off, thirty-four states have to apply for a convention to deliberate on a common subject matter agreed to by each of their legislatures and expressed in their applications to Congress. Deliberations are restricted to the expressed subject matter in the applications, and any convention proposal outside this restriction is invalid. Any proposal sent to Congress by the convention requires a vote of approval by a majority of the convention delegations. Finally, and perhaps most important, any proposed amendment from the convention sent to the states by Congress for ratification requires approval by three-fourths of the states before becoming law. Failure to approve *by only thirteen states* dooms any proposed amendment. With a bar this high to clear, the only "runaway" is by those fleeing from the facts.

Exploring theory and means for *We the People* to effect constitutional change to rebalance governmental institutions will prove critical in the years ahead. In the absence of the package approach advocated by the Convention of States Project, the state-convention amendments process described earlier in this chapter will require repeating until this Great Experiment in self-governance is secure.

BALANCING THE FEDERAL BUDGET

Using a constitutional amendment to prevent Congress from turning the United States into Greece has received widespread support from the public for at least forty years. Previous chapters have dealt with why Congress refuses to enact this law, so we will move on to discussing the attempt to restore fiscal sanity to our federal government through a balanced budget amendment.

Most versions of a balanced budget amendment (BBA) would hold federal expenditures to no more than the revenues in that same year, unless a supermajority in both houses of Congress approved an exception. National emergencies—such as wars, major recessions, or financial crises—would trigger this exception. This approach is fairly straightforward, but the devil, of course, is in the details.

The arguments generally made in support of a BBA are that American households and most state governments operate on a principle of balancing their books. Why should the federal government be an exception? Critics of a BBA, often correctly, point out problems with this comparison. Families do not always live solely on their income in a given year, frequently relying on loans and savings accounts to make ends meet. Similarly, many states allow for borrowing often in the form of bonds. And many officials rightfully question how "balanced" most state budgets truly are.

Many proponents of a balanced budget amendment concede the problems of "straight-jacketing" federal officials' fiscal policies and the fact that many "balanced-budget" states are also well on their way to insolvency. Yet they rightfully point out the willful stupidity of continuing our current profligacy with no attempt to control it. The problems that might accompany a BBA pale in comparison to the calamity we already face with the current fiscal chaos in Washington. In our present crisis, rejecting spending constraints out of fear of creating other problems is akin to a five-hundred-pound diabetic refusing to diet because it might lead to anorexia.

Real political leadership in Washington could begin the process of solving the nation's deficit spending and debt without a BBA. But where are these fiscal leaders? We have relied on their magical appearance for decades now, with the result being only disappointment and a tsunami of debt. The fiscal leadership I have observed has been outside the nation's capital, often among state legislators—who represent everyday Americans terrified of the nation's financial bedlam and disgusted at the federal government's robbing their children and grandchildren's futures.

The state legislators and amendments-convention delegates will have to sort through the complexities of how best to place restraints on federal spending. This may be difficult, but that is what real political leadership is all about—responsibly addressing complex issues and offering practicable, long-term solutions. These legislators' very willingness to apply for a convention to address this issue better qualifies them than members of Congress, who are content with continuing to kick the can down the ever-shortening road.

Professor Sabato's examination of a BBA in *A More Perfect Constitution* rightly points out the complexities and potential problems of this arbitrary restraint. Still, he ends his analysis with an admonition the nation should consider:

> But whatever the details, a Balanced Budget Amendment in the Constitution will be a powerful symbol that the nation values fiscal responsibility. The principle is vital—a principle about which all parents should think when they ponder their children's senior years, and which all teachers should consider when they look at their

students. These children and students may judge us harshly, and justifiably so, if we fail in this basic test of character, discipline, and foresight on their behalf.[30]

A constitutional amendment for a balanced budget will at least give some career politicians an excuse to make the correct hard choice. The excuse will be that now the Constitution says they must, so they can fall back on this. They will be able to tell their various pressure groups, "It's not my fault that I voted against this or that spending measure. I had to because of the balanced budget amendment." A true balanced budget amendment will prod some politicians to make the hard choices that they are unwilling to make without this restrictive measure.

It will take courage for a convention of states to place fiscal restraints on the federal government. These controls may create new challenges. Moreover, a balanced budget amendment by itself will not be near enough to save the nation from the cynical manipulations of a corrupted Congress. Its true value may be somewhat symbolic, but even a half measure to end the current financial folly is better than the current paralysis in the face of disaster.

TERM LIMITS ON CONGRESS

Another restraint on the federal government, limiting the years of service in the U.S. House and Senate, might have eliminated the need for a balanced budget amendment if this measure had been enacted two decades ago. By now a fresh group of citizen legislators in Congress would likely have addressed our nation's financial nightmare with responsible action. I well remember Congress's cynical attempts to propose term limits in my first year in the House (covered in chapter 1). Careerist leaders in Congress opposed self-imposed limitations as much then as they do now. No question, this cure for the disease of Washington's "politics as usual" will only happen through an amendments convention or the threat of one.

Ideas for term limits vary, with some proposing a maximum of six terms in the House and two terms in the Senate. Some proponents of term limits prefer a ceiling on total years of service in Congress, allowing more flexibility as to the years in either chamber. For example, an eighteen-year limit would allow three terms in the Senate, or nine terms in the House, or some combination thereof. Whatever plan is chosen at an amendments convention, lifetime congressional careers like that of Michigan's John Dingell (in the House from 1955 to 2015) would thankfully be relegated to an absurdity in the nation's past.

Conservative commentator George Will made a strong case for a term-limits amendment as far back as the early 1990s with his book *Restoration*. With his usual thoroughness, Will provided statistics and facts to bolster his work's thesis that "the fundamental ailment of American politics is not a function of partisanship—not any ideological difference between Democrats and Republicans. Rather, the problem is rooted in the nature of the contemporary political class regardless of party. That class exploits the modern state to make incumbency almost unassailable."[31]

This exploitation of the modern state that Will decries promotes Washington's irrational "culture of spending," often a result of government officials lobbying for bigger government. The author offers as evidence a 1990 academic study featuring witnesses who testified about federal programs at fourteen House and Senate hearings. Of the 1,060 witnesses who testified, 1,014 favored funding for these programs. Of these 1,014 who spoke for this spending, 63 percent were federal administrators and government officials—"government itself acting as an interest group."[32] This was more than a quarter century ago, when 70 percent of the country favored term limits on Congress—and when our national debt was about one-fifth of current levels.[33]

So why is the normal political process of "voting the rascals out" failing? The ballot box seemed to work well enough until the last forty years or so. The difference today resides in the size and scope of the federal government, which has ballooned over the last five decades. As Will described this new political playing field:

> Back then, there were many areas of life that government, especially the federal government, was at least hesitant about regulating, subsidizing, taxing or otherwise bringing under its sway. Today there are few such

areas. Now there are few limits to the areas in which legislators can operate to confer the favors that are the currency for purchasing perpetual incumbency. That currency has considerable purchasing power.[34]

This purchasing power has increased the average tenure of U.S. representatives from about four years in the first two Congresses of the twentieth century to ten years in the three most recent sessions. The Senate has seen similar careerism, steadily increasing from an average of fewer than five years in the 1880s to more than thirteen years in recent Congresses. Overall congressional tenure increases when representatives from the House gravitate to the Senate. Thus, dual careerism in Congress is at an all-time high, with 53 percent of current senators (2015–2017) having previously served in the House. Underscoring the purchasing power of incumbency, these political aristocrats have maneuvered to cling to their perquisites and power at a time when public approval of Congress is at record-setting lows.[35]

I believe one of the strongest—and most enlightening—arguments for term limits ever made was inadvertently given by Representative Debbie Wasserman Schultz in January 2016. Responding to criticism that her actions as Democratic National Committee chairwoman were self-serving, the Florida congresswoman offered this revealing nugget: "If I were only interested in advancing myself, I would only be a member of Congress, and I could focus on myself 100% of the time."[36] Sadly for America, that is how many of our national officials view their service in Washington.

My own years in Congress, where I term-limited myself, allow me to speak with more authority than most on this need to term-limit our national legislators. Yes, we will lose some experienced and unselfish representatives and senators, but not before they have had a chance to provide experienced service to our national government. Moreover, the national benefit of eliminating self-serving and corrupted officials will more than offset the loss of the few term-limited "virtuous" officials in Congress. In addition, the sanitizing effect of term limits may attract more principled leaders to Congress, many of whom may have declined to serve the nation in the past.

RESTRAINTS ON THE FEDERAL JUDICIARY

Fiscal restraints and term limits on Congress would go far to rebalance power in the federal government, but a limitation on the influence of federal judges would also help. Chapter 7 illustrates how the "discovered" interpretations of the Constitution by the courts led the nation down the slippery slope to an overreaching federal leviathan that limits liberty, stifles economic growth, and saps the American spirit.

In *Federalist* No. 78 Alexander Hamilton described the judiciary as the "least dangerous" branch of government, but that was long before the initial creeping and later galloping activism shown by the courts in the nineteenth and twentieth centuries. A fifteen-year term limit on federal judges, including those on the Supreme Court, would ensure a judiciary more in touch with reality and alleviate long-term philosophical bias.

Limiting the federal judiciary has been a sort of "third-rail issue" for constitutional reformers, but the politicized, overreaching court decisions—especially over the last few decades—have brought calls for better balance to this governmental institution. Professor Sabato boldly addressed these judicial transgressions and the need for reform in *A More Perfect Constitution*:

> Without the need for reappointment or review, [federal judges] are free to "evolve," changing philosophies to some degree and discarding the suit of clothes they wore to gain appointment. Without any effective checks, they can "discover" interpretations not found in the Constitution's text in order to validate their own personal and political choices. In mandating their own opinions in sweeping judgments that sometimes lack convincing legal foundations, they write themselves into the history books and curry favor with the media and academic elites—all the while ignoring original intent and casting off the wise restraints of prudence and caution.[37]

The appointment process of federal judges now appears more concerned with perpetuating big government—or trying to prevent it—than with interpreting foundational law. Who can argue with a straight face that recent appointments to the Supreme Court are not the long-term installation of a political view or cultural trend? It may be difficult to take the politics out of these appointments, but term limits would reduce the national burden of an activist jurist's personal bias and motivation for decades on end.

Well before his appointment to the Supreme Court in 2005, John Roberts argued for a fifteen-year limit on Supreme Court judges. The Framers "adopted life tenure at a time when people simply did not live as long as they do now," Roberts stated. "A judge insulated from the normal currents of life for 25 or 30 years was a rarity then but is becoming commonplace today. Setting a term of, say, 15 years would ensure that federal judges would not lose all touch with reality through decades of ivory tower existence."[38]

The lifetime tenure of Supreme Court justices and federal judges has become outmoded, and only an amendment to the Constitution will ameliorate this polarization of the judiciary along partisan and philosophical lines. A nonrenewable, fifteen-year term for all federal judges would help. This allows a long enough period for judges to utilize their accumulated wisdom and experience, but limits the time to evolve a different philosophy than the one held at his or her appointment.

Term limits on federal judges is certainly not the only idea being floated to restrain an overreaching federal judiciary. Some authorities have argued for an amendment to allow a congressional override of court decisions with a supermajority vote, thus removing some federal policies from court decisions and placing them in the political process. Obviously, careful deliberation is needed before this kind of change. Another consideration: the salutary effects of fiscal limits on the government and a less self-interested Congress may combine to provide the serendipitous effect of removing much of the politics and activism from the courts.

ROLLING BACK THE BLOATED BUREAUCRACY

The above three proposed restraints on the federal government would directly rebalance some of the institutions of the legislative and judicial branches of the federal government. The vast administrative state—an unofficial "fourth branch" of government—also sorely needs rebalancing. Technically a part of the executive branch, this jungle of bureaucracies and regulators must be suppressed. The administrative state mushroomed over the last forty years and now wields enormous unofficial and extraconstitutional power over the economy and society. As relentless as the kudzu scourge, these federal bureaucracies are probably immune to reform except by constitutional amendment.

The clumsy, heavy hand of government bureaucracy was spawned and nurtured partly by ambitious, overreaching presidents and partly by a pandering, irresponsible Congress. The national legislature acquiesced to this expansion of big government by ceding its legislative authority and neglecting its oversight of federal programs. The 440 federal agencies and their 1.4 million federal workers provide a constituency for elected officials in Washington and a government fiefdom unanswerable to the voters.[39]

Where to start restraining this leviathan? Two recent books by noted political commentators Philip K. Howard and Mark Levin point the way. In Howard's book, *The Rule of Nobody*, the author explains how government bureaucracy, federal regulation, and outmoded law not only gobble taxpayer dollars, but also contribute to broken government. "The same onerous process for passing a new law is required to amend or repeal old laws," he explained in a recent *Wall Street Journal* article, "with one additional hurdle: Existing programs are defended by armies of special interests. . . . That's why Congress can't get rid of New Deal agricultural subsidies, 75 years after the crisis ended."[40]

Howard calls for a constitutional amendment imposing a "sunset law" of ten to fifteen years on all laws that impact the budget. This amendment would provide Congress with the new structure and incentive to eliminate outmoded laws and programs. The amendment would require a private, independent review of old laws and regulations before reauthorization. "The political sensitivity of these programs is why a mandatory sunset is essential; it would prevent Congress from continuing to kick the can down the road," Howard argues.

Former Reagan administration attorney Mark Levin offers a similar but more stringent amendment to limit the federal bureaucracy, including a requirement that all federal agencies expire unless reauthorized every three years by a majority vote of Congress. The amendment, explained in his book *The Liberty Amendments*, would also require review and approval by a joint committee of Congress for any executive-branch regulation "exceeding an economic burden of $100 million."[41]

Levin's sunset law and executive limitation are meant not only to reduce the expensive, bloated administrative state currently centered in Washington. He promotes this amendment also as a means to stop the violation of the separation of powers, which stems from executive agencies usurping Congress's legislative authority and control of the public purse.

Sunset laws such as those advocated earlier would force Congress to do what it has been entrusted to do by the voters—provide oversight of federal programs and public funds. The teeming swamp of interest groups and constituencies in Washington sorely need this kind of restraint. The administrative state has outgrown its keepers. Privately, some in Congress probably welcome some kind of amendment that sunsets programs unless proved cost-effective. They know a gauntlet of pressure groups would never allow this kind of legislation to be enacted by Congress. Only *We the People* through our state legislators can effect this change.

WE THE PEOPLE CAN CHANGE WASHINGTON

For the past forty years or so, Washington has been changing America. It is time that Americans start changing Washington. Amendments for this change, as stated earlier in the chapter, are primarily about limiting the reach and power of the federal government. These amendments are constitutional measures to return more limited governance through a rebalancing of some of our governing institutions. This is not a rejection of our foundational laws; this is an embrace of these laws *as they were originally intended*. Our current dysfunction and division result from departing from the original constitution, with its core principles of limited government, free markets, and broad individual liberties.

The amendment proposals in this chapter are hardly a comprehensive listing of current ideas to rein in the federal government and safeguard America's future. Both Larry Sabato's and Mark Levin's books, cited earlier, provide more grist for this thought mill. Other, similar books are available, and many innovators in our state and national legislatures have even more ideas. Whatever proposed measures emerge from the marketplace of amendment ideas in the near future, most probably should and will be directed at rolling back our runaway federal government. Our current national debt and dysfunction obviates the need to rebalance our national governing institutions in ways to reduce Washington's debilitating effects.

While the needed amendments have much to do with directly limiting federal government, some of the indirect results of this may be as important. Dispersing the money and influence that is now centered in Washington can go far to improve the attitude and tone in the capital. So much of the rancor and partisanship in the federal government stems from the fight for money and power, and often has little to do with actual governance. Shrinking the political spoils system will enable Congress to better focus on governing for the betterment of the nation.

Many Americans believe our current dysfunction and national angst unique and shocking, but I believe the Framers would be unsurprised at our current state. They lived through one of the more tumultuous periods in the history of Western civilization. These uncommon men had a long perspective on government and a realistic view of human nature. The constitutional republic they founded may have been unique in history at the time, but the philosophy behind it drew on the "experience of the ages." The two millennia of history absorbed by the Founders gave them an insight into what lay ahead for a country of self-ruling people. They knew much about "times that try men's souls"[42] and governments of fallible men who do not always act in the people's best interest.

The Framers planned for answers to flawed government with Article V in the U.S. Constitution. This provided for changes in the nation's foundational laws in two ways: through federal officials in the nation's capital and through state officials closer to the people. The first method was undoubtedly preferred by the Framers. They knew, however, that the second method would likely become necessary. Their only surprise at our current unhappy condition would probably be that the states had not resorted to this second method before now.

As a check on powerful, ambitious leaders in the nation's capital, an Article V convention of states walks hand in hand with federalism. James Madison believed this concept of shared power between the states and the national government to be fundamental to his ingenious governing system of checks and balances. The Framers listened, debated, and eventually concurred. Convention-of-states amendments not only uphold and demonstrate federalist tenets. They also confirm the most fundamental principle of American republicanism: *We the People* as the source of all governmental power.

This book is largely about urging the people to exercise that power through their state representatives to mend their broken federal government. The people have both a constitutional means and natural right to do so. Several of the later chapters are meant to demystify this process of the states meeting in convention to act in the long-term interest of the people. That is how this constitutional republic came into being in 1787. This chapter was aimed at showing the inherent safety of the established procedures of the states' delegates meeting in convention to propose constitutional amendments. Of course, the final safety mechanism to this amendment process rests with the people themselves through the ratification process.

When our national representatives continually fail us, as a self-governing people we should embrace proposed changes in the Constitution through Article V convention amendments. As the closest representatives of the people in our federal system, state legislators should readily accept their responsibility to act in the best interests of the people. It takes courage from the legislatures, but failure to act in the face of national crisis would be a dereliction of these state representatives' duty—a duty not only to the citizens of their states but also to their fellow Americans nationwide.

I am optimistic that the state legislators will act. Many already have with their applications to Congress. The Great Experiment has come too far to unravel with only a whimper of uncertainty. I choose to believe Americans—of all colors, philosophies, and backgrounds—still mean to govern themselves. I hope and pray they truly do.

4

THE CURRENT QUEST FOR AN
ARTICLE V CONVENTION

It is clear that we must rely on the states to force Congress to act on our [balanced budget] amendment. Fortunately, our Nation's Founders gave us the means to amend the Constitution through action of state legislatures. . . . That is the only strategy that will work.

—RONALD REAGAN

THIS IS AMERICA!" on-air personality Rick Santelli shouted the morning of February 19, 2009, on CNBC's morning television program *Squawk Box.* "How many of you people want to pay for your neighbor's mortgage that has an extra bathroom and can't pay their bills? . . . President Obama, are you listening?"

Santelli continued his rant: "Cuba used to have mansions and a relatively decent economy. They moved from the individual to the collective. Now, they're driving '54 Chevys, maybe the last great car to come out of Detroit."[1]

The CNBC personality delivered his unscripted diatribe from

the floor of the Chicago Board of Trade as traders around Santelli applauded. The bemused host of *Squawk Box*, Joe Kernen, played along nervously, not sure where the show was headed.

"We're thinking of having a Chicago tea party in July," Santelli announced, still in full-rant mode. "All you capitalists that want to show up to Lake Michigan, I'm gonna start organizing." By that time the floor traders were cheering and whistling.

The seasoned CNBC personality had been angered by recent news of President Obama's $275 billion mortgage bailout for delinquent home-owners. The president planned to loosen restrictions on Fannie Mae and Freddie Mac and allow refinancing for many struggling with their mortgage payments. The homeowner bailout came on the heels of the nearly $1 trillion economic stimulus bill Obama had signed in February.

Santelli's fifteen minutes of fame went viral. His rant resonated with many Americans upset by the president's generosity with taxpayer money to help those whom many viewed as irresponsible homebuyers. The "tea party" that the CNBC personality called for in July happened well before summer. Carrying signs that read, "Stop Bankrupting America" and the like, thousands of Americans in Chicago and across the nation participated in tea party demonstrations on April 15, national tax day. Santelli's televised editorial tapped into a vein of anger and concern at the federal government's profligate spending. His call to action was answered by the roar of the nascent Tea Party movement.

A few scattered Tea Party events had occurred before the now-famous CNBC segment, but a deluge of protests followed. Disturbed at the enormous federal expenditures in 2008 and 2009 and the related spiraling national debt, Americans coalesced under the Tea Party banner. What began as a taxpayer revolt grew into a political movement. The Tea Party attracted primarily conservatives and Republicans angry at federal spending and growth.

The movement soon found a receptive audience in Florida. With no state income tax, Florida is a haven for retirees and those trying to limit tax liabilities. In 2010 the state elected a Tea Party favorite named

Marco Rubio to the U.S. Senate. Earlier that same year, Florida became the first state in twenty-seven years to apply to Congress for a balanced-budget convention. More states soon followed.

Although the Tea Party was not officially linked to the reenergized campaign for a balanced budget amendment, both movements found common purpose in a stiff pushback against government intrusion, overspending, and debt. Many became active in both causes. The first major campaign for an Article V convention in the twenty-first century was under way.

The Tea Party movement, which began in 2009, echoed loudly in the 2016 election of Donald Trump. The energy and determination of the same kind of working-class Americans voiced their anger both at Trump campaign rallies and at the ballot box.

In 2012, I publicly called the Tea Party movement one of the best things to happen in the nation. I defended those in the movement against charges of extremism and racism. Most of the intelligentsia failed to understand that Tea Party members were ordinary Americans fed up with the tax-and-spend mentality in Washington. Or maybe the media pundits understood all too well and cynically chose to portray angry taxpayers as a bunch of whackos. My "rumble" speech denouncing ear-marks from the Senate floor in October 2005 exactly described the Tea Party before it emerged nationally, and CBS News later reported that I had been called the "Godfather of the Tea Party."[2] Although I never formally declared myself a member, I took this label as a compliment.

After retiring from the Senate in December 2014, I began advising the Convention of States Project (COS) in their push to encourage state legislatures to petition for an amendments convention. By then a number of states had followed Florida's lead with an Article V petition to Congress. COS is now one of four major advocacy groups working with the states to propose amendments.

Much of the spirit and energy of the current-generation campaigns for an amendments convention share a common purpose with the convention drives from the 1960s through the 1980s—resistance to Washington's growing power and intrusiveness. Chapter 7 reviews how the courts laid the foundation for the expansion of government and its power through broad interpretations of the Constitution. Since the 1960s the nation has witnessed a large onslaught from a burgeoning central government and the resultant national unrest. The states' motivation to amend the Constitution stems largely from a desire to counter this trend toward bigger government. The 1960s drive centered on Washington's forced reapportionment of the states' legislative districts. The balanced budget amendment campaign emerged soon afterward, in the mid-1970s.

With continual resistance to federal growth and intrusion since the mid-1960s, little wonder the nation is now into its third major campaign for an amendments convention. This current drive is led by different groups with varying amendment goals. Each group, however, shares the common purpose of pushing back against federal power and dysfunction. I have become familiar with the players in the various amendment drives and their strategies to get thirty-four states to petition Congress. It is important to assess these campaigns and measure the nation's progress toward salutary constitutional change.

To evaluate the success or failure of the modern-era amendments campaigns and to determine the number of state filings now active, we need to establish some evaluative criteria. Cited often earlier in this book, legal scholar Robert Natelson may be unsurpassed in research and analysis of the origins of the Article V amendments convention. Thus, we will use two of his published opinions on the validity of state applications for a convention: (1) only applications that address a similar general topic aggregate toward the two-thirds requirement for a convention call, and (2) unrescinded applications do not grow "stale" with the passage of time.[3]

Using these criteria as of May 2016, we can classify forty-four state applications for an Article V convention that are (1) still active, (2) currently being promoted, and (3) agreeable with at least three other similar applications. These forty-four applications can be sorted by four general topics, and an identifiable group is promoting an amendment proposal for each. The subject matter of three of these four general topics overlaps, but following Natelson's opinion, applications with overlapping but varying subject matter are not aggregable.[4] Following is a review of the four advocacy groups, the amendment subject matter of each, and the status of each group's campaign.

THE BALANCED BUDGET AMENDMENT TASK FORCE

The current campaign for a balanced budget amendments convention is in many respects a continuation of the earlier effort from the 1970s and 1980s. Fifteen of the thirty-two states that petitioned Congress for a convention in that period had not rescinded their applications as of May 2016. When Florida applied in 2010, the primary advocacy group for a balanced budget amendment—the Balanced Budget Amendment Task Force (BBATF)—hailed this modern-era application as an addition to the petitions from the earlier campaign.[5] BBATF would no doubt be happy to have Congress propose a balanced budget amendment, but hopes for this have long faded. BBATF has focused efforts to achieve their goal through an amendments convention of the states for the single subject of balancing the federal budget.

The BBATF advocacy group was launched when Florida businessman and civic leader David Biddulph served as host for a 2008 conference in Florida. Original cofounders at this conference included National Taxpayers Union president Pete Sepp, economics professor Barry W. Poulson, and West Virginian Scott Rogers, who would serve as BBATF executive director. The group soon combined efforts with Florida economic-policy adviser Bill Fruth, who was advocating for an amendments convention with his book, *10 Amendments for Freedom*.[6]

BBATF has become a collection of national organizations, state groups, and individual advocates, all united by their common goal of a balanced budget amendment to the Constitution. The group claims ties with fiscal conservatives back to the 1950s, when conservative state legislators began discussion on a balanced budget convention. The BBATF primarily blames runaway-convention fearmongering by Democratic Speaker of the House Tip O'Neill in the 1980s for the failure of the Carter–Reagan-era drive for a convention. The group similarly faults the John Birch Society's scare tactics for later rescissions by more than a dozen states.[7]

Three affiliated organizations provide key support to BBATF's efforts. The National Federation of Independent Business (NFIB) has helped with its lobbying efforts with state legislatures. Ninety percent of the business organization's three hundred thousand members are in favor of a balanced budget amendment. The American Legislative Exchange Council (ALEC) has provided a forum for state legislators to share ideas and discuss strategies for a balanced budget amendment. Conservative legislators and private-sector representatives gather at the annual ALEC meetings to discuss a range of ideas and legislative initiatives. The Heartland Institute, a conservative public-policy group based in Chicago, uses its considerable influence to aid BBATF's work.[8] Several other affiliated grassroots groups provide a solid ground game.

BBATF's modern campaign for a balanced budget convention has had a string of successes since the application by Florida in 2010. Alabama followed with an application in 2011, reversing its earlier rescission of 1988. New Hampshire followed in 2012, just two years after it had rescinded its application from the late 1970s. No states applied for a balanced budget convention in 2013, but five states in 2014 made this a banner year for BBATF efforts. Two of these states, Michigan and Ohio, were new converts. Neither had been part of the thirty-two applications from the Carter–Reagan years. The other three applicants that year—Georgia, Louisiana, and Tennessee—reversed their earlier rescissions.

The year 2015 brought three more states back into the fold following their rescissions from more than a decade earlier. North Dakota's, South Dakota's, and Utah's petitions stated their intention that these applications be aggregated with the other states' applications for a balanced budget amendment. This continued the trend of "intended aggregation" stated in several earlier petitions. The 2015 applications also clearly limited their subject matter to that of balancing the federal budget.[9] This brought the overall total at year-end to twenty-seven state applications with specific wording for a balanced budget convention.

Going into 2016, the BBATF resolution was active in Massachusetts, Oklahoma, and South Carolina. Early in the year, the group's proposal was introduced in five new states: Arizona, Kentucky, Virginia, West Virginia, and Wyoming. The West Virginia legislature approved a petition in mid-March followed by Oklahoma in late April. Several other likely states failed to approve. Some of these states carried over into 2017. Following Delaware's unsurprising rescission in spring, the official count for BBATF topped out at twenty-eight states by May 2016.[10]

Although BBATF is an ally against government growth, I have a couple of key concerns about their campaign. First off, many of these state applications for a balanced budget amendment use dissimilar wording and may face considerable legal challenges. Even if this campaign reaches the required thirty-four applications, time-consuming legal actions may grind on for years with an undetermined outcome.

More problematic, a balanced budget amendment alone will not solve our nation's considerable difficulties. It may send a symbolic message that fiscal responsibility matters, but Congress—trust my sixteen years of experience here—would find numerous ways to weasel out of spending limits. Even the states currently with balanced budget amendments cheat. No question, Washington would be the biggest cheater of all. Moreover, passing a balanced budget amendment fails to address the need to limit an overreaching administrative state that interferes in our lives and limits our freedoms. It also does nothing to limit judicial activism, which is a major problem in the loss of our freedoms.

THE CONVENTION OF STATES PROJECT

Begun in 2013 under the aegis of Citizens for Self-Governance (CSG), the Convention of States Project (COS) was conceived by constitutional lawyer Michael Farris and former Tea Party leader Mark Meckler. Farris is the president of Patrick Henry College in Virginia, and Meckler is a California attorney and founder of CSG. Although alarmed by federal profligacy and allied with BBATF, COS believes the problem with the federal government exceeds mere spending and debt. Thus, the COS resolution advocates for a multi-subject amendments convention "to impose fiscal restraints on the federal government, limit the power and jurisdiction of the federal government, and limit the terms of office of its officials."[11]

As threatening as the nation's fiscal problems are, my years in Congress have convinced me that the problems in Washington go beyond spending and debt. Probably about 40 percent of Washington's dysfunction could be fixed with a balanced budget amendment, but that still leaves the nation with sizable concerns—a careerist mentality in Congress and extraconstitutional federal authority. After leaving Congress I put my support behind COS as an adviser.

Organized on a grassroots strategy, COS targeted forty state legislatures and recruited district captains for each of the approximately three thousand house districts in these forty states. Each district captain is tasked with recruiting one hundred volunteers in his or her respective district. The district volunteers serve as lobbyists at state legislative committee hearings and rally support for the COS resolution. The Citizens for Self-Governance organization provides funding for COS, and the group's half million or so supporters give COS a potent force at the local and national level.[12]

COS hit the ground running in 2014, introducing its resolution in fifteen of its targeted states. Its interactive website and educational events went far to promote the entire Article V convention movement nationwide. Also promoting both the Article V movement and COS in particular was the endorsement of radio talk-show host Mark Levin, whose book *The Liberty Amendments* received widespread attention in 2014. Georgia became the first state in the nation to adopt the COS resolution that year. Alaska and Florida soon followed. With the approval of their COS resolutions, all three states had both multiple-subject and single-subject (balanced budget amendment) applications in Congress. Just as important as garnering these three state applications, the group fleshed out its grassroots organizations in all fifty states.[13]

In 2015, Alabama passed the COS resolution, and the COS application was filed in an additional twenty-one states. Nineteen of thirty-six states passed the resolution in initial committee votes. Three senate chambers and eight house chambers passed the resolution on a floor vote.[14]

Going into 2016, the COS resolution was active in sixteen state legislatures. By mid-March the COS resolution had passed in Tennessee and Indiana, and Oklahoma and Louisiana brought the total to eight states by late May. The measure was active in about two dozen other states. It should be noted that six of the states that had passed the COS resolution by spring 2016 also had a balanced budget amendment application in Congress.[15]

By the end of the regular 2016 legislative sessions, the COS resolution had been passed by eighteen state houses and eleven state senates. Making use of their extensive grassroots network, the group secured petitions in June 2016 for 100 percent of the state house districts across the nation, with these petitions to be delivered to the respective state legislators. Building on its strong grassroots efforts in the states and its impressive progress in 2016, COS anticipated even more success in 2017.

WOLF PAC—FREE AND FAIR ELECTIONS

Started in 2011 by progressive political activist and Internet talk show host Cenk Uygur, Wolf-PAC, which fights for "Free & Fair Elections" according to its website,[16] advocates for an amendment convention to overturn the Supreme Court's campaign finance decision in *Citizens United v. FEC* protecting corporate contributions. I am not a supporter of the Wolf-PAC drive, but the group's efforts should be noted as part of the overall national amendments campaign. The group makes heavy use of the Internet, including progress updates through Uygur's online talk show, *The Young Turks*.[17]

Decrying the money in U.S. political campaigns, Wolf-PAC has a strategy to "fight fire with fire" by asking donors to sign on to a ten-dollar-per-month pledge. The group organizes volunteers in legislative districts throughout the states. These grassroots volunteers lobby legislators to support the Free and Fair Elections amendments resolution. The exact wording for this resolution remained elusive by early 2017, but its purpose was to "take away the massive influence that money has over our political process."[18]

Over the last several years, the group has persuaded four states to back their cause with applications for convention—Vermont, California, Illinois, and New Jersey. To garner the required thirty-four state applications, Wolf-PAC will have to appeal to some of the more conservative state legislatures, which now hold sway in a majority of states. The group's leadership seems disinclined to lobby support for their amendments drive from conservative Republican states, so their chances for success appear remote.[19]

Wolf-PAC started 2016 with its resolution active in eight states. By mid-May the resolution was active in eleven states but had added no new applications.[20]

Again, I do not support Wolf-PAC's proposed amendment because I believe Wolf-PAC is taking the wrong approach by trying to overturn the *Citizens United* decision. If successful, they would return a regulatory approach to controlling corporate political contributions. Complete transparency of political contributions works much better, as Virginia's campaign finance laws have proved over the years. In Virginia political donors can give as much as they want, but everyone knows what they give. The state's elections have avoided much of the dirty politics associated with states that attempt to limit donations.

Regarding Wolf-PAC supporters, I do find it noteworthy to mention the four states applying for the Free and Fair Elections amendment. None of the states behind this proposal have ever supported a balanced budget amendment to control the reckless spending of the federal government. Indeed, the California Legislature held hearings in 1979 to discredit the balanced budget amendment convention and to disavow the process as uncontrollable. It will be interesting to see if these four states suddenly join the "runaway convention" club if thirty-four states file applications to balance the budget, term-limit Congress, or rein in Washington.

COMPACT FOR AMERICA

The rather complex strategy of the Compact for America supporters involves the combining of four state legislative acts into one, producing a simultaneous application for a balanced budget convention and ratification of the amendment. The group hopes to gain support by eliminating concerns over the fabled runaway convention. This "all-in-one" strategy was designed largely by Nick Dranias, former general counsel and constitutional policy director for the Goldwater Institute, a conservative think tank based in Phoenix, Arizona. Dranias began working full-time for the Compact for America Educational Fund, Inc. in fall 2014.[21]

The Compact approach is called a hybrid Article V convention movement, as it involves two pieces of legislation. The first is a state legislative bill for a convention application for a balanced budget amendment with the wording of the proposed amendment in the petition to Congress. The bill also appoints the governor of the applying state as a delegate to the convention and adopts the rules of the assembly, precluding deviation from an up-or-down vote on the amendment proposal. At the same time the bill's approval ratifies in advance the balanced budget amendment proposal anticipated from Congress. The second piece of legislation is through a resolution by Congress approving the thirty-eight states' mechanism for proposing amendments, calling the convention, and referring the proposed amendment to the states for ratification—which was preapproved in their applications. Lots of moving parts here.[22]

Due to the complexity of its approach, the Compact has spent much of its efforts on educating state legislatures. This measured approach might bring rewards in the long run. Four of the targeted sixteen states have passed bills supporting the Compact: Arkansas, Georgia,

Mississippi, and North Dakota. It was active in only four other states by May 2016. With its assumption of unauthorized powers, the Compact strategy probably faces legal challenges. Additionally, the Constitution does not allow a compact without approval by Congress.[23]

Despite these challenges, it has received support from syndicated columnist George Will and judicial analyst Judge Andrew Napolitano.[24] I wish the best for the Compact but harbor doubts about this "all-in-one" strategy. My concerns stem from some of the analyses by renowned Article V authority Robert Natelson, cited previously. Natelson believes that the Compact approach overstates the powers of the states to control the process of an amendment proposal through a convention:

> The Founding-Era records may be ambiguous, but there is no ambiguity in the courts' position. Federal and state tribunals—including the Supreme Court—have ruled repeatedly and uniformly that the amendment authority exercised by legislatures and conventions comes from Article V, not from the states' reserved powers [under the Tenth Amendment]. Further courts have ruled almost as uniformly that trying to use state law to control the process, or aspects of the process, in advance is unconstitutional.[25]

Natelson cites the 1995 Supreme Court decision *U.S. Term Limits v. Thornton* as a more recent example of court rulings unfavorable to the Compact approach. The 1995 case determined that powers the states did not have before the Constitution cannot be "reserved" to the states by the Tenth Amendment. Clearly, the states' powers to make a "binding application" to Congress for an amendments convention could not have existed before the existence of both the Constitution and Congress. I readily admit my Natelsonian leanings regarding the legal nuances of the Article V amendments process, as few, if any, legal scholars have the former law professor's credibility on this subject. Thus, I share his concerns that if the courts strike down the Compact approach, the entire Article V movement could be harmed.[26]

But a more definitive reason why the Compact approach is probably doomed lies in its requirement that Congress approve this proposing mechanism. The entire process for an amendments convention is necessitated by congressional recalcitrance. It's a way of bypassing a Congress that opposes these constitutional changes. If Congress opposes a balanced budget amendment—which they repeatedly have—they will never approve the Compact mechanism.

In summary of the advocacy groups named in this chapter (more information on each can be found in appendix 2 on page 203), the Balanced Budget Amendment Task Force may be closest to reaching an amendments convention, but related campaigns to stop federal overreach show promise. Those of us who support the Convention of States campaign welcome a balanced budget amendment (one of the COS goals) but also believe that the extensive problems with the federal government require more changes to fundamental law to rebalance government institutions. Finally, the Compact for America could prove problematic for the Article V movement. Success by the Compact in the legislatures could lead to failure in the courts, I believe, and bring discredit to the other campaigns' efforts to rein in the federal government.

INFORMATION SOURCES ABOUT AN ARTICLE V CONVENTION

Greatly aiding the modern amendment campaigns, the Internet has provided ready access to information about an Article V amendment convention. Advocacy and educational groups have established numerous websites with articles, records, and facts. This has also served the various legislative groups in their coordination and planning for such an event. Appendix 3 on page 205 lists and provides website addresses for a number of key information sites. Some of these are reviewed in the paragraphs that follow. Much of the information on these websites is in portable document format (PDF) and can be downloaded and stored.

Advocates of an Article V convention owe a debt of gratitude to the Friends of the Article V Convention (FOAVC)—one of the first groups to establish an online reference resource about Article V and the various convention campaigns. Bill Walker, the public face of

FOAVC, maintains that enough states have already applied to warrant a convention call by Congress. Walker filed federal lawsuits in 2000 and 2004 to force Congress to act, but the merits of the cases have not been resolved. Judge Thomas E. Brennan, former chief justice of the Michigan Supreme Court, also played a key role in FOAVC's development. Brennan has advocated for an Article V convention since 1982 and recently authored *The Article V Amendatory Constitutional Convention*, a book advocating and explaining the uses of an Article V amendments convention. The FOAVC is non-partisan and supports no specific amendment.[27]

Another excellent resource for Article V researchers and enthusiasts is the Article V Library—an online source of documentation related to Article V applications. Started and maintained by South Carolinian Robert Biggerstaff, this sizable repository of Article V information was meant to provide what Congress failed to disclose over the more than two centuries of state applications since 1789. The information on the site is searchable, making this reference source even more useful to researchers.

Perhaps embarrassed into action by the Article V Library, Congress finally abandoned its secretive way of recording (or failing to record) Article V applications by the states. Sponsored by U.S. Representative Steve Stivers of Ohio, an amendment to House Rules passed on a floor vote in January 2015, making available to the public Article V filings by the states. The rule change assigned the U.S. House Clerk's Office the responsibility of posting these applications on the clerk's official website. Scans of these original documents are organized by subject, state of origin, and year of receipt. The rule change also created a process for the official receipt of these petitions through the chairman of the House Judiciary Committee. By late March 2016, the site listed twenty-four state filings from 2012 through 2016. It did not include the applications for a balanced budget amendment from the 1970s and 1980s, which many authorities on Article V maintain still to be valid.[28]

A project of the nonpartisan Independence Institute in Denver, the Article V Information Center provides a bounty of articles, online research, and legal analysis by Robert Natelson, the preeminent Article V legal researcher. Few authorities come close to Natelson's heroic efforts to shed light on the Article V process and to debunk the myth of the inevitable "runaway convention" at an amendments conclave. Beginning in 2010, the retired law professor began publishing groundbreaking legal research on the Article V amendment convention. He continues to add to his already voluminous repository of useful articles and vital scholarship as the director of the Article V Information Center. Natelson's considerable store of work is easily accessed and downloaded as PDF files from the center's website.[29]

The websites of three of the leading advocacy groups for an amendments convention also provide a trove of videos, articles, research, and more. The longer established of these is the Balanced Budget Amendments Task Force site, but the Convention of States Project and Compact for America sites have caught up quickly. I admit my bias for favoring the Convention of States site over the other two. The interactivity of my affiliated group's site facilitates easy communication between site visitors and COS staff members.

A number of the legislative groups (discussed momentarily) planning for an Article V convention also sponsor websites with useful information. The State Legislators Article V Caucus website posts a monthly newsletter of current news related to an amendments convention, along with useful links to other sources. The Assembly of State Legislators' websites includes their important work on defining the rules and procedures for a convention of states. The COS Caucus website has several videos related to legislature debates and floor speeches related to Article V applications.

One of the most useful sources of information about the efforts and progress of the groups advocating for an Article V convention is the work of Georgia attorney David Guldenschuh. His monthly progress report (sometimes twice monthly), which began in 2015, evaluates the successes and failures of the advocacy groups' efforts through the committees and chambers of the state legislatures. This ingeniously simple, one-page report provides an invaluable snapshot of the Article V campaigns in the nation. It is available as a clickable link and PDF on the home page of the website for the State Legislators Article V Caucus. Or, the report can be received via e-mail on a regular basis by contacting David Guldenschuh at dfg@guldenschuhlaw.com and requesting to join his mailing list. (See appendix 4 on page 207)

The preceding summary of information sources related to an Article V convention is not intended to be definitive. Other sources exist and new ones are added regularly. This is nonetheless a solid start for researchers, convention advocates, legislators, and anyone interested in the Article V convention and efforts to promote one. These information sources provide a better understanding of the Article V convention movement and should greatly aid cooperation and coordination among the various advocacy and legislature groups.

STATE LEGISLATURES' PREPARATIONS FOR A CONVENTION

State legislators have organized several national organizations to promote and plan for an Article V convention. Each of these organizations has a different focus, and some legislators have membership in more than one. With the growth of these groups over the last several years, newer ones may be active by the time this book is published.

Workshops and training seminars by the American Legislative Exchange Council (ALEC) greatly promoted the formation of Article V–oriented groups of legislators. ALEC is a nonprofit organization that supports federalism, limited government, and free-market enterprise. Providing a forum for legislators to discuss and plan model legislation to support conservative principles, ALEC was a natural rally point for legislators interested in an amendments convention to stop government overreach.

Soon after the annual ALEC meeting in December 2013 in Chicago, the State Legislators Article V Caucus was formed. The Article V Caucus's stated purpose was "to re-establish federalism as our Founders intended, and limit the runaway growth of the Federal Government."

The group's founding members were all Republicans. The caucus views an amendments convention as the surest pathway to their goal. By early 2016 the group claimed membership of more than ninety state legislators in thirty-two states.[30]

The Assembly of State Legislatures (ASL) formed about the same time as the Article V Caucus. The ASL considers itself a bipartisan group of state legislators that promotes cooperation among the states to solve national problems. Oklahoma legislators Gary Banz and Senator Rob Standridge, both personal friends of mine, have been active with the group since its beginning. Banz serves on the executive committee, and Standridge has attended all their meetings. At their initial gathering in December 2013, more than one hundred legislators met at Mount Vernon in Virginia to plan for an Article V convention. A committee was assigned the task of drafting model rules for an amendments convention. If a convention becomes imminent, the committee is also to coordinate action with Congress and plan for the gathering's administration.

The ASL met twice in 2014, at Indianapolis in June and outside Washington, D.C., in December. The group met in Salt Lake City in November 2015 to draft a set of model rules for a convention and in June 2016 to make final edits to their proposed convention rules. Despite a heavily conservative membership, the group has steadfastly maintained a bipartisan approach. Three Democratic legislators sit on the ASL executive committee, and the group has maintained its independence from advocacy groups.[31]

During the annual ALEC meeting in San Diego in July 2015, a group of legislators organized to plan for an amendments convention. The Federal Assembly of State Presiding Officers formed to promote a "one state/one vote/one amendment" policy for an amendments convention. Coordinating with the Balanced Budget Amendment Task Force, the assembly has invited the senate president and house speaker from each state to go on record in favor of this policy.[32]

Further attempting to settle some of the procedures at an amendments convention, by early 2016 seven states had adopted "faithful delegate" legislation to limit their future representatives' authority. This action is meant to address "runaway convention" concerns. Professor Natelson might argue that this is an unnecessary precaution, as actions by delegates outside their commissioned authority would be invalid and nonbinding. Nonetheless, these steps by the legislatures underscore their efforts to ease concerns.

A summary listing of these groups of legislators and their website addresses can be found in appendix 5 on page 208.

THE KEY TO CONVENTION: ADVOCACY-GROUP/ LEGISLATURE COOPERATION

As stated in the previous chapter, public resentment of federal overreach has been widespread since the late 1960s, producing several campaigns for an amendments convention over the last several decades of the twentieth century. Since 2010 we have seen the emergence of not one but several simultaneous amendments campaigns to limit the central government. As the 2016 presidential primary races demonstrated, the level of public dissatisfaction with dysfunctional federal government and establishment politicians continues to grow.

Perhaps foremost, the Article V movement needs to show the nation that a convention of states can meet, stay on task, and go home—all while adhering to a policy of one vote per state for one amendment. With the achievement of this landmark event in American democracy, all the scaremongers and naysayers are suddenly silenced. A new era of revived federalism and self-governance begins. If more changes are needed to rebalance the institutions of government, *We the People*— acting through our state legislators—can then stand on a strong precedent to overcome resistance to another convention of states.

In May 2014 while debating Andy Schlafly of Eagle Forum, Convention of States co-founder Michael Farris made this same point. While Schlafly argued for winning supermajorities in Congress to pass laws to limit the government, Farris advocated for the more efficient approach through Article V and underscored the benefits of getting an initial amendment convention successfully concluded. "The best thing we can possibly do is to validate this [convention] process on something the American public is united behind," Farris stated. "People want to fix the fiscal problems, and then we can come right back after it. Once we validate this process, we can use it again to fix [other problems]."[33]

The ultimate goals for the COS are "to impose fiscal restraints on the federal government, limit the power and jurisdiction of the federal government, and limit the terms of office of its officials." A severability-aggregation provision in the COS resolution ensures that the topic of "fiscal restraints on the federal government" aggregates with the BBATF's resolution to impose fiscal restraints through a balanced budget amendment. Similar to the resolutions passed by Georgia and Oklahoma, wording for the COS resolution like the following ensures this aggregation:

> BE IT FURTHER RESOLVED that this application shall be deemed an application for a convention to address each or all of the subjects herein stated. For the purposes of determining whether two-thirds of the states have applied for a convention addressing any of the subjects stated herein, this application is to be aggregated separately with the applications of any other state legislatures for the single subjects of balancing the federal budget and/or imposing other fiscal restraints on the federal government, limiting the power and jurisdiction of the federal government, or limiting the terms of federal officials.[34]

My home state of Oklahoma is a good example of a successful result from cooperation between advocacy groups and the legislature combined with a strong educational campaign. The state is also a prime example of how even a conservative state can be adversely affected by fearmongering from groups such as the John Birch Society and Eagle Forum. Renewed efforts for an amendments convention began in the Oklahoma Legislature around 2010, led in the state senate by Josh Brecheen and in the house by Gary Banz. Rob Standridge later became the standard-bearer in the upper chamber. While the state ranked high among those pushing back against federal overreach, the lack of information about an Article V convention worked to the advantage of those who spread fear about potential abuses to the Constitution. Understandably, it was easier for a busy state legislator to vote against a convention resolution in the midst of uncertainty.

A strong campaign to educate both the public and the state legislators in Oklahoma paved the way to ultimate success. I concentrated on the legislators, speaking to them in groups and often one-on-one. Banz and Standridge worked tirelessly to educate their fellow legislators and the public in general on the need for restraints on the federal government and the process of an Article V convention of states. These efforts were coordinated with leaders from the Balanced Budget Amendments Task Force and the Convention of States Project.

Standridge said he believed the corner was turned in 2015 "when we really built a strong foundation of knowledge about an amendments convention." Much of this foundation was laid in numerous debates and talks across the state. "You can't be afraid to debate opponents in the lion's den," Standridge advised. "I pounded home the point that only an amendments convention can work to fix Washington, and of course I had to slay a lot of dragons—hollow fears of an uncontrollable convention."[35]

Officials from BBATF and COS spoke to various groups in Oklahoma and even debated representatives from the Birch Society and Eagle Forum. COS leader Michael Farris's 2015 visit to the state to join Standridge in a debate with noted opponents of an amendments convention greatly helped to better educate many, Standridge recalled. "If a few key advocates will canvas the state and debate anyone, anytime, it will get results," the state senator said. "They don't need to make it vitriolic. The facts are on the side of those supporting an amendments convention."[36] Educating the public is obviously a key to success.

WHY AN ARTICLE V CONVENTION APPEARS IMMINENT

After failed attempts at an Article V convention over the last two-hundred-plus years, many doubt that current efforts by state legislators will fare better. One of the more authoritative doubters is Judge Thomas Brennan, who helped establish the Friends of the Article V Convention website. Not that Judge Brennan would be unhappy to see an amendments convention. He vaulted to national prominence as an Article V–convention proponent in 1982 with his groundbreaking journal article "Return to Philadelphia: A Case for Calling of an Amendatory Convention under Article 5 of the Federal Constitution."[37]

Yet after decades of advocacy and disappointment, sadly, Judge Brennan lost faith in our state legislators. Frustrated, he established Convention USA, an organization promoting an amendments convention of citizens acting outside their state legislatures—and outside the authority of Article V, most would contend. Convention USA advocates amendments to stop governmental overreach and rebalance power between Washington and the states. I applaud Judge Brennan and Convention USA's advocacy for these constitutional changes. Yet I disagree with this esteemed jurist's pessimism regarding our state legislatures. From my view, the outlook has never been better for an Article V convention, possibly within the next several years.

Improving this outlook, first off, is the peak level of dissatisfaction with the federal government and nationwide contempt for congressional cronyism and careerism. Again, the 2016 presidential election clearly demonstrated this. Public disdain for establishment politicians and irresponsible government has energized many Americans. This record dissatisfaction comes after public polls for fiscal restraints and term limits on Congress have remained as high as 85 percent since the 1980s.

The Article V convention drive in the 1970s and 1980s had only one primary advocacy group, the National Taxpayers Union, which pushed solely for a balanced budget amendment. Energized by the heightened public outrage, multiple advocacy and legislature groups are now actively pursuing an amendments convention. These groups are backing several different amendments proposals, all with a common goal of stopping big government and curbing corruption in Washington. These multiple efforts reflect the public's surging support for an Article V convention.

A second trend working in favor of an amendments convention is the gnawing fear of an economic meltdown in America. The push to balance the federal budget in the 1970s and 1980s may have been as much about limiting federal growth and power as it was about fiscal restraint. These goals still have strong support, but the staggering national debt has injected a new urgency into the call for fiscal restraint. The fiscal crisis is painfully real and magnifies the outcry for responsible governance—a reform that a corrupted, career-oriented Congress shows no sign of providing. New attempts by Congress to derail an impending balanced budget convention—like the Gramm–Rudman–Hollings Balanced Budget Act of 1985—will not fool the public this time around.

A third development aiding an amendments convention is the communications revolution wrought by the Internet. With the advocacy-group websites and e-mail now pervasive in our interconnected world, campaigns can be much more easily coordinated than in the past. These technological innovations provide a needed cohesion to counter the geographic dispersion of the legislatures and advocacy groups. It is a tribute to past legislators and advocates—who networked without modern communication technology—that the three major campaigns of the last century battled to within one or two states of forcing a convention call by Congress. The Internet and e-mail provide current advocates with a great advantage.

Another key development is seen in the growth of more conservative legislatures—partly a reflection of dissatisfaction with federal overreach at the expense of state government. These conservative gains at the state level represent a move toward fiscal and social conservatism and away from the fiscal profligacy and social turmoil seen over the last decade. After the November 2016 elections, the Republicans held the governorship and both houses of the legislature in twenty-five states, in contrast to only six of these "trifectas" by the Democratic Party. The Republicans controlled sixty-eight of the ninety-nine chambers of the state legislators. The Democrats held only thirty-one. Plus, thirty-three of the state governors will be Republicans in 2017.[38]

The Article V convention movement is not the exclusive domain of Republicans, but much of the movement against government growth is. Hence, we see the continuing gains made by the Republican Party in the states. This bodes well for the current amendment drives to restrain the federal government.

Finally, the exorcism of the "runaway convention" demon by legal scholars such as Robert Natelson now allows an intellectually honest discussion about a convention of states. Fearmongering by amendment opponents played a crucial role in the defeat of the last two nearly successful convention campaigns. Deployment of these dishonest tactics can now be rebutted by factual information, thanks to Professor Natelson and several others.

As difficult as the final leg of the journey to an Article V convention may be, I maintain that Judge Brennan's assessment of the state legislators is unduly pessimistic. As mentioned in this chapter, a number of positive developments are pointing toward reaching the thirty-four-state goal. Thus, while I disagree with the good judge's gloomy assessment of our state legislators, I heartily concur with the importance he assigns to the campaign for a convention of states in his well-reasoned 2014 book, *The Article V Amendatory Constitutional Convention: Keeping the Republic in the Twenty-First Century.* "And yet [a convention] is an adventure of the heart for those who love the United States of America and revere her unique place in the history of human civilization," eighty-four-year-old Brennan wrote: "It may just be our last chance to save the Republic."[39]

Take heart, noble judge. We may yet see it.

5

ARTICLE V: THE FOUNDERS' GIFT TO THE PEOPLE

If in the opinion of the people the distribution or modification of the constitutional powers be in any particular wrong, let it be corrected by an amendment in the way which the Constitution designates.

— GEORGE WASHINGTON

ALTHOUGH HER TWELVE SISTER STATES had ratified the new U.S. Constitution by the end of 1789, the small state of Rhode Island and Providence Plantations refrained from joining the new national government. The state's resistance to national authority traced back to 1782, when the Rhode Island Assembly rejected a proposed amendment to the Articles of Confederation granting Congress the power to collect a 5 percent duty on imports. With an economy dependent on sea commerce, the state balked at this anti-trade policy.

Moreover, leaders argued, the burden of direct taxation to support state government would necessarily increase if import duties were surrendered to Congress. Rhode Island's sole rejection led to the amendment's failure, as unanimous approval of amendments by the states was required to change any of the Articles of Confederation.

By early 1790, contemporaries in surrounding states attributed the New England state's reluctance to join the Union as a scheme by "Rogue Island" debtors to defraud creditors. Financial matters concerned Rhode Island leaders, but their failure to ratify the Constitution involved more than private debts. Loss of state sovereignty threatened these men.

Pressure to ratify the Constitution continued to build inside and outside the state. Convening in the U.S. capital in New York City, the new Congress threatened to treat Rhode Island as a foreign government, which would entail a duty on the state's goods. The Rhode Island Assembly finally voted to hold a ratification convention in March 1790 in South Kingston.[1]

Tedious debate began among the sixty or so members of the convention on March 1. Many were upset that slavery would be allowed by the new federal government. Fearful as much of what was in the Constitution as what had been left out, the delegates agreed to discuss issues with parts of the text during deliberations. As the various articles in the document were read aloud, Revolutionary War hero William Barton interrupted after Article V of the Constitution was heard. He told his colleagues they were "altogether going one side" by focusing only on the negative.

"This clause," said Barton of Article V, "ought to be written in letters of gold. We ought to observe the excellencies of the Constitution. There is a fair opportunity furnished *for amendments provided by the states.*"[2]

Not all present were as sanguine as Barton. State Anti-Federalists insisted on twelve amendments to the new Constitution as a condition of ratification. The convention approved the addition of these protections of state and individual rights. Still unwilling to risk a vote for ratification, the Anti-Federalists managed to avoid the issue by parliamentary maneuver. The convention adjourned with plans to meet again on May 24 in Newport.

By the time the delegates reconvened in Newport, the town of Providence had seceded from the state with an ultimatum: ratify the Constitution without the required amendments or the major seaport would not rejoin the state. The delegates approved the new framework by a narrow two-vote margin on May 29.[3]

Meeting the requirement of Providence, the convention listed no constitutional amendments as a condition for ratification. The wary delegates did, however, attach some twenty-one suggested amendments to their ratification proclamation before its delivery to the new government in New York City. In this proclamation they appealed to future Rhode Island congressional representatives to "exert all their influence, and use all reasonable means" to have these amendments added to the Constitution.

The leaders of this smallest and most vulnerable of the thirteen states placed at the top of this list their most fervently desired amendment. It read: "The United States shall guarantee to each State its sovereignty, freedom and independence, and every power, jurisdiction and right, which is not by this constitution expressly delegated to the United States."[4]

Having served sixteen years in Congress, I now look back at many of those first citizens of the fledgling United States with the utmost respect. The ratification of the new Constitution occurred amid the pride of hard-won independence and satisfaction in the establishment of a new republic. Yet even in those intoxicating times of new nationalism, the leaders of Rhode Island showed a sober presence of mind. Their concern over forfeiture of some of their state's rights and of potential oppression by the new federal government was well justified, as clearly shown by the turn of events two centuries later.

The proposed amendment at the top of their list underscored their fears of a powerful central administration in the nation's capital. The wording would place a crucial limitation on the new federal government, reserving "every power, jurisdiction and right" to the thirteen states that the Constitution did not "expressly" delegate to the higher state. As men of trade and commerce in the smallest of the states, these leaders had an innate and ultimately prescient sense of how the larger federal government might override and diminish the weaker individual state governments.

This proposed amendment bears a striking similarity to the Tenth Amendment to the Constitution, adopted late in 1791 as part of the Bill of Rights demanded by many during the ratification process. The Tenth Amendment, of course, reserves all powers to the several states or to the people except those the Constitution delegates to the federal government or prohibits to the states. The Rhode Island ratifiers of the Constitution would be dismayed and doubtless outraged at how weak this limitation on federal power would prove during much of the twentieth century and afterward.

Yet just as striking to me as these ratifiers' concerns over a dominating central government was Col. William Barton's joy and relief at the recognition of Article V's protection to the states and the people. As his fellow Rhode Islanders expressed grave concern over the powers granted in the Constitution to this new federal government, Barton rejoiced in the safety feature of Article V, the key parts that read:

> The Congress, whenever two-thirds of both Houses shall deem it necessary, shall propose Amendments to this Constitution, or, *on the application of the Legislatures of two thirds of the several States, shall call a Convention for proposing Amendments,* [emphasis added] which, in either Case, shall be valid to all Intents and Purposes, as Part of this Constitution, when ratified by the Legislatures of three fourths of the several States, or by Conventions in three fourths thereof, as one of the other Mode of Ratification may be proposed by the Congress. . . .

With the inclusion of the Article V provision in the Constitution, power to propose amendments to the nation's foundational laws is granted both to Congress and to an amendments convention of the states. These conventions are made up of groups of delegates sent by the various states. The ratification process, however, remains the same: Three-fourths of the states must approve proposed amendments before they become a part of the Constitution.

I, too, rejoice in this constitutional right of the people to propose amendments through their state representatives. All Americans who believe in government by the people should celebrate this right. I came to appreciate the importance of the convention clause in Article V after witnessing during my years in Congress the unconstitutional growth of government that threatens the liberties and properties of Americans present and future. Since the nation's elected representatives in Washington generally champion big government, the burden now falls on the people to save their country from financial ruin and federal oppression. The convention clause in Article V grants the state legislatures the legal authority and an orderly procedure to propose amendments.

My jaundiced view of Congress and the unresponsive, overreaching federal government aligns me with the generation of wary Rhode Islanders in 1790. These early Americans guardedly assented to the Constitution and the new national government, but only with the reassurance of the constitutional right of the states to amend the Constitution. More than two hundred years later, it is now the present generation's dire need and responsibility to exercise Colonel Barton's highly regarded right of the people to govern themselves through an amendments convention of the states.

Although the failure to act with an amendments convention could be catastrophic in our current national debt crisis, some national leaders and opinion shapers have expressed uncertainty and alarm about the process and potential outcome. Questions have been raised about the scope of an amendments convention, the required wording of state applications to trigger a convention call by Congress, and the procedural rules for these types of conventions. Moreover, concerns have been raised about the delegates of these conventions proposing ill-conceived, wholesale changes to the Constitution and an inexplicable ratification of these proposals by the required three-fourths of the states. From my observations, these concerns have been raised by groups and individuals either ignorant of the history behind governing conventions in America's formative years or intent on defeating attempts at self-government by the people.

Much of the confusion and concern about an Article V amendments convention can be assuaged by a better understanding of the Framers' long tradition of conventions and their well-developed system of protocols for these gatherings. This progress in republican rule dates back to the seventeenth century and reflects a profound respect for the liberties of the people and their natural right of self-governance. Frequent use of these conventions popularized and routinized these important assemblies. Let us now review these historical advancements in self-rule by the English-speaking peoples of Europe and North America, and how this history guides us as precedent.

A CENTURY OF CONVENTIONS BEFORE 1787

Well before the Federal Convention of 1787, generations of Americans had participated in conventions and grown accustomed to this mode of self-government outside regular colonial and state legislatures. Sometimes elected and sometimes appointed, these ad hoc representative assemblies generally addressed a specific, pressing issue that the regular legislative bodies were either ill suited or unwilling to undertake. Typical of this method of self-governance, the Federal Convention of 1787 (later known as the Constitutional Convention) was called by the states—not by the Articles Congress—to address the dysfunctional government under the Articles of Confederation. The requirement of unanimous approval by the states under the Articles greatly impeded salutary amendments.

The history of self-government by the English-speaking peoples through a legal tradition of conventions is well documented in Russell Caplan's scholarly narrative, *Constitutional Brinksmanship*. Prompted by interest after thirty-two states applied to Congress for an amendments convention in the early 1980s, this much-needed work filled a void with its publication in 1988. Caplan's book was the first systematic study of the convention clause in Article V of the Constitution. His careful research and objective presentation stands in contrast to convention alarmists whose bias shows in their poorly informed opinions. Much of the author's research is combined in this chapter with more recent scholarship by legal historian Robert Natelson.[5] Natelson has done much since 2010 to synthesize legal insight with Caplan's work and other research from founding-era documents.

The concept of conventions for self-governance has deep roots in British-American history. Following the end of the English Interregnum under Oliver Cromwell, a "convention Parliament" recalled the royal Stuart line to rule England in 1660. This assembly was followed by another convention Parliament in 1689. This conclave adopted the English Bill of Rights and put William and Mary on the throne in the bloodless Glorious Revolution.[6]

This mode of self-rule was certainly not lost on the English colonies of North America. In 1689, at least four intra-colony conventions were called to replace unpopular governments. In the century before the drafting of Article V at the Federal Convention of 1787, at least twenty-one multi-colony conventions were called. During and after the American Revolution, another eleven multi-state conventions met between 1776 and 1786. These numerous conventions set a clear precedent for the amendment-convention provision in Article V. Thus, the customs and procedures for these kinds of gatherings were well established by 1787.[7]

Historians have studied four of these conventions extensively, and records show a remarkable consistency in protocol and terminology. The convention "call" was the request, usually by single or multiple colonies or states, inviting some or all of the affiliated governments to an ad hoc assembly. This call was accompanied by the topic or topics for the proposed convention, whose body of members would act as a problem-solving task force.[8]

A "general convention" drew its name from the broad call for all the colonies or states to meet. The "general" qualifier had no reference to the subject matter of the assembly. A "partial convention" restricted the call to a region of the colonies or the new country. Alleged authorities have mistakenly claimed that Article V indicates a convention with an agenda of general or wide-ranging topics, rather than a meeting open to all the states. Historical evidence shows the "general" qualifier in the founding era convention calls referred to the colonies or states summoned, not the issue or issues to be addressed.[9]

In contrast to the usual narrowly focused assemblies, a convention with delegates authorized to deliberate on a broad range of subject matter was called a "plenipotentiary" gathering.[10] This term would apply to the Federal Convention of 1787, according to Natelson. The facts, as will be shown, are on Natelson's side in this controversy over the authority of the delegates at the Great Convention to address a broad range of issues.

Representatives sent to conventions were formally titled "commissioners," but they were often informally referred to as "delegates." The term "commissioner" referenced the delegate's commission or credentials, which specified the topic for the convention and the official scope of the delegate's authority. This commission could be limited by special (sometimes secret) instructions from the colony or state that authorized the delegate.[11]

Before the American Revolution, many of the multi-colony conventions were called to bolster colonial defenses against the threat of American Indian tribes or French troops from New France (later called Canada). The Albany Congress, called in 1754, became the most noted of these conventions before 1765. Twenty-five delegates from eight colonies met in Albany in the colony of New York to discuss the improvement of relations with the six nations of the Iroquois Confederacy. The call came from the royal lieutenant governor of New York, James DeLancey. Like most of the conventions in the colonies before 1787, the Albany Congress ("congress" and "convention" were interchangeable terms in the eighteenth century) was a limited convention rather than plenipotentiary.[12]

The next multi-colony convention called was the Stamp Act Congress in 1765. The lower house of the colonial legislature of Massachusetts issued this general call, and nine of the thirteen colonies sent "committees," or groups of commissioners. The language of the call was somewhat broad but still limited the commission of the delegates "to Consult togather [*sic*] on the present circumstances of the Colonies and the Difficulties to which they are and must be reduced by the operation of the late Acts of Parliment [*sic*]," with taxation by the Stamp Act prominent on the agenda.[13]

The language and procedures at the Stamp Act Congress served as a prototype for subsequent general conventions in the colonies and states. Confirming the interchangeability of "congress" and "convention," a number of contemporary writings referred to the Stamp Act Congress as a "convention." Each colony issued its own credentials to its commissioners. Some of these delegates were authorized by their respective colonies only to consult at the convention; others were given full powers to participate in deciding the assembly's course of action. Procedural rules were determined by the participants. The assembly selected two of the delegates by ballot to officiate at the convention, but then reverted to a one-vote-per-colony rule to determine any action. After three weeks of deliberation, the Stamp Act Congress issued four documents: a declaration of the colonies' rights and separate pieces of correspondence to the British king, the House of Lords, and the House of Commons.[14]

Another key inter-colonial convention, the Continental Congress of 1774, was called by the New York Committee of Correspondence in a circular letter to all thirteen of the American colonies. These committees of correspondence had been established to facilitate communication between the colonies during the growing crisis with their British rulers. With all thirteen colonies called, this was a "general" convention. Most of the fifty-six delegates from the twelve colonial governments represented were commissioned by the lower house of their respective legislatures or by colonial conventions.

Reflecting the urgency of the crisis, this meeting of the first Continental Congress may have been the most nearly "plenipotentiary" of the intercolonial and interstate conventions before 1787. All the delegates except those of Rhode Island had been commissioned with authority to consult on a wide range of subjects and "to bind their respective colonies to collective decisions" regarding the impasse with Britain. An unusually strong authorization, this power "to bind" their respective states to decisions extended the commissions of these delegates beyond proposing. The Rhode Island delegation's commission, however, was restricted to "consulting." The rules and procedures for the meeting closely followed the protocols from the Stamp Act Congress.[15]

The convention adjourned with no legally binding decisions on the colonies. Notably, the recommendations and petitions constrained action to the narrow credentials of the Rhode Island delegates. The assembly ended with a conditional call for a second convention to meet on May 10, 1775. By that time fighting had begun in Massachusetts, and the second Continental Congress became the de facto government of the colonies. During the Revolutionary War, a number of multistate conventions were held, with delegates sent by a number of the now-independent states of America. None were general conventions. The various calls for these gatherings went out from the new state governments to as few as three states and as many as ten.[16]

From the outset, many of the founders were profoundly dissatisfied with the weak government under the Articles of Confederation, which the last colony ratified in 1781. With the oppressive British government strongly on the Founders' minds, the new central government had been severely limited by its few powers to raise revenue and conduct the nation's business. In contrast to the British system of rule, the former colonies were given authority under the Articles to act more as sovereign nations, soon a source of consternation to many of the young nation's leaders in the Confederation Congress.

This frustrating state of affairs quickly became intolerable. A potential solution would have been to amend the Articles to strike a balance between an effective national government and the desires of the states to maintain considerable autonomy. The main obstacle to this, however, was the Articles' requirement of unanimous consent by the thirteen quarrelsome states. No national constitution in world history had included a formal provision for amendment until the Articles, yet this stringent requirement of unanimity nearly mooted this advancement in self-governance. At the Federal Convention in 1787, Virginia delegate Charles Pinckney succinctly explained the unhappy result of the provision's requirement: "It is to this unanimous consent, the depressed situation of the Union is undoubtedly owing."[17]

The Founders' long history and familiarity with ad hoc governing conventions to address difficult issues outside the regular legislative process quickly emerged as a safe and well-established means to effect the needed changes. In 1782 the New York Legislature passed a resolution appealing to the Confederation Congress to call a "General Convention of the States, specially authorised [sic] to revise and amend the Confederation, reserving a Right to the respective Legislatures, to ratify their determinations." It should be noted that the authorized revisions and amendments appeared to be directed at the Confederation government and not at the Articles, the laws of governance.[18]

With no action by Congress, the Massachusetts Legislature followed New York's call with a resolution in July 1785 asking Congress to call a general convention of the states to amend the Articles of Confederation. Unlike New York's authorization, these revisions were directed at the Articles and not the Confederation. Massachusetts followed up this resolution with a circular letter to the states, describing its communication to Congress as an "application to the United States in Congress assembled." The state's employment of the word *application* in 1785 would closely correspond to its usage in the wording of the convention clause in Article V, written two years later. Still, the recalcitrant Congress took no steps for a general convention.[19]

Seeking greater interstate cooperation in commercial matters, the Virginia legislators took matters in their own hands. The Virginians adopted a resolution in January 1786, calling a general convention "to take into consideration the trade of the United States; to examine the relative situations and trade of the States; [and] to consider how far a uniform system in their commercial regulations may be necessary." A circular letter went out to the other states, fixing the date of the conclave on September 4, 1786, in Annapolis, Maryland.

Seven states commissioned delegates, but only five state committees arrived in Annapolis at the designated time for the convention. The credentials of the delegates corresponded with the subject matter of the call. Skeptical of the acceptability of this minority of states crafting commercial regulations for all, the Annapolis convention adjourned on September 14 without commercial recommendations—but with a pointed suggestion to the five states that had commissioned the delegates:[20]

> Your Commissioners, with the most respectful deference, beg leave to suggest their unanimous conviction, that it may essentially tend to advance the interests of the union, if the States, by whom they have been respectively delegated, would themselves concur, and use their endeavours to procure the concurrence of the other States, in the appointment of Commissioners, to meet at Philadelphia on the second Monday in May next, to take into consideration the situation of the United States, to devise such further provisions as shall appear to them necessary to render the constitution of the Federal Government adequate to the exigencies of the Union; and to report such an Act for that purpose to the United States in Congress assembled, as when agreed to, by them, and afterwards confirmed by the Legislatures of every State, will effectually provide for the same.[21]

Most important, this missive is obviously addressed to the "States, by whom they [had] been respectively delegated." The commissioners to the Annapolis convention urged that these five states "use their endeavours to procure the concurrence of the other States" to meet in Philadelphia in May 1787. Nowhere in this communication is any further appeal to Congress to take action on a convention of the states. Nor could Congress make a legally binding call if it received such a request. Under the Articles of Confederation, the weak Congress had no expressed right to order the states to convene. It could make a nonbinding call or recommend such a convention, but no more than that.

To that point, Congress merely issued a resolution early in 1787 that "in the opinion of Congress it is expedient" that the convention be held as recommended (or perhaps called) by the Annapolis convention.[22]

Moreover, Congress's mere opinion on the convention came several months after the Virginia and New Jersey legislatures, prompted by the Annapolis communiqué, had already made a formal call to the states to convene in Philadelphia. The call from these two states late in 1786 may even have been redundant, as the earlier statement by the Annapolis convention recommending the Philadelphia conclave arguably may have represented a formal call to a general convention.[23] More clear is the minimal role Congress had in instigating the Federal Convention: Congress had no authority to make a legally binding call for a convention and merely offered a concurring opinion well after the formal call for a general convention had already gone out.

Madison wrote Washington the day of Congress's resolution in February 1787 that the national legislature was divided and embarrassed over getting involved, and some legislators were not sure if their resolution would help or hinder the upcoming Philadelphia conclave. Later that year in Philadelphia, Virginia delegate George Mason offered his opinion on the authority of the Great Convention: "I consider the federal government as in some measure dissolved by the meeting of this Convention."[24]

In light of this compelling evidence, it amazes that allegedly knowledgeable sources state that Congress called and limited the Federal Convention in Philadelphia. More may be afoot than historical ignorance. A further review of the origins of the Philadelphia Convention helps dispel another historical myth—that long-standing hobgoblin of a "runaway convention" in 1787.

As discussed earlier, the established protocol for conventions during the colonial period and afterward had been for the colony or state to empower its representatives with documents called "commissions." Thus, these representatives were formally titled commissioners and informally referenced as delegates. The commission from the governing officials specified the topic of the convention the delegate was to attend and the scope of his authority. Delegates were expected to honor their commissions, and actions or recommendations beyond the limits of their authority were considered "unratifiable" and legally void.[25]

With the Confederation Congress having little or no legal standing in the convention process, what was the expressed authority granted by the various states' commissions to their delegations to the Federal Convention in 1787? Closely following the Annapolis Convention's wording in its recommendation, Virginia's appointment of commissioners authorized "Alterations and farther Provisions as may be necessary to render the Foederal [sic] Constitution adequate." This reference to the "Federal Constitution" should not be understood as limited to the Articles of Confederation. During the late eighteenth century, the prevailing definition for "constitution" was the political makeup or governing system of a nation. Thus, the wording in the Annapolis Convention recommendation ("to render the constitution of the Federal Government adequate") restated by Virginia's commission to its delegates referred more likely to the national system of governance, not the Articles of Confederation.[26]

At the same time Virginia authorized its delegates for the Philadelphia Convention late in 1786, New Jersey commissioned several delegates "for the purpose of taking into Consideration the state of the Union, as to trade and other important objects, and of devising such other provisions as shall appear to be necessary to render the Constitution of the Federal Government adequate to the exigencies thereof." Pennsylvania acted about this same time with commissions similar to those of the Virginia delegation. By February 1787, North Carolina, New Hampshire, Delaware, and Georgia had commissioned delegations with broad powers to propose reforms that were not limited to changes in the Articles of Confederation.[27]

In late February, a congressional committee moved that the Confederation Congress recommend that the states send delegates to the Philadelphia Convention with authority to prepare "such farther provisions as shall render the same adequate to the exigencies of the

Union." Citing instructions from their state, the New York congressional delegation objected and offered wording that would limit the convention's proposals to "revising the Articles of Confederation." As Natelson has pointed out, "their insistence on that wording confirms that people understood that the convention recommended by the delegates at Annapolis, endorsed by seven states, and promoted by congressional committee was *not* limited to proposing changes in the Articles."[28]

After a postponement, new wording from Massachusetts was subsequently adopted. The approved resolution by Congress was the milder "opinion" that the convention in Philadelphia be limited to revisions in the Articles, which were to be approved by Congress and confirmed by the states. Congress's opinion had little influence, as none of the seven previously commissioned delegations received any changes to their authority. To the contrary, the number of states favoring a plenipotentiary convention soon grew larger. Connecticut, Maryland, and South Carolina granted broad authority to their newly commissioned delegates.

Ultimately, only New York and Massachusetts commissioned their delegates with restrictions that limited their proposals to revisions of the Articles. Later that year, as the Philadelphia Convention began proposing changes outside the scope of these two states' commissions, all but three of these two states' delegates dutifully left the convention. Of the thirty-nine delegates who signed the proposed constitution in September 1787, only two delegates from Massachusetts and one from New York (Alexander Hamilton) exceeded their authority from their respective states. Thirty-six of the thirty-nine acted within the authority of their commissions.[29] The resolution by the convention on its final day, September 17, called for presenting their proposal in a document to Congress for forwarding to the states for approval by special conventions. Signed by the assembly's presiding officer, George Washington, the resolution said nothing about congressional approval of the new laws.[30]

Eighteen of the delegates who proposed the new constitution were also members of the Confederation Congress, so they hurried to New York for the upcoming congressional session. Meeting two weeks after the Philadelphia Convention was adjourned, Congress voted unanimously to send the convention's recommended "report" to the states for consideration by special conventions, not by their legislatures. The resolution authorizing the document's transmittal to the states did not use the word "constitution." This action was Congress's only substantive contribution to these new foundational laws of governance. Note that Congress took no vote of approval on the new laws, as this would be the purview of the state conventions.[31]

The only authority clearly exceeded at the Federal Convention in Philadelphia was the participation of the two delegates from Massachusetts and the one from New York. This arguably became moot with the ratification of the Constitution by the required two-thirds of states in summer 1788. As the legal tradition in self-governance by convention dictated, the overwhelming majority of delegates acted within their state-authorized commissions to propose changes in the Confederation government beyond amendments to the Articles. The only "runaway" aspect of the Great Convention of 1787 is in the imaginations of the fearmongers who have no faith in the American people's ability to govern themselves.

The Philadelphia Convention had been necessitated by the difficulty of getting unanimous consent from the states to change the flawed Articles, so the delegates writing the new constitution would ensure that the amendment process would be more practicable. Furthermore, the legal precedent of using general conventions of states to propose needed change in governance had proven vital to assembling the delegates to deliberate and recommend. These and other lessons in self-governance were not lost on the Framers that summer in Philadelphia. American revolutionary thinkers made history by codifying a safety feature for their constitutional republic in the new foundational laws. We know this constitutional protection as Article V of the U.S. Constitution.

From the preceding it can be seen that the Federal Convention was not a creature of the Confederation Congress. Moreover, the overwhelming majority of the state delegates acted within their commissioned authority in the writing of the proposed constitution. Let us now look at the theory and purpose of the writing of the Article V provision.

FORGING ARTICLE V AT THE GREAT CONVENTION

Two weeks after deliberations at the Federal Convention began in May 1787, Virginia delegate and governor Edmund Randolph rose to offer the Virginia Plan as a blueprint for the new foundational laws of the nation. This plan had been primarily developed by James Madison and included his creative idea of three separate branches of government to balance out power. The Virginia Plan was presented in a series of fifteen resolutions that day. Before Randolph sat down, it was obvious that this was a plan for an entirely new government, not merely revisions to the Articles.[32]

The plan's thirteenth resolution included the wording "that provision ought to be made for the amendment of the Articles of Union whensoever it shall seem necessary, and that the assent of the National Legislature ought not to be required thereto."[33] This brief resolution is noteworthy in several respects. First, the idea of codifying a procedure for changing the proposed constitution was first proffered at the convention from the plan developed by the great political genius himself, James Madison—the Framer behind divided government to safeguard the liberties of the people. Second, the term applied to the laws for which the amendment process was directed was "Articles of Union," not "Articles of Confederation." This appeared to signal that the convention was not to be limited to amending the old Articles. And finally, in this initial proposal for an amendments mechanism, Congress was to have no role in the approval of these changes to the new foundational laws. This would be constitutional change closer to the people themselves.

The legal tradition of amending laws of governance was not as widespread in the colonies and young states as the practice of calling conventions. An amending mechanism had been formalized into written law in 1682 for William Penn's colonial charter, Frame of Government of Pennsylvania, but the other colonies generally saw their charters of government as inviolate. The American Revolution did much to change this view. Jefferson's *Declaration of Independence* conveyed the ideal in Revolutionary America that governments existed to secure fundamental rights of the people and drew their legitimacy from popular consent. Under this revolutionary premise, many of the new states codified a formal means to alter their foundational laws. The Articles of Confederation, of course, had included a mechanism for amendment, albeit with the impracticable requirement of unanimity of the states.[34]

By the time of the Federal Convention, nine of the thirteen new states had codified a mode of amendment in their constitutions. Three methods were adopted to effect these changes. Four states allowed for amendments to be enacted through their legislatures; three allowed amendments only through state conventions; and two could alter their constitutions through a "council of censors" that periodically reviewed these laws. Thus when the Federal Convention met, the Framers had a record of experience for preparing an amendments mechanism in the new constitution.[35]

Following Randolph's initial resolution for an amendments provision in late May, the issue was taken up on June 5. Responding to a delegate who saw no use for this mechanism, Elbridge Gerry of Massachusetts rose to defend it. Citing the novelty of the proposed republican government, he foresaw a potential need to make changes to the constitution. Besides, he noted, the experience with the states that had an amendments provision outside their legislatures had caused no problems. But debate on the provision was postponed.[36]

Deliberation continued on June 11. Several delegates argued that an amendments provision might be unnecessary and that it would be improper to exclude Congress if it were enacted. Yet Virginia delegate George Mason defended both the amendment provision and excluding Congress from the approval process. It was inevitable that some defects in the constitution would need correction, he said, and a formal process would be better "than to trust to chance or violence." He also argued for excluding a required assent by Congress to congressional amendments "because they may abuse their power, and refuse their consent on that very account." Edmund Randolph voiced his agreement with Mason. The delegates voted unanimously to include a provision for amendment in the proposed constitution but nothing beyond that.[37]

In late July the convention adjourned until August 6 to allow time for the Committee of Detail to prepare a draft of the laws that had been proposed through late July. When the delegates reconvened, the committee's spare wording for the amendments provision was presented as Article XIX: "On the application of the Legislatures of two thirds of the States in the Union, for an amendment of this Constitution, the Legislature of the United States shall call a Convention for that purpose." The states were apparently to be granted sole authority to propose and approve amendments. Congress would have no role other than to call the convention. The article was approved on August 30.[38]

On September 10, just one week before the convention ended, delegate Gerry voiced concern that states might call conventions and obtain amendments that "bind the Union to innovations that may subvert the State-Constitutions altogether." He asked the delegates to reconsider the previously passed measure. Alexander Hamilton seconded the motion and asserted that Congress should also be empowered to call an amendments convention with a two-thirds vote of each branch. He saw no danger in this, as the "people would finally decide in the case." Madison expressed concern over the lack of procedural guidelines in the article. The delegates voted to reconsider the amendments article as previously approved.[39]

Wording was added to the article allowing Congress to propose amendments with a two-thirds vote by both chambers and subject to ratification of the states. Pennsylvania's James Wilson moved to require two-thirds of the states to approve amendments before they became binding. The motion was defeated, whereupon Wilson changed the ratification requirement to three-fourths of the states. The requirement was unanimously approved. Madison apparently rewrote the article, allowing Congress to propose amendments and deleting the wording about Congress calling "a Convention for that purpose." He moved to take up the newly worded measure. After the motion was seconded, South Carolina's John Rutledge objected to the article without wording to protect slavery from future amendment. Madison's new wording allowing congressional proposal of amendments and deleting state amendments conventions was approved, but a vote to add Rutledge's protection of slavery was postponed.[40]

Reviewing the new draft of the amendments article on September 15, Connecticut delegate Roger Sherman argued to expand the proviso protecting slavery to include a guarantee that no state could be deprived of equal representation in the Senate. About this same time, George Mason observed that the language requiring Congress to call a convention of the states upon application of two-thirds of the states had been omitted in the latest draft of this provision, which had been reclassified as Article V. Calling the article's new wording "exceptionable and dangerous," Mason contended that without the previous wording requiring Congress to call an amendments convention with the requisite applications, "no amendments of the proper kind would ever be obtained by the people, if the Government should become oppressive," as he believed ultimately "would be the case."[41]

The original wording requiring Congress to call an amendments convention after application by two-thirds of the states was added to the article and unanimously approved. This "state application and convention" process was reinserted to restrain Congress if it abused its powers. The proviso protecting equal representation of the states in the Senate was also endorsed in the final wording for Article V.[42]

George Mason deserves recognition for his championing of the right of the states to propose amendments, as ultimately codified in Article V. He pushed for this states-rights issue during deliberations in June, and then in mid-September pushed for the state-application-and-convention process that required a congressional convention call on application by two-thirds of the states. Mason's alarm at this omission and its subsequent addition occurred on the final day of substantive deliberations at the convention. (See the final wording of Article V in appendix 1 on page 202.)

By providing opportunities for both Congress and the states to propose amendments to the Constitution, Article V reflects the Madisonian principle of shared power between the national government and the states. The required supermajorities for proposal and ratification also strike a balance between a potential for reform and stability in government. Without the safeguards of the amendments provision in Article V, the new Constitution may never have been ratified by the wary citizens of the new United States.

ARTICLE V DURING THE RATIFICATION DEBATE

The states had commissioned delegates to the Federal Convention to provide a stronger, more effective central government. Afterward, the state ratification debates would center largely on whether the Framers had given too much authority to the federal government. Everyone understood that the new constitutional powers allotted to the national authority reduced the liberties and rights of the states and the people. Shared power truly was a zero-sum game. Adding to the political tempest, a kind of class-warfare aspect to the ratification debates emerged. Some of the Anti-Federalists contended that the new laws had been drafted by elitists who meant to establish "two orders in the society, one comprehending the opulent and great, the other the poor and illiterate."[43] Fierce arguments roiled the polity of the new nation.

Many of the Anti-Federalists wanted to include in the proposed constitution written guarantees for the rights of the people and the states. Some state leaders insisted that their ratifications be conditional. If the amendments guaranteeing basic rights and liberties were not proposed by the new Congress, these representatives reserved a right to rescind their ratification. A number of prominent national figures, several having served at the Federal Convention, recommended another convention of the states to include these guarantees. Most of the Framers strongly opposed another plenipotentiary assembly. Exhaustion from their lengthy ordeal in summer 1787 was not the only reason; many feared another convention might undo the remarkable legislation already achieved.[44]

The Article V provision that codified an orderly process to amend the proposed constitution quickly assumed a key role in the successful argument for ratification of the new laws. Those concerned that the proposed constitution failed to include expressed guarantees of basic rights and liberties were eventually mollified by the amendments mechanism that would allow these alterations. Madison initially saw no reason to call for future amendments guaranteeing basic rights, yet he understood how fears of an overreaching government could be abated by expressed guarantees of basic rights. He supported future amendments as a strategy to encourage ratification. Article V would be the tool to enact these changes.

In a January 1788 *Federalist* essay promoting ratification, Madison stated that amendments to the constitution would be inevitable, and Article V would facilitate these changes with a process neither too difficult nor too easy. He also lauded the parity of the states and Congress in this process: "It moreover equally enables the general and the state governments *to originate* the amendments of errors as they may be pointed out by the experience of one side or the other."[45]

In another of the *Federalist* essays urging ratification, Alexander Hamilton gave high marks to Article V as a means to limit "persons delegated to the administration of the national government" who "will always be disinclined to yield up any portion of the authority of which they were once possessed." Although Hamilton stated that he gave little weight to these concerns at the time, any future attempts by federal officials to thwart amendments would be futile. "[T]he national rulers, whenever nine states [two-thirds] concur, will have no option on the subject. . . . The words of this article are peremptory. The congress 'shall call a convention.' Nothing in this particular is left to discretion. Of consequence all the declamation about the disinclination to a change, vanishes in air. . . . We may safely rely on the disposition of the state legislatures to erect barriers against the encroachments of the national authority."[46]

George Washington's own state of Virginia witnessed one of the fiercest ratification debates in June 1788. As the various state debates intensified that year, the future first president promoted ratification with a letter from his home at Mount Vernon, assuring that shortcomings in the constitution could be readily amended after ratification. "That the Constitution will admit of amendments is acknowledged by its warmest advocates," he wrote.[47]

A delegate to the Virginia ratifying convention, Madison battled with Anti-Federalist Patrick Henry, a firebrand in the pre–Revolutionary War years. When Henry warned delegates of the difficulty of getting future amendments to the proposed constitution, Madison counterargued that getting three-fourths of the states to approve amendments would be far easier than obtaining the unanimity required under the Articles. In a tight 89–79 vote, Virginia ratified on June 25, gratifying Madison, who believed that his home state had brought the new government into being as the ninth to approve the new Constitution. New Hampshire, however, had taken the honors four days earlier.[48]

The old patriot Henry, who staunchly opposed the centralized authority in the Constitution, was gracious in defeat after Virginia ratified the new framework. He drew solace from the amendments mechanism guaranteed with Article V. "I will be a peaceful citizen," he told still-angry Anti-Federalists in his state. "My head, my hand, and my heart, shall be at liberty to retrieve the loss of liberty and remove the defects of that system in a constitutional way." Henry worked hard "in a constitutional way" as provided by Article V, with some of Virginia's recommended amendments later reflected in the Bill of Rights.[49]

The Anti-Federalists were strong in New York, and the state's belated ratification came after the Constitution had been endorsed by the required nine states. During New York's bitter debates, one of the delegates to the state ratifying convention, Samuel Jones, left to future generations one of the most enlightening explanations of how the Framers may have viewed uses for Article V:

The reason why there are two modes of obtaining amendments prescribed in the constitution I suppose to be this—it could not be known to the framers of the constitution, whether there was too much power given or too little; they therefore prescribed a mode by which Congress might procure more, if in the operation of the government it was found necessary; and they prescribed for the states a mode of restraining powers of the government, if upon trial it should be found they had given too much.[50]

The first mode delegate Jones referenced was a proposed amendment by Congress, contingent on the approval of three-fourths of the states either by their legislatures or by state conventions. This requirement was to ensure that the federal government received no more authority than that granted by the Framers *unless* a supermajority of the states consented to these additional powers. (Few of the Framers envisioned a future where federal courts allowed the government to maneuver around this constitutional protection.) The second mode referenced by Jones was of course the state-application-and-convention process, which the delegate believed would be employed for "restraining powers of the government." Like Alexander Hamilton, Jones apparently put little trust in the willingness of federal officials to voluntarily relinquish authority.

For amending the Constitution, an argument can be made that Article V grants more power to the people's state representatives than to their federal representatives. Congress must request consent from the states for increased constitutional authority for the central government, yet the states on their own volition can propose and approve constitutional limits on the powers of the federal government. This check on centralized power would be expected from founding-era lawmakers, who believed that governments drew authority only from the consent of the governed. The state legislatures better reflect the people's needs and desires than does the distant national legislature. Thus, republican ideals of self-rule lay at the very core of Article V. Little wonder so many self-interested federal officials and government-enthralled progressives have long discouraged and slandered an amendments convention by the states.

TEXT AND HISTORY TO GUIDE US

Just two months after the initial Congress of the United States met in March 1789, the first application for an amendments convention of the states was filed with the clerk of the House of Representatives. Virginia legislators, no doubt led by Patrick Henry, were eager to "secure to ourselves and our posterity the great and unalienable rights of mankind," as their application grandiosely stated. The next day, the clerk received a second application for an amendments convention. With wording similar to Virginia's petition, the New York legislators were also eager to propose amendments at a convention. They were as reluctant as their Southern sister state to rely on the "slow forms of Congressional discussion."[51]

These first two applications were dutifully filed to await the arrival of others from the requisite two-thirds of the states, whereupon Congress would be constitutionally bound to "call a Convention for proposing Amendments." Additional applications never came. Hoping to avoid another convention that might undo work from the Federal Convention two years earlier, Virginia representative James Madison quickly drafted nineteen amendments for Congress to consider. They had been distilled from the many recommendations from the states.[52]

From Madison's drafts, Congress proposed twelve amendments in fall 1789. By December 1791 ten of them had been ratified by the required three-fourths of the state legislatures. These first ten amendments approved by the states became the Bill of Rights—expressed constitutional guarantees of personal rights and liberties demanded by the states at the time of ratification. The Bill of Rights would not be the last legislation initiated by the states using the "prodding effect" of Article V's convention clause to impel action from an intractable Congress.

Madison need not have worried about upheaval from another convention. The people were satisfied with their guarantees under the first ten amendments. A calm settled over the young nation. Further assuring domestic tranquility had an amendments convention been called, the codification of the founding-era convention procedure in the Constitution would have limited the subject matter of the conclave: *under Article V, the framework created by the Founders cannot be rewritten;*

it can only be amended with specific instructions by the authorizing states.

No other reasonable conclusion than the preceding can be drawn from Robert Natelson's extensive research of the convention process used in eighteenth-century America and the wording in the construction of Article V. "During the Founding Era, a proposing convention could be plenipotentiary or limited," Natelson explained. "Article V clarifies that neither the states nor Congress may call plenipotentiary conventions under Article V, because that Article authorizes only amendments to 'this Constitution,' and, further, it proscribes certain amendments."[53] Thus references to a modern-era amendments convention as a "constitutional convention" or a "con-con" are inaccurate.

No less an authority than James Madison, the principal author of Article V, confirmed Natelson's conclusion that the convention clause limits the subject matter of an amendments convention. In a letter to Virginia state legislator George Lee Turberville after the Constitution had been ratified, Madison stated that "if first principles are to be recurred to," a convention call with unlimited subject matter required "unanimous consent" of all the states. From all appearances this refers to a "constitutional convention" like the Federal Convention of 1787. On the other hand, "if the forms of the Constitution are to be pursued," Madison continued, an amendments convention with limited subject matter could be assembled after "previous application of 2/3 of the State legislatures." Case closed—by the very words of the father of the Constitution.[54]

One of Russell Caplan's key contributions from his systematic study of the convention clause is its direct link to the well-established protocols and procedures established before and during the founding era by the colonies and new states. With this prior connection, modern-era amendments conventions are guided both by the limits under Article V and legal precedent:

> The pre-1787 interstate conventions had been governed by commissions—the credentials issued to the delegates by home state legislatures—and the 1789 applications of Virginia and New York, reflecting that origin, speak of deputizing the convention delegates

with the powers necessary to consider appropriate amendments. The applications submitted under Article V, therefore, are the descendents of the pre-1787 convention commissions.[55]

Further clarifying procedures and limiting wholesale changes to the Constitution, Russell's careful research of legal precedents leads to this guide for state applications for an amendments convention: "Despite the nebulous quality of article V's phrase 'a Convention for proposing Amendments,' applications must evidently specify particular amendments, and a convention need be called only if the requisite number of applications agree in text or subject matter with regard to at least one amendment."[56]

For more than two hundred years, our constitutional gift from the founders has been available as a safety feature to check the power of the federal government and to make needed amendments to our foundational laws—especially when our elected officials cannot or will not. I was only vaguely aware of the Article V endowment when I entered Congress in 1995. Like many Americans, I relied on Congress for corrective measures and never believed the people would need to use this constitutional power.

My time as a U.S. representative and senator, however, convinced me otherwise. I witnessed the corruption, self-interest, and party interest that have rendered our elected officials incapable of acting in the people's long-term interest. I have left Washington and Congress behind. My efforts now are directed at thoughtful, targeted action by an amendments convention to rebalance our system of governance. *We the People* need to reassert control of our nation's future.

Unnecessary concerns over the state-application-and-convention process have discouraged a much-needed amendments convention the last several decades, and this unease is on the right as well as the left. Russell Caplan's and Robert Natelson's research cited earlier assures us of the orderliness and safety of this process. Most assuring of all is the requirement that three-fourths of the states—currently thirty-eight out of fifty—agree to any proposals before enactment. This virtually guarantees a supermajority of the citizens in favor of any amendment. This rigorous political constraint serves as the ultimate safeguard against radical and undesired changes to the nation's foundational laws.

With voices from the past, our founders call upon us to employ this republican measure. "We may safely rely on the disposition of the state legislatures to erect barriers against the encroachments of the national authority," Hamilton wrote of the safety feature of Article V in his defense of the new Constitution.[57] We should consider it the duty of members of the state legislatures and all liberty-loving Americans to work for an amendments convention. It is the best means to ensure the American promise for future generations.

This chapter should be read with relief and gratitude. The Founders' gift of Article V provides the people with a safe, orderly means to effect changes in our national government. Bringing about these changes lies at the heart of republicanism, as the people ultimately decide the direction of the country. The power in the federal government emanates from the people and can be limited or taken back by the people by constitutional means.

The people's right to exercise this option is guaranteed by Article V despite disinclination of federal officials "to yield up any portion of the authority of which they were once possessed," as Hamilton wrote. The wording of Article V is preemptory: ". . . on the application of the Legislatures of two-thirds of the several states, [Congress] shall call a Convention for proposing Amendments." As Natelson accurately described the state-application-and-convention process, it is the "federal analogue of the state voter initiative, whereby the electorate can bypass the legislature by adapting laws or amending the state constitution."[58]

Moreover, the Framers would argue, Congress's failure to deal with both our nation's debt crisis and bureaucratic limitations on Americans' freedoms are precisely the circumstances for which the convention clause was created. The people's reluctance to use this right leaves our foundational laws incomplete and jeopardizes the republic. Concerned

Americans are increasingly coming to this conclusion.

An understanding of how our Constitution was originally designed to limit our federal government and prevent the corruption and dysfunction currently experienced is explored in the next chapter.

6

LIMITED GOVERNMENT FOR A SELF-RULING PEOPLE

It is hardly too strong to say that the Constitution was made to guard the people against the dangers of good intentions. There are men in all ages who mean to govern well, but they mean to govern. They promise to be good masters, but they mean to be masters.

— DANIEL WEBSTER

IN 1842, A TWENTY-YEAR-OLD DARTMOUTH COLLEGE STUDENT had the good fortune to meet an aging veteran of the American Revolution— ninety-one-year-old Levi Preston from Danvers, Massachusetts. Preston had spent his life as a small farmer, distinguished in his community mostly by his role as a twenty-four-year-old minuteman in 1775. Early in the revolution, Preston's militia unit fought against British troops near Concord, Massachusetts, and he went on to attain the rank of captain during the eight-year conflict.

The Dartmouth student, Mellen Chamberlain, would have a notable career as a judge, member of the Massachusetts Legislature, historian, and head of the Boston Public Library system. Chamberlain's conversation with Preston must have made quite an impression on the young scholar, as fifty-two years later he wrote about it in a historical essay published in his book about the political life of John Adams.

Asking Preston why he and his comrades took up arms against the British, the youthful Chamberlain expected a familiar response about the origins of the American Revolution. Were the colonists motivated by British oppression, unfair tax policy, or libertarian principles? No, Preston said, none of those things were on their minds when his militia fought the British on that April morning in 1775.

"Well, then, what was the matter?" Chamberlain asked. "And what did you mean in going to the fight?"

"Young man," Preston replied, "what we meant in going for those red-coats was this: we always had governed ourselves, and we always meant to. They didn't mean we should."[1]

The Revolutionary War veteran's simple response reduced the war between the colonists and their British overseers to a struggle over the right of a people to rule themselves. He could not have better captured the essence of this revolutionary event in world history.

By standards of the age, the British crown had not been particularly oppressive to its North American colonies. Over a century or more of "benign neglect," Great Britain had allowed the prosperous colonists a level of independence that had nurtured the natural desires of a people to govern themselves. The crown's attempts to reassert authority over the freethinking Americans in the 1760s met a resistance both surprising and unreasonable to the British.

In the eighteenth-century world of Western civilization, ideas of government were changing. The European Enlightenment principles of natural rights and consent of the governed had rooted deeply along the eastern seaboard of North America. Attempts to firmly control these colonists by a distant ruler would naturally be resisted by American leaders inspired by these Enlightenment ideals. As Levi Preston explained, the American colonists had been governing themselves for some time, and they did not intend for this to end by royal decree. This was indeed a *revolutionary* way of thinking.

With America's newly won independence, its well-read leaders understood something entirely new had happened on the world scene. "The foundation of our Empire was not laid in the gloomy age of Ignorance and Superstition, but at an Epoch when the rights of mankind were better understood and more clearly defined, than at any former period," George Washington said at the end of the revolution.[2] The wording on the young country's Great Seal—"*Novus ordo seclorum*" (a new order of the ages)—reflected this concept. The political world, at least along the eastern seaboard of North America, would be much different now: no more centralized, autocratic government dominating an exploited and oppressed people.

The republican system of government designed by the Founders in 1787 was to embody this key difference. As such, it would provide as much self-governance by the people as possible while maintaining an effective central government. With the emphasis on governing power in the hands of the people through elected representatives, the federal government as intended by the Founders would be inherently limited. The U.S. Constitution would codify these limits.

Levi Preston's generation fought for self-rule and wrote a constitution for a decentralized, limited government. The "new order of the ages" established by these revolutionaries was to disperse government into the hands of the people. Yet ambitious men and court rulings changed this in the twentieth century, reestablishing an "old order" of strong, central government and a diminished people. Americans now suffer grievously from these reactionary changes.

Early in this book, I chronicled how my experiences in Congress shaped my understanding of how the natural desire of career politicians to attain and hold power puts personal and party interests ahead of the public good. A result of this has been the seemingly inexorable march of big government and the attendant loss of wealth and liberties of the American people. This growth of government and diminishment of the American people directly contradicts the original intent of the Founders as just outlined.

This chapter will review the Founders' efforts to establish a government by the people and limited in its central authority. These efforts culminated in the adoption of the Constitution, still intact more than two centuries later although battered and bruised by ambitious politicians and misguided jurists. The next chapter will show how the federal government took on powers not granted in the Constitution and how this unbalanced our system of government. We saw the result of this in the previous chapters: massive growth in government, political corruption and factionalism, and skyrocketing national debt.

These problems can be disheartening, but we have shown earlier how *We the People* can use our constitutional right in Article V to amend the Constitution in ways to dramatically rein in our extravagant, intrusive government and to significantly protect and expand our opportunities and freedoms. This is a process of "rebalancing" the federal government—making changes to the institutions that direct Washington's power and responsibilities.

To better understand how amendments to the Constitution can rebalance our federal government and ameliorate the dysfunction of a corrupted government, we need some lessons from history. The first will be a review of how our foundational laws were originally designed to limit Washington's power and work to the nation's felicity. In the next chapter, we will look at how our government drifted—and sometimes lurched—away from this constitutional framework and so far out of balance.

Carefully following the guidelines of the Constitution is not blind obedience to the "dead hands" of the nation's founders. Disregarding the wisdom and experience used to mold this framework can lead to dire consequences, as illustrated in earlier chapters. Our constitutional "superstructure," as Madison called it, was never designed for the far-ranging powers and responsibilities amassed by the federal government over the last century. Since Washington's role far exceeds the framework into which it was designed to function, we are plagued with political corruption and social disharmony. This political corruption leads to the everyday waste, fraud and duplication in government, perhaps as much as one-third of annual spending in Washington. These are the very governmental dysfunctions from an oversized federal government that the Constitution was designed to avoid.

The text of the Constitution limits our government to fit the framework for governance ratified in 1788 and amended over time as needs arose. The founders designed these constitutional guidelines to maximize the people's "life, liberty, and pursuit of happiness." Yet it often works to the advantage of factional interests and Washington careerists when the government operates outside its constitutional framework—which it has been taking to extremes for the past eighty years or so. Let us look now at how our federal government was originally designed to function under our foundational system of laws, the U.S. Constitution.

THE SUPERSTRUCTURE OF A MORE PERFECT UNION

The Constitution of 1787 was not the first set of laws that governed the thirteen states along the eastern seacoast of North America. These rebellious British colonies had declared their independence in 1776 and ratified the Articles of Confederation as their loose system of governance in 1781. This league of states was poorly served by the Articles system, which allowed each of the former colonies to act as sovereign entities. To provide a stronger, more effective federal government, twelve of the states authorized representatives to amend these laws through a convention of states in May 1787 in Philadelphia.[3]

The gathering for the Federal Convention at the Pennsylvania State House, a national shrine now called Independence Hall, included some of the same men who had signed the Declaration of Independence at the site eleven years earlier. One of the writers of the Great Declaration, John Adams, declared the convention's work "the greatest single efforts of national deliberation that the world has ever seen." Another of the declaration's writers, Thomas Jefferson, called the gathering "an assembly of demigods." Neither of these founders, however, was present at this convocation of distinguished early Americans in spring and summer 1787. Both were serving their country abroad, Adams as minister to Great Britain and Jefferson as minister to France.[4]

Adams and Jefferson would doubtless have added gravitas to the convention, but the gathering assembled a plethora of prominent and experienced legislators. Americans in 1787 probably had more experience writing constitutions than any group of people in world history. Meeting in conventions over the previous dozen years, these mostly citizen-legislators had written their various state constitutions and the Articles of Confederation. They would put this invaluable experience to good use.[5]

Two of the more prominent delegates in attendance were James Madison of Virginia and Alexander Hamilton of New York. Both would play a crucial role in campaigning for the ratification of the convention's proposed constitution after adjournment in September. Most prepared of the delegates was Madison, who sat daily in front of the proceedings, meticulously recording the speakers. The bookish thirty-six-year-old had spent the previous year studying the governing laws of ancient republics and confederacies. In letters to Jefferson and George Washington, who would preside at the assembly, Madison outlined his thoughts for a governing framework for a republic. Many of the political theorist's ideas would be translated into the unique set of foundational laws that have lasted more than 225 years and served as a model for other nations' constitutions.[6]

The great conclave in Philadelphia in summer 1787 deliberated on and drafted new foundational laws to replace the Articles of Confederation. Some key questions to be answered were: How much power would be given to the newly invigorated central government? How would the strength of the federal government be kept in check? How much power would be retained by the states? How were the people to be represented in the new Congress? Would legalized slavery be continued?

The final document approved by the Convention in September was a compromise reached after lengthy debate and often-tempestuous argument. Serving as a delegate from Pennsylvania, the eighty-one-year-old Benjamin Franklin probably best expressed the thoughts of most present when he spoke on the final day of the Great Convention:

I doubt too whether any other Convention we can obtain, may be able to make a better Constitution. For when you assemble a number of men to have the advantage of their joint wisdom, you inevitably assemble with those men, all their prejudices, their passions, their errors of opinion, their local interests, and their selfish views. From such an assembly can a perfect production be expected? It therefore astonishes me, Sir, to find this system approaching so near to perfection as it does.[7]

As the presiding officer of the assembly, Washington sent the proposed constitution to Congress with a resolution expressing the "opinion" of the convention that the new laws be sent to the states for ratification by special state conventions, rather than by their legislatures.[8] Congress agreed, and the proposal for a new governing framework was forwarded to the states for consideration.

This set off another round of deliberations on the new laws, this one by the people in the states. Most of the delegates at the Philadelphia Convention had concluded that the loose confederation of states had needed more than an "alteration" to their laws of governance; the country would be better served by a whole new framework. The delegates generally supported the concept of a federation—a stronger central government that shared power with the several states. So, proponents of the new laws became known as "Federalists." Those opposed, many with self-serving interests and who benefited from the weak Articles of Confederation government, were called "Anti-Federalists."

Fortunately for posterity, this public debate between the two camps played out in a series of printed essays from both sides. The leading writers for the Federalist view were former convention delegates Madison and Hamilton, and a third, John Jay, who had not been sent as a delegate to the convention due to strong anti-Federalist sentiments among his state's leaders. As was the custom of the time, these three founders wrote under a pen name, Publius, and their essays were widely published. Their arguments for the document's ratification and explication of its merits were well preserved as essays included in a later publication called *The Federalist*—described by constitutional scholars Michael S. Paulsen and Luke Paulsen as "a work that has come to be regarded as the most important American contribution to political theory in our nation's history."[9]

As these dueling essays were read and discussed by the highly literate American citizenry, one by one the states began to ratify the new "Constitution of the United States." A major objection of the Anti-Federalists was overcome when Federalists leaders agreed to propose a number of amendments to the Constitution to serve as a "bill of rights" as soon as the new government was installed. These amendments would be an ironclad guarantee for the liberties of individuals and states.[10]

The Anti-Federalists had been concerned that the stronger central government would overreach its authority and limit the people's hard-won rights and freedoms. The Federalists at first protested that these protections in a bill of rights were unnecessary since the new government "could only do those things that the Constitution said it could do; therefore, under a system of limited powers, there was no need for a bill of rights." Later, seeing no harm in agreeing to written guarantees for individual and state's rights and liberties, the Federalists promised to propose these as the first order of business for the new government.[11]

In summer 1788 New Hampshire became the ninth state to ratify the Constitution, providing the required two-thirds majority of the thirteen states. The *united States* of America under the Articles of Confederation became the *United States* of America under the U.S. Constitution. New York and Virginia followed later that summer, and North Carolina came aboard in fall 1789. Tiny Rhode Island, feeling vulnerable and threatened by the larger states, failed to ratify until March 1790, more than a year after the new Congress was seated at Federal Hall in New York City.

With this Constitution now ratified by all the states, just what did the Americans possess with their new government? "A republic, if you can keep it," Benjamin Franklin is said to have replied—and warned—when asked at the Great Convention's closing. Would this framework of governance, as the Constitution's opening words aspire, "form a more perfect Union, establish Justice, insure domestic Tranquility, provide for the common defence, promote the general Welfare, and secure the Blessings of Liberty to ourselves and our Posterity"?[12]

To ensure the survival of the new government with its unique set of foundational laws, the Framers of the Constitution had studied past republican forms of government. None of them survived long. The mistakes of those failed states could be instructional. The delegates also had the advantage of a close look at two other worthy but flawed forms of national government: their current system under the Articles of Confederation and the British parliamentary system. They borrowed the better elements of both and rejected the rest. Incorporating the liberal Enlightenment tenets of the natural rights of man and limited government, the Framers also compromised and innovated.

One of the prime innovators was James Madison. "More than any other Founder, Madison questioned the conventional wisdom of the age concerning majority rule, the proper size for a republic, and the role of factions in society," wrote historian Gordon Wood. "His thinking about the problems of creating republican governments and his writing of the Virginia Plan in 1787, which became the working model for the Constitution, constituted one of the most creative moments in the history of American politics."[13]

The superstructure of the United States government ratified by the thirteen original states is upheld by four fundamental supports, or pillars. First, the foundational laws for the government are *written*, an innovation in the eighteenth century. This provides clear wording and is meant to avoid legal and political dispute. Second, the form of government is *republican:* the people rule themselves through elected representatives. Third, a *separation of powers* in the central administration acts as a check on the usurpation of power by any of the three branches of government: the legislative, the executive, and the judicial. And finally, the principle of *federalism* requires the sharing of power between the states and the national government.

The Constitution's clearly written wording and organization by articles and sections seems entirely logical and natural to us now. Yet the fully recorded foundational laws of the new republic were unique at the time. Many eighteenth-century countries were governed by what an absolute ruler decreed on any given day. Others, like Great Britain, mixed monarchical rule with heavy influence by legal tradition.

The writing in the Constitution was to bind the actions of the government by the words, phrases, and structure of the document. Early chief justice John Marshall called these new laws "the greatest improvement on political institutions—a written constitution" and said the idea of departing from the guidance of these words would be absurd. Yet, as will be demonstrated in the next chapter, Marshall himself would violate his own words with his loose interpretations of foundational law. In their 2015 book, *The Constitution: An Introduction*, Michael Paulsen and Luke Paulsen emphasize the "written-ness" of these laws: "The whole point of a written constitution—the great American advance in political science—was to set forth clearly and absolutely what government could and could not do."[14]

No branch of government and none of the people's representatives were to legitimately act against the wording in the Constitution. These officials were to be bound by oath to support and defend these written laws. As Paulsen and Paulsen explain: "Thus, the idea of a written constitution is closely tied to the idea of *constitutional* supremacy: ***In America, no branch of the government is supreme*** [emphasis added]. The government as a whole is not supreme. The *Constitution* is supreme. *It is the written Constitution that prevails over every other source of authority in the United States* [emphasis in original]."[15]

Yet while I was in Congress, I saw daily violations of the oath by officials to support and defend the Constitution. I saw it by members of Congress, by federal judges, and by the executive branch. If these officials adhered to their oath to uphold the Constitution, they could not vote for or enable so much of our present government that violates the enumerated powers of Congress. As subordinate to the Constitution as the branches of government were supposed to be, ambitious officials have made a mockery of this foundational tenet.

The second pillar of the new government, its *republican* nature, endows the American people with the right to rule themselves through elected representatives. Although these agents perform the duties of governance, all power both in the government and its officers originates from the people. This distinction of power vested in the citizens permeates the wording of the Constitution. The first three words of the Constitution—*We the People*—underscore the primacy of this tenet. Lincoln later echoed this principle of popular rule in his Gettysburg Address when he described a government "of the people, by the people, for the people."

Why did the Founders mold an indirect democracy in the form of a republic rather than more of a direct democracy? Besides practical reasons of time and distance, they also feared a tyranny different from that of a grasping central government—a tyranny of the masses who might vote themselves the properties of others or limit minority freedoms. Also, channeling the will of the people through "virtuous" elected officials was hoped to moderate the views of the people and better protect the rights and liberties of minorities within the republic. As Franklin allegedly explained, "Democracy is two wolves and a lamb voting on what to have for lunch. Liberty is a well-armed lamb contesting the vote."

Further codifying republicanism in the Constitution, the granting of titles of nobility by the national government or the states is forbidden in Article I, Sections 9 and 10. To ensure compliance with republicanism throughout the nation, Article IV, Section 4 guarantees republican forms of government in all the states.

Madison emphasized the people's primacy in their government in *Federalist* No. 39, but he also credited republicanism with another benefit: a means of controlling factionalism. In his essay No. 10, the political theorist touted republicanism as a means to overcome the poisonous effects of factionalism through its ability to govern a large population over a widespread area. This would allow a larger pool from which to select patriotic, public-spirited representatives, and a more diverse range of interests to discourage collusion by factions.

Madison considered a "great object" of this new political experiment to be the securing of both the public good and private rights from the dangers of factionalism while preserving popular government. The carefully designed republican form of government would be critical to attaining this goal. He defined factionalism in essay No. 10 as "a number of citizens, whether amounting to a majority or minority of the whole, who are united and actuated by some common impulse of passion, or of interest, adverse to the rights of other citizens, or to the permanent and aggregate interests of the community." The vice of self-interested groups occurs naturally in a free society, Madison contended, so an object of government must be to control factionalism's ill effects rather than futile attempts to eliminate them altogether.[16]

The lawmaker believed that different abilities among individuals to acquire properties often divided society into factions, but tendency toward factionalism appeared to be inherent in human nature:

> A zeal for different opinions concerning religion, concerning government, and many other points, as well of speculation as of practice; an attachment to different leaders, ambitiously contending for pre-eminence and power; or to persons of other descriptions, whose fortunes have been interesting to the human passions, have, in turn, divided mankind into parties, inflamed them with mutual animosity, and rendered them much more disposed to vex and oppress each other, than to co-operate for their common good.[17]

Still, the republican form of limited government ruled by the Constitution, Madison asserted, could control the omnipresent scourge of factionalism. To completely eradicate it would be asking too much of any set of man-made laws. But have the miseries of factionalism been contained by Madison's ideas of limited government? With pandering politicians slicing and dicing our current society by race, creed, color, sex, national origin, and sexual orientation, factionalism runs rampant and uncontrolled. How could it not in a government that has so far exceeded its originally limited role?

The poster boy for the ill effects of factionalism in America could be former Nevada senator Harry Reid. In the run-up to the 2012 presidential election, Reid stood on the Senate floor and stated that presidential contender Mitt Romney had paid no taxes in the decade preceding 2012. When his smear later brought accusations of McCarthyite tactics, Reid shrugged his fabrication off. He justified his behavior afterward with the statement "Romney didn't win, did he?" What better example could be found to illustrate Madison's warning of the bad effects of and the need to control factionalism in politics?[18]

The two most important foundational supports of the Constitution were supposed to be the *separation of powers*—the division of power among the branches of government; and *federalism*—the division of power between the central authority and the various states. Both of these concepts are concerned with allocation of power. This allocation is a vital consideration for the preservation of freedom and liberty in a republic. The Founders took great care in writing a Constitution that would protect the people from the menacing power of central authority. Madison's explanation of the need for this precaution is one of the more profound statements on government:

> But what is government itself, but the greatest of all reflections on human nature? If men were angels, no government would be necessary. If angels were to govern men, neither external nor internal controls on government would be necessary. In framing a government, which is to be administered by men over men, the greatest difficulty lies in this: you must first enable the government to control the governed; and in the next place oblige it to control itself. A dependence on the people is, no doubt, the primary control on the government; but experience has taught mankind *the necessity of auxiliary precautions.* [19]

The old Articles government had been too weak, so the Framers faced the dual task of strengthening central authority while maximizing the liberties of the people and the states. Here the genius of Madison came to the fore as evinced in his use of the concept of separation of powers. This was not a wholly new idea at the time. The Baron de Montesquieu had praised the concept, and the British system made use of divisions of power. Madison proposed a system for the new republican government that combined his Calvinist understanding of the fallibility of human nature with the concept of separate powers. With federal authority divided into three distinct branches, government officials' natural ambition and quest for power would be used to act as an inherent check on centralized power.

As a further delineation of power, authority in the legislative branch is divided between the House and the Senate. The significance of these divisions at the federal level as "auxiliary precautions" can hardly be overstated. In Paulsen and Paulsen's words: "This system of separate, independent branches, exercising some separate and some shared powers, and each armed with some power to check and balance the others, is perhaps the most important structural feature of the Constitution."[20]

In Madison's system the bane of personal ambition would actually be turned against itself. The self-interest of national officers acts as a legal means to resist encroachment from other self-interested officials. Although driven by personal motives, the actions of one official to prevent overreach by another works to the public good. "Ambition must be made to counteract ambition," Madison stated. "The interest of the man, must be connected with the constitutional rights of the place."[21]

While separation of powers is applied horizontally at the national level to control concentrated power, the concept is applied vertically in the relationship of the federal government with the several states. This lies at the heart of the Constitution's *federalism*—the sharing of power between the central authority in Washington and the governments of the lower states. Federalism's "double security" for the people's liberty added to the uniqueness of the Founder's system.

In the "compound republic of America," Madison said, the powers surrendered by the people would be "divided between two distinct governments," federal and state, and then subdivided among the various governmental branches of both bodies. "Hence a double security arises to the rights of the people. The different governments will control each other; at the same time each will be controlled by itself."[22]

Yet has not this original sharing of power between the federal government and the states been transformed into a haughty Washington overlord dictating to a diminished lot of subservient state governments? Have not ambitious politicians and progressive-minded judges made a mockery of Madison's "double security" on the rights of the people? Of course they have, and I witnessed it nearly every day I served in the House and Senate.

Beyond this vertical division of power, Paulsen and Paulsen describe three key features of federalism, and each in different ways was to protect the rights of the people. The first of these limits central government control to the "enumerated powers" in the Constitution. The authority of the federal government is specifically listed and limited by the written words in Article I, Section 8. "The powers delegated by the proposed constitution to the federal government, are few and defined," Madison argued in *Federalist* No. 45. "Those which are to remain in the state governments, are numerous and indefinite." Furthermore, the Constitution granted discretion to the states to make their own laws to govern their citizens. Finally, the Tenth Amendment was made a part of the Bill of Rights, which states, "The powers not granted to the national government, nor prohibited to the states, are reserved to the states respectively, or to the people."

The "few and defined" powers of the federal government, however, have been expanded by proponents of central authority into a mutant offspring of the Founders' vision. What better example of this distortion of original intent than the $1.4 billion in guns, ammunition, and military-style equipment purchased over the last decade by federal agencies outside the armed services? The two hundred thousand armed federal workers outside the military and authorized to arrest U.S. citizens outnumber the uniformed men and women of the U.S. Marine Corps. Thus, an army of federal officials with police powers exists today in a nation that originally restricted this authority to state and local jurisdiction.[23]

The second key feature of federalism was to be the mutual check on power by the state and national government. The Senate in some ways serves as a representative of the states, with each state receiving two representatives in the upper chamber regardless of population. The states are to operate their own governments virtually independent of the federal state, and usurpation of power by the national government can be contested by the states. Likewise, the federal government can call to account states in violation of the Constitution.

The third feature of federalism is the Constitution's creation of a "more perfect Union." This union is both of and for *We the People* and binds all the states to the supreme Constitution. It also provides an effective national government, the need for which had everything to do with the calling of the Federal Convention in 1787.

The constitutional principles of "written-ness," republicanism, separation of powers, and federalism provide the framework for the interior furnishings of the U.S. Constitution. Paramount in these principles, a republican form of government—by the people and with all governmental power emanating from the people—by definition was to limit central authority. The principle of "few and defined" powers allotted to the federal government in Article I, Section 8, was to further restrict the power of Washington and leave much in the hands of the states and the people. With this framework, Madison and the Framers hoped to preserve the new republic for posterity by preventing government overreach and containing the ills of factionalism and partisanship. Yet our current state of affairs mocks our Founders' hopes.

LEVI PRESTON'S FADING SPIRIT OF '76

For a long period after the Great Convention of 1787, the unique system of foundational laws may have worked better than most of its originators had even dared to hope. The United States came of age in the nineteenth century, becoming the leading industrial power in the world by 1900.

The Union even survived a cataclysmic civil war from 1861 to 1865. The desperate compromise over legalized slavery at the Constitutional Convention in 1787 was expunged by the Thirteenth Amendment, banning slavery. The words of the entire Constitution could now more fully embody the ideals of the Declaration of Independence.

Blessed with an abundance of natural resources and unfettered by government restraints, America's economic engine roared in the last half of the nineteenth century. The Founders understood the intimate connection between political freedom and economic growth. It was no coincidence that the year 1776 saw both the signing of the Declaration of Independence and the publication of Scottish economist Adam Smith's *The Wealth of Nations*. Jefferson's Great Declaration speaks of the "unalienable Rights" of "Life, Liberty, and the pursuit of Happiness." Smith's timeless treatise explains how in an economy unfettered by government intrusions and suffused with freedoms for individuals to pursue their own self-interest, an "invisible hand" in the marketplace works to maximize gains to individuals and *to society as a whole*.

Yet even with America's early successes, a few cracks in the wall of the republic appeared almost from the start. As the decades went by, some of these weaknesses became more obvious, and even after a repair here and there, problems continued. During the balance of the twentieth century, corruption, factionalism, and dysfunction grew—side by side with the size and scope of federal power.

My alarm over these problems by 1994 led me to Washington for six years in the House of Representatives and a return for ten years in the Senate. I saw the uncontrolled spending from factionalism, the bitter partisanship, and the unwillingness of Washington officials to address critical problems for the public good. I fought all of these hard for many years. By the time I left the Senate at the end of 2014, I realized that our federal government would not and probably could not fix these problems. The source of Washington's power—the people—would have to save their republic.

What went wrong? How did so much power become centralized

in the nation's capital? How did our federal government—contrary to the concept of a republican form of governance—expand and become so intrusive in almost every aspect of American society? Why do the people's representatives in Congress each year authorize the expenditure of several hundred billion dollars of the people's money on waste, fraud, and duplication and directly contrary to the public good? Did the Founders pass down a flawed Constitution?

I contend that the Constitution, while an imperfect work, never let the nation down. The people, often in the form of ambitious men and special-interest groups, just asked a lot of the federal government, and certainly far too much after the 1920s. To accommodate those requests, Washington overstepped its enumerated powers, often with the help of strained court rulings. This has been especially so over the last eighty years, opening a Pandora's box of factional mischief and political corruption. The powers and responsibilities of the federal government increased, but no changes were made to the national institutions directing those powers and responsibilities. This unbalanced the republican system of government outlined in the Constitution and led to an unwholesome growth in government and to corruption as an institutionalized feature in Washington.

The term "corruption" as used in this book should not be construed as necessarily illegal activity. Its uses here are best understood as exploitation of federal power for self- or party interest and contrary to the public good. To reduce opportunities for corruption, the Madisonian system for the Constitution had limited the federal government to "few and defined" powers. Individuals and groups wielding those powers would be controlled by the separation of powers and the checks and balances operating on the system's varied institutions. When the federal government is granted or takes on new powers without adjustments to the system to control exploitation by self-interested parties, the resultant political corruption is predictable. The young nation soon witnessed this unpleasantness. The next chapter shows how much of this happened through court rulings.

7

A JUDICIAL FOUNDATION FOR BIG GOVERNMENT

The Union: Who are its real friends? . . . Not those who study, by arbitrary inter-pretations and insidious precedents, to pervert the limited government of the Union, into a government of unlimited discretion, contrary to the will and subversive of the authority of the people.

— JAMES MADISON

JUST A FEW MONTHS AFTER the Affordable Care Act was signed into law by President Obama, I questioned Supreme Court nominee Elena Kagan at her confirmation hearing in summer 2010. Already on my mind was a Supreme Court ruling from nearly seventy years earlier and its support for the expansive new health care law. I cut straight to the chase.

"If I wanted to sponsor a bill and it said, 'Americans, you have to eat three vegetables and three fruits every day,'" I queried Kagan, "and I got it through Congress, and that's now the law of the land, got to do it, does that violate the Commerce Clause?"

"Sounds like a dumb law," she replied, humorously sidestepping my question.

"Yeah," I responded, "but I got one that's real similar to it that I think is equally dumb. I'm not going to mention which it is."[1]

After more back-and-forth on whether the government could use court interpretations of the Constitution's commerce clause to impose dietary rules on Americans to cut health care costs, she never directly answered my original question. She did, however, hint at such sweeping governmental powers with an explanation of how in the past the Supreme Court had broadly interpreted the commerce clause to apply to regulation of nearly any commercial channel that substantially affected interstate commerce.

With my allotted time running out, I reminded Kagan that several of the primary authors and interpreters of our Constitution would have disagreed with court expansions of the commerce clause. The Supreme Court's rebuke to the framers of the Constitution has encouraged government overreach, I said, and paved the way for our nation's $1.6 trillion annual deficit.

"Well, Senator Coburn . . . a few points," she replied, then lectured for a minute or so. Finally, she concluded, "And I guess the third point is . . . that $1.6 trillion deficit may be an enormous problem. It may be an enormous problem. But I don't think it's a problem for courts to solve; I think it's a problem for the political process to solve."[2]

On examination, this was a revealing response. This erudite legal scholar and now Supreme Court associate justice essentially said that the "enormous problem" facilitated by judicial activists who circumvent the political process with strained legal interpretations should be addressed by . . . *the political process.* So, activist courts can make a muck of things by loosely interpreting the Constitution (created by a political process) and facilitating government overreach, but when it comes to cleaning up the mess, "it's a problem for the political process to solve."

How did we get here? What has caused the wealthiest nation in history to saddle future generations with untold trillions in public debt? We will take a look at that in this chapter.

In chapter 1, I chronicled how my experiences in Congress shaped my understanding of how the natural desire of career politicians to

attain and hold power leads them to place personal and party interests ahead of the public good. A result of this has been the seemingly
inexorable march of progressive big government and the attendant loss
of wealth and liberties of the American people. In the previous chapter
we reviewed the writing of the Constitution, which established a limited
central government for a self-ruling people. This chapter will show how
the federal government took on powers not granted in the Constitution
and how this unbalanced our republican system of government. In the
first chapter, I described from firsthand experience the results of this
imbalance: massive growth in government, political corruption and
factionalism, and skyrocketing national debt. The problems created by
big government were also analyzed in an earlier chapter.

Although the drift promoted by activist jurors away from limited
government and federalism can be disheartening, earlier chapters have
shown how *We the People* can use our constitutional right in Article V
to amend the Constitution in ways to control our extravagant, intrusive
government. These changes through amendments can significantly
protect and expand our opportunities and freedoms. This is a process of
"rebalancing" the federal government—making constitutional changes
to the institutions that direct Washington's power and responsibilities.

Let us now look at how our government wandered so far from its
original constitutional framework.

AMBITIOUS OFFICIALS PUSH FOR BIGGER GOVERNMENT

Pressure began early in our republic for the federal government to do
more than constitutional powers granted, and certainly more than some
of the Founders could find in the expressed wording of the Constitution.
As the first secretary of the Treasury, Alexander Hamilton proposed that
the federal government charter a Bank of the United States to stabilize
the credit of the new country and to manage financial transactions. He
persuaded President Washington to sign this into law after Congress
approved this legislation early in 1791.

With this action, the new president acted against the advice of secretary of state Thomas Jefferson, Virginia representative James Madison, and attorney general Edmund Randolph. Madison argued in Congress against this bill. He called it an "unconstitutional assertion of federal power" as the Constitution "did not expressly grant the federal government the authority to charter a bank." Both Jefferson and Randolph argued against the bill's constitutionality, "contending that the Tenth Amendment to the Constitution left all powers not specifically delegated to the Congress to the states or the people."[3]

Hamilton countered with a state paper to the president that "made a powerful case for a broad construction of the Constitution that resounded through subsequent decades of American history." The Treasury secretary argued that Article I, Section 8 of the Constitution gave Congress the right to make all laws "necessary and proper" (the means) to the execution of the legislature's specified powers (the end). Hamilton asserted that without this "implied power" of means, the federal government would be greatly weakened. Washington was won over. The First Bank of the United States was granted a twenty-year charter.[4]

Corruption quickly followed. Before the bank's chartering, Hamilton proposed establishing the country's creditworthiness by using the proposed banking institution to redeem the country's debt securities from the Revolutionary War at full face value. With this insider knowledge, his assistant secretary resigned from the Treasury at the end of 1791 and with his partners began buying up government paper at a discount in hopes of profiting later. Attempting to corner the market on these securities, they overextended their credit lines at the bank. When they failed to pay their creditors, a panic led to a run on the bank. Only adept stewardship by Hamilton staved off an early financial disaster for the country.

With both appalled by these events, Madison wrote to Jefferson that Hamilton's financial system had upset the balance in the government. What was to have checked this executive overreach to create the bank, which enabled acquisition of special information by a faction of treasury insiders? The legislative branch should have prevented this under the

Madisonian system, its namesake reasoned. Yet this new, extraconstitutional banking institution had influenced even some in Congress by facilitating their own personal investments in bank shares. The officials acted in their own interest rather than the public good—our primary meaning of "corruption" in this book.[5]

Political analyst Jay Cost wrote in *A Republic No More* about how this and other overreach by the federal government unbalances our constitutional system and leads to corruption. Of this seminal event in the early 1790s, Cost said:

> For the style of corruption bred by the Bank will recur time and again: ambitious national leaders see some problem that the existing powers granted under the plain meaning of the Constitution do not allow; they expand those powers successfully; this may or may not solve the problem, but it disrupts the balance the Constitution hopes to achieve; and it lends itself to corruption as one faction or another can take advantage of the new weaknesses of the system. . . . Such innovations in governmental power—once successfully claimed—are virtually irrevocable.[6]

Despite the early near panic, the First Bank of the United States was ultimately beneficial in the early economic development of the country. It proved such an unqualified success for national expansion that even President Madison chartered the Second Bank of the United States in 1816. Twenty-five years earlier Madison had argued against the First Bank's twenty-year charter, but he could not deny the economic benefits of this institution in the crucial early years of the country. He continued this extraconstitutional power of government.

The bank's long-term effects for expansion of congressional power and federal government might have been contained except for a Supreme Court ruling on its constitutionality in 1819. Leading to this court ruling, the Maryland Legislature had levied a tax on the Baltimore branch of the bank related to significant embezzlement by the cashier, James M'Culloh, and several other officials. The entire matter ended up before the Supreme Court with Congress's power to create the bank at issue. Descending the slippery slope, the Marshall Court upheld the constitutionality of congressional incorporation of the bank. More disturbing was the grant of such sweeping powers to Congress in the wording of this ruling.

In the resounding *McCulloch v. Maryland* ruling, Chief Justice Marshall applied a broad construction to the wording of the Constitution's necessary and proper clause in Article I, Section 8. While the Constitution had not expressly mentioned the right of Congress to incorporate the bank, it was "implied" by the clause, Marshall wrote in his opinion. The clause authorized Congress to use a means—incorporating the bank—merely "appropriate" and not necessarily "indispensible" in the exercise of specified powers. The ruling in *McCulloch* was the Marshall Court's first decree to expand the power of the federal government.[7]

In this ruling, Marshall also contrasted the Framers' use of the word "necessary" with their use of "absolutely necessary" in another part of the Constitution. From this difference, Marshall concluded that the "necessary" in the Necessary and Proper Clause could be equated with "convenient." Madison, who had chartered the Second Bank in 1816, was suddenly aroused and greatly concerned by Marshall's loose interpretation of the Constitution. Reverting to his 1791 position, Madison said that Marshall's opinion granted to Congress "a legislative discretion . . . to which no practical limit can be assigned." According to legal scholar Randy Barnett, "history seems to have borne out Madison's and others' expressed concern for the integrity of the enumerated powers scheme. *With rare exception, the enumeration of powers has largely been vitiated as a limitation on the scope of the national government, owing in no small measure to the influence of Justice Marshall's opinion in* McCulloch."[8]

The point here is not that the bank's innovation alone was destructive to the country. To the contrary, the bank aided the country's economic development. These events, however, illustrate how ambitious leaders and the courts—often with good intentions—granted extraconstitutional powers to the federal government from the beginning and, moreover, how this unbalanced the republican system and eventually corrupted government. The Supreme Court ruling on the necessary and proper clause is just the first in a long line of interpretations that, intentionally or not, encouraged expansion of federal power and growth of government—and ultimately limited our freedoms.

Throughout history, changing conditions in America have prompted a new form of governmental action or program, and too often this has occurred without expressed constitutional authority. Sometimes this expansion of government has had serious consequences; sometimes not. Seldom, however, have federal leaders considered how additional federal power can unbalance the system of governance. Two centuries later, we see the unhappy result of these incremental and sometimes sudden moves away from limited government in our country, epitomized by our $20 trillion and counting national debt and $143 trillion in unfunded liabilities.

Another commercial dispute soon led the activist Marshall Court into another decision with long-range implications for increased federal power and bigger, more intrusive government. Around 1820, The New York Legislature granted an exclusive franchise for steamboat trade in the state. The company licensed businessman Aaron Ogden to oversee trade from New York with the New Jersey shore. A former partner of Ogden's, Thomas Gibbons, challenged the monopoly granted by the New York franchise.

The case of *Gibbons v. Ogden* reached the Supreme Court in 1824. The Marshall Court ruled that the federal government had the power to "regulate commerce among the several states." Thus, the monopoly granted by New York could not be applied to trade along the Jersey shoreline. Once again, the Court's finding would have been of little consequence if limited to this case. Yet the legal theory and wording for this ruling by Chief Justice Marshall would again grant new power to the federal government.[9]

"Commerce, undoubtedly, is traffic," Marshall opined, "but it is something more; it is intercourse." The jurist hedged his words a bit

later in the opinion, narrowing—ever so slightly—the court's definition of commerce to "commercial intercourse." Marshall then turned
to another part of the commerce clause in Article I, Section 8, which
granted federal power to regulate commerce "among the several states."
Marshall defined the word "among" as "intermingled with," and wandered further afield with his opinion on Congress's power to regulate
commerce within a single state. As legal analyst Adam Freedman has
stated, "But Marshall planted another time bomb in his famous opinion:
he noted that Congress could regulate a state's internal commerce whenever that commerce might 'affect other States.' . . . In cases like *Gibbons*,
Marshall set the standard for later generations of activist judges. His
description of the commerce clause was dictated not by the text or by
logic but by his desire *to achieve a result*."[10]

Legal scholar Randy Barnett has published one of the most extensive analyses of the commerce clause and a thorough indictment of the
Marshall Court for its activism in the *Gibbons* ruling. Barnett takes issue
with Marshall's redefining "commerce" outside of its common usage
in the period, which was reserved to "trade or exchange" and exclusive
of manufacturing or agriculture. Marshall's overly broad construction included his reasoning that "among the states" in the commerce
clause could be construed as "concerns more states than one." Barnett
summarizes: "This substitution of language has been used to justify
extending the power of Congress from regulating commerce that actually moves between the states to commerce that occurs within a state
and has external effects." With this single ruling, the Marshall Court
broadened the meaning of "commerce" far from its common usage and
its intent by the Founders. This extended Congress's regulatory powers
for this new, broader activity from "among the states" to within a single
state. The real harm from this ruling would not come for more than
a century, but the groundwork had been laid for more court mischief
and increased federal power.[11]

Intentionally activist or not, John Marshall arrogantly left his
imprint on the nation's highest court. Perhaps he would have repudiated

his *Gibbons* opinion if he could have attended Elena Kagan's Senate confirmation hearing and heard her defend government overreach with past court interpretations of the commerce clause. Marshall's increase in federal power without institutional offsets—often difficult to come by—helped unbalance the nation's system of governance. With this imbalance the door opened for corruption—exploitation of federal power by self-interested officials and results contrary to the long-term public good.

Despite these court tendencies to enhance federal power in the nation's early decades, the federal government was limited to a small role. The economy continued to grow with little regulation, and the individual states maintained a strong position as a counterbalance to the national state. Centered on the slavery issue, eleven Southern states' secession from the Union brought on the Civil War in 1861. This struggle ended with a weakening of states' rights and a strengthening of Washington's power—much of this in the executive branch.

Still, the limited federal government largely maintained a laissez-faire policy regarding economic and social issues as the nation settled the West and began industrialization on a massive scale. In the decades after the Civil War, the governments' primary involvement in the economy involved actions to enhance national commerce, as exemplified by its role in the building of the transcontinental railroad. It should be noted, however, even this short-term role in the railway's construction led to one of the largest financial scandals in the nation's history. The government offered free land as incentive to the two companies chartered to establish the rail line, and one of these, the Union Pacific Railroad Company, set up Credit Mobilier of America to do the work. Fraudulent overcharges for construction and conflicts of interest between stockholders of both railroad companies and government officials embarrassed President Grant's administration. Once again, an increase in federal authority without an institutional counterbalance led to corruption, with costs borne by private interests and the American public.

With money to be made during industrialization and the settlement of the West, Gilded Age politics brimmed with corruption. Yet much of the money changing hands was private money and local government funds. The Tammany Hall officials in New York took local corruption to new heights, and similar big-city political machines practiced patronage and cronyism. The federal government was still too small to siphon much from the national economy or from the people. During an economic panic in the mid-1890s, the modest U.S. government actually borrowed $65 million in gold from investment banker John Pierpont Morgan and his associates to restore public confidence in the gold standard.

THE POTENT MIX OF PROGRESSIVISM AND JUDICIAL ACTIVISM
The long era of small government came to an end with the rise of the progressives at the turn of the century. Industrialization had changed the social and economic landscape in the last decades of the nineteenth century, and many in the working class felt exploited and powerless. They looked to government to level the playing field in the marketplace, and the progressive presidents—Theodore Roosevelt, William Howard Taft, and Woodrow Wilson—used new federal power to regulate big business and redistribute some of the country's new wealth with a progressive federal income tax. This tax was made practicable by ratification of the Sixteenth Amendment in 1913. This would have major implications for future government growth and economic regulation.

Americans cannot be faulted for seeking help from government after the social and economic upheaval brought by industrialization. In a republic like ours, the political process can be a major avenue for relief from large-scale distress. Still, government is run by politicians and officials with largely the same ambitions and self-interests as society as a whole. A constitutional system like ours can be readily exploited when the federal government is seen as a solution to a problem better solved in the private sector or with state and local government. For better and for worse, Americans became accustomed to a federal government more active in the economy and society during the era of the progressive presidents.

Another amendment to the constitution during these progressive years is worth a quick review. The Seventeenth Amendment involved a change in a government institution, allowing the direct election of U.S. senators by their respective state voters. As originally written in the Constitution, senators were elected by their state legislatures—a method thought by the Founders to provide a higher quality of representatives and as a tenet of federalism. By late in the nineteenth century, lengthy vacancies were common in the U.S. Senate owing to political deadlock in many state legislatures. Also, many of those in the Senate were seen as corrupt pawns of big business, as they were often elected through bribery of state legislators.

A number of state governments began petitioning Congress for an Article V amendments convention to propose the direct election of U.S. senators by citizens. After twenty-five of the states applied, Congress took note and passed the proposed amendment in 1912. The amendment's potential harm to federalism aside, here is a classic example of *We the People* exercising their constitutional right to address an imbalance in a government institution—vacancies and corruption in the U.S. Senate. We will revisit this affair in detail in the next chapter.

After a brief, conservative renaissance in the 1920s, the miseries of the Great Depression and Franklin Roosevelt's New Deal programs forged an alliance of activist courts and big government—a combination that for the next eighty years greatly enhanced the power of the federal government and ballooned a bureaucracy of programs, services and entitlements. With this burgeoning and activist government came the waste, fraud, duplication, and dependence that have saddled future generations with government debt of $20 trillion and $143 trillion in unfunded liabilities. The framework intended to limit the powers of the federal government has undergone wrenching change in these years, unbalancing the republican system of governance and promoting corruption in Washington. The long-term public good has suffered grievously.

Initially, the courts rejected Roosevelt's New Deal programs. In particular, government intrusion into the private sector was rebuked.

But after the retirement of one Supreme Court associate justice and a change in the attitude of another, Roosevelt and the progressives finally had the Court they needed by 1937. And this was in time to fend off the challenge to the administration's Social Security Act, which had become law in August 1935. Regarded as the "cornerstone of his administration" by the president himself, the act's validation and legal opinion by the Supreme Court would add a similar cornerstone in judicial activism.

A shareholder of the Edison Electric Illuminating Company sought to avoid the company's payroll deductions and contributions required by the new Social Security Act. Ultimately, the Supreme Court upheld the constitutionality of the act in *Helvering v. Davis* as a spending power of the federal government to provide for the "general welfare" of the country. The flaw in the ruling, according to a strict reading of the Constitution, is that the clause in Article I, Section 8 gives power to Congress only "to lay and collect Taxes . . . for the common Defence and General Welfare of the United States." There is no expressed "spending power" in the general welfare clause.[12]

A revealing story lies behind the Roosevelt administration's decision to proceed with the Social Security Act despite concerns over its constitutionality. At a Washington tea party late in 1934, Secretary of Labor Frances Perkins expressed these doubts about the proposed legislation to Supreme Court associate justice (later chief justice) Harlan Stone. "Upon hearing this, the Justice looked around to see if anyone was listening, leaned over to her, and putting his hand up to his mouth, whispered, 'The taxing power of the Federal Government, my dear, the taxing power is sufficient for everything you want and need.' The Secretary excitedly returned to her staff and announced she had made up her mind, they would base the new program on the government's power to tax."[13]

Yet it was not just the taxing power of Congress that carried the day in the Supreme Court. The decision granted the government new authority to spend tax revenues for the country's "general welfare." "Congress may spend money in aid of the general welfare," the *Helvering v. Davis* decision opined. "The conception of the spending power advocated by Hamilton has prevailed over that of Madison." In his argument with Madison over the creation of the Bank of the United States, Hamilton had contended that the Constitution in Article I, Section 8 granted the federal government "implied powers" to promote the general welfare of the country. Legal analyst Adam Freedman has criticized this ruling's boost to congressional power under the general welfare clause: "Congress would be limited to its Article I powers— unless it wanted to spend money, in which case it could do whatever it wanted." So, the general welfare clause would serve nicely for future congressional maneuvering.[14]

While conceding the public good from a retirement pension program like Social Security, one can also criticize the legal contortion and broad reading of congressional power related to the enactment of this law. While one public good may come from a broad interpretation of government power, years later a public harm may result from another law using this same legal precedent. So, criticism of judicial activism is often better directed at its potential for future harm rather than its initial objective.

The federal government would maneuver mightily after the 1930s, potently armed with legal precedents from rulings related to the necessary and proper, commerce, and general welfare clauses. Using these prior rulings in 1942 led to one of the most egregious cases of judicial activism. The power-constraining meaning of "commerce among the states" had been weakened somewhat back in 1824 with the *Gibbons* ruling; this constraint of congressional regulatory power would now be eviscerated in a case regarding an Ohio wheat farmer.

Roscoe Filburn went to court to defend his cultivation of eleven acres of wheat more than he was allowed under guidelines established by the New Deal's Agricultural Adjustment Act of 1938. Administered by local officials as a price support, the federal law set individual quotas on crops and livestock. Filburn argued that he had no intention of marketing the wheat. Its use would be confined to meal for his livestock and for personal consumption. No commerce among the states involved here, he reasoned, so no federal power to regulate. The Supreme Court, however, cited in *Wickard v. Filburn* the *Gibbons* definition of commerce to deny the family farmer the right to produce those crops for personal use. Congress's regulatory power of "commerce among the states" had been interpreted in 1824 by Chief Justice Marshall as commerce "intermingled with" other states, the Court stated in 1942, and thus "is not confined in its exercise to the regulation of commerce among the States."[15]

What made this case truly a landmark was its potent combination of the necessary and proper clause and the commerce clause to justify the expansive regulatory powers of Congress and to extend those powers to activities in individual states. With this one-two punch by the Court, the *Wickard* ruling dramatically increased federal power to regulate activities only indirectly related to commerce. ***It was a grant of government authority undreamed of by the Framers in 1787.*** Just as important, the opportunities for corruption in government created by this imbalance—increased federal power without institutional counterbalance—was magnified.[16]

A section in Cost's *A Republic No More* summarizes the long-term consequences of the New Deal legislation and court rulings, only a small part of which was covered earlier:

> The New Deal was an explosion in the size and scope of government, far beyond what the country had previously experienced at any point during peacetime and certainly more than what the Framers had ever envisioned. . . . The point here is not to criticize the principle of industrial regulation, to promote a laissez-faire view of political economy, or to argue against social welfare provisions like Social Security. The point, rather, is that such programs must be evaluated within the context of the particular government that is implementing them, and the American government was never designed with such actions in mind. It was meant to balance power among institutions . . . Of course, there was no turning back after the New Deal. These powers were here to stay, and so was the corruption they bred.[17]

The New Deal ushered in a new era of government growth. Washington would now be an active promoter of social welfare, so it was unsurprising that health care for the elderly and the poor would be high on the agenda for progressive-minded American leaders. Initial planners for Social Security had considered involving the government in health care, but that big step would not be taken until President Lyndon Johnson's Great Society programs of the 1960s. In 1966 two amendments were made to the Social Security Act, beginning the programs of Medicare and Medicaid. These two health care initiatives would now be piggybacked onto the already court-sanctioned Social Security Act.

As a practicing physician for twenty-five years and a member of Congress for sixteen, I have seen Medicare from several perspectives. Social benefits aside, the government's subsidization of health care insurance for the elderly has been and will continue to be a major driver of spending and national debt. I advocate consumer choice and a market-based approach to make this program more cost-effective, but cost controls on this budget-buster are peripheral to our discussion here on the growth of government and its power. My involvement with this program as a physician and congressman informs my earlier critique on the growth of federal power and its attendant corruption on our system of governance.

As Cost explained in *A Republic No More*, the major waste and abuse in this expensive government program does not stem from villainy, despite some bad actors in this system. The real problem is a federal government ill suited (and unwilling, I would add) to oversee these kinds of programs. "Medicare has been in crisis off and on, since the early 1970s," Cost wrote. "These crises have been predictable yet unavoidable because they stem from a simple problem: Medicare provides benefits to factions within society that are extremely adept at ensuring those benefits continue, despite the obvious problems they pose to the public good." The thesis of Cost's book "is that the power of government has grown much too vast for the institutions designed to manage it."[18] Again, I contend, institutional changes are needed to counter the imbalance in the system and to better control government.

From Medicare, it was only a small step for Washington to shower us with the benefits of the Affordable Care Act—signed into law by President Obama in March 2010 and fulfilling a century-long progressive dream. We have now come full circle to Elena Kagan's Senate confirmation hearing and my questions to her about the expanded, extraconstitutional powers of the federal government. As a legal scholar, Kagan cleverly and correctly pointed to the courts' past broad interpretations of the commerce clause to justify the federal government's regulation of just about anything in society—including a theoretical requirement for Americans to eat three servings of fruits and vegetables each day.

Two years later I wrote about the pending Supreme Court decision on the constitutionality of the Affordable Care Act's individual mandate: "If the Court decides Congress has the power to force consumers to buy health insurance and, by implication, eat their fruits and vegetables, the last vestiges of the Commerce Clause's limitations on government interfering with the market will be washed away."[19] Yet the Supreme Court did not use Congress's sweeping power under the commerce clause to uphold the individual mandate to purchase health insurance under the Affordable Care Act. The Court found another sweeping power—the taxing authority of the federal government. Remember Associate Justice Stone whispering to Labor Secretary Frances Perkins at the tea party? Where there's a will to expand government, there's always a way.

From this chapter's review of court outreach in service of government overreach, it is not hard to understand how Congress's latest misadventure into health care was sanctioned by the Supreme Court's *NFIB v. Sebelius* ruling in 2012 and with *King v. Burwell* in 2015. And one can easily guess which side of the Court Associate Justice Kagan joined in both decisions.

The preceding narrative on the growth of federal power and government goes beyond a criticism of the social and economic goals of this expansion. Our federal government *should* respond to some public needs in times of great peril and unusual deprivation. Yet reliance on the government for wants and needs attainable through the people's initiative saps the economic and social vitality of the republic. Thus, this book is meant to promote a more limited government.

Also, our review on governmental power and overreach underscores how the judicial activists over the years deserve opprobrium for their readiness to read more into the Constitution than our system of governance can responsibly handle. *The cases discussed earlier in this chapter demonstrate the federal court system's allegiance more to central authority than to the ultimate source of that authority—the American people and the Constitution.* Ultimately, allegiance to this authority is required for a republic to survive. Men and women of the courts can be influenced by social movements as much as any of us. Jurists inevitably stray from the Constitution when they put more confidence in the prevailing attitudes of their times than in the Founders' "experience of all ages."

Associate Justice Antonin Scalia well articulated the argument for using constitutional text and history to guide jurisprudence, rather than the value judgments of fallible men and women of the court. Legal decisions based on subjective value judgments supersede the democratic process, he argued, and should remain outside the process of jurisprudence. "The people know that their value judgments are quite as good as those taught in any law school—maybe better," Scalia wrote in a 1992 Supreme Court decision.[20]

From an opposite perspective, jurists should forsake the principle of *stare decisis*, or settled law, as a means to perpetuate "constitutional tradition" from prior decisions unmoored to the Constitution. Judicial interest in settled law should never require a rigid adherence to past decisions hinged on social trends. "The 'constitutional tradition' that we are now told to worship stands for a federal regime of unlimited jurisdiction," Adam Freedman wrote. "It stands for a government by unelected, unaccountable, and unremovable bureaucrats. . . . To paraphrase Yogi Berra, tradition ain't what it used to be."[21]

INSTITUTIONAL CHANGES TO REBALANCE THE SYSTEM

Most important, the preceding account is intended to provide a useful understanding of how our system of republican governance is thrown out of balance when jurists allow Washington to take on powers and functions outside the constitutional framework. I am a medical doctor by training, certainly not a constitutional attorney, so legal scholars may view my analysis as quaint and lacking nuance. Yet some of these same learned men and women of the court, it should be noted, have facilitated the enhanced federal power and expansive government that foment the kind of corruption and dysfunction that we now have in our nation's capital—and that jeopardize the future of the republic.

The American people instinctively know when their nation's leaders in the courts and in Congress are straying from the foundational laws that have made this country a beacon of opportunity and freedom. This kind of immense political power wielded by a handful of progressive elites in the nation's court system is both illiberal and undemocratic. It is time for *We the People* to exercise our constitutional powers. The rebalancing of the system will require targeted institutional changes to contain the political ambition and factionalism that now thrive in our unbalanced system.

This chapter has given a brief narrative of how some of our national leaders forsook the Framers' guidelines for limited government and promoted an unbalanced, overreaching federal government. Previous chapters have shown the results of this unbalanced government and how an Article V amendments convention can be used to rebalance the institutions of government.

Although opponents of amendments conventions portray a potential gathering of state delegations as unnatural and even dangerous, conventions of the states and attempts to convene an Article V amendments convention have a lengthy tradition in American history. Much can be learned with a review of past state conventions and of applications by the states for an Article V convention. The next chapter recounts this history.

8

LESSONS FROM PAST CONVENTIONS AND APPLICATIONS

I will venture to add that to me the convention mode seems preferable, in that it allows amendments to originate with the people themselves; instead of only permitting them to take or reject propositions originated by others, not especially chosen for the purpose, and which might not be precisely such as they would wish to accept or refuse.

— ABRAHAM LINCOLN

FROM 1975 TO 1983, THIRTY-TWO STATES filed applications for an amendments convention to consider a federal balanced budget. Just two states short of the thirty-four required, the National Taxpayers Union–led drive appeared on the verge of triggering a congressional call for a convention of states. By September 1984 the Michigan Senate had approved a petition and the state's lower house was poised to concur. The final push to reach thirty-four states would likely be in the conservative state of Montana, which was set to pass a state referendum for an application in November.[1]

Although odds favored the nation's first Article V amendments convention in the mid-1980s, events turned against it. Before the Michigan House of Representatives voted, the measure first had to clear a nine-person committee. Ten-year veteran of the Michigan Legislature Ruth McNamee would cast the decisive vote on September 13. The night before the committee met, a Reagan White House aide called to urge her "yes" vote.

Yet, to the consternation of many of her Republican colleagues, McNamee voted against the measure. The 4–5-committee vote doomed the state's attempt to become the thirty-third to apply to Congress for a budget-related amendments convention. "I felt this resolution creates a risk," the legislator said just after her decisive vote. "This is not a good political climate for a *constitutional convention*."[2]

The failure in Michigan dispirited convention organizers, and this would be as close as the nation came to seeing an amendments convention for a balanced budget proposal. McNamee had fallen for the canard that the gathering of states would be a "constitutional convention." She was not alone in her mistaken belief. President Jimmy Carter called the convention drive "extremely dangerous" and warned that the Constitution "could be amended en masse with multitudes of amendments." Many on the left and some on the right echoed the president. Some of these opponents were benighted; others were disingenuous.[3]

Now here we are, more than thirty years later and with an "extremely dangerous" national debt of $20 trillion. The nation is certainly less financially stable than three decades ago, but hopefully becoming better informed on what an amendments convention can and cannot do. Chapter 5 described how our Founders endowed the people with this constitutional gift to deal with major national issues such as our frightening national debt.

Since the nation's founding, American political leaders have considered a convention of states to address specific problems, to resolve constitutional deadlock, and to ameliorate federal dysfunction. The usefulness of this republican process has become obscured by the mists of time—and more recently by dishonest advocates of big government—but a review of its uses after the nation's founding further clarifies its utility and safety.

CONVENTIONS BEFORE THE CIVIL WAR CRISIS

Fears of federal encroachment on individual rights and liberties had been relieved by ratification of the Bill of Rights in 1791—amendments proposed by Congress partly in response to state applications for an amendments convention. No state would apply to Congress for a convention until several decades later, but the republican tradition of conventions continued to play a political role in the nation's early history.

The threat of war with France agitated politics during John Adams's presidency, and the arguably unconstitutional Alien and Sedition Acts of 1798 granted broad authority to the Federalist government. Some of this new authority forbade criticism of Congress or the president. Now aligned with the political party out of power, Democratic-Republicans James Madison and Thomas Jefferson anonymously authored resolutions by the Virginia and Kentucky legislatures that brashly condemned these new federal powers. Madison's Virginia Resolution called for cooperation from other states to resist the new laws. Jefferson's Kentucky Resolution first broached the idea of "nullification" of federal laws that states considered an infringement on their prerogatives.[4]

These controversial resolutions were not well received by the other twelve states. (Vermont had joined the Union in 1791 as the fourteenth state.) The Massachusetts Legislature recommended an Article V convention as an alternative to nullification. Madison suddenly grew more interested in this constitutional provision as a way for states to push back against extraconstitutional federal authority. Answering charges that the Virginia Legislature had acted unconstitutionally with its resolution, Madison asserted late in 1799 that to rescind the offending Alien and Sedition Acts the states "might, by an application to Congress, have obtained a Convention for the same object."[5]

The unpopular Alien and Sedition Acts were allowed to expire in

1801, and by then Madison had become an outspoken proponent of the Article V convention as a check on overreaching federal power. This constitutional right of the states to propose amendments should be the tool for states to "interpose" against federal abuse, he contended, not "nullification," which would later be falsely attributed to him. Madison would further clarify his position in subsequent writings.[6]

A decade later as the War of 1812 ground to a stalemate, the New England states bordered on secession in their opposition to the war. In 1814 some of the Federalist leaders in New England recommended a "partial" convention of states to moderate some of the antiwar extremism in the region and to express their grievances to the national government. Twenty-six delegates from New England states gathered in December 1814 in Hartford, Connecticut. Much of the New Englanders' ire was directed at the "Virginia Dynasty" of presidents in the White House, which they blamed for the war.[7]

The Hartford Convention issued a report to Congress in early January with seven recommended amendments to the Constitution, many reflecting the region's anger at Virginia's political dominance of the young nation. Since the convention had met outside the authority of Article V, their proposed amendments had no legal force. With their report, however, the delegates included a contingent call for another convention of states in June 1815. This assembly would also be outside the Article V framework unless three fourths of the states applied to Congress for this convention.

If the war continued, a resolution in the report stated, "it will in the opinion of this Convention be expedient for the Legislatures of the several States to appoint Delegates to another Convention, to meet at Boston, in the State of Massachusetts, on the third Thursday of June next with such powers and instructions as the exigency of a crisis so momentous may require." The Hartford Convention's report to Congress arrived at about the same time as news that the Treaty of Ghent had concluded the war. The crisis passed.[8]

After the war a newly cohesive United States put political squabbles behind for nearly a decade, but the Era of Good Feelings ended by the mid-1820s. Exacerbated by the slavery issue, the country's sectional divide grew. In 1828 the Southern states vehemently opposed new tariff law that they believed unfair to the region. South Carolina brandished the state-nullification doctrine outlined by Jefferson's Kentucky Resolution a quarter century earlier. This doctrine held that states had a right to reject federal laws within their borders unless this action was reversed by an amendment to the Constitution. Drawing his inspiration from both the Virginia and Kentucky resolutions, South Carolinian John C. Calhoun championed this nullification doctrine—he preferred to call it "interposition"—while protesting the recently enacted tariff law.[9]

The aging James Madison publicly denied in late 1830 that his writings of a quarter century earlier supported nullification. Agreeing with a previous opinion by the now-deceased Thomas Jefferson, Madison argued that an Article V convention was the proper forum to settle disputes over power between the states and an overreaching federal government. An amendments convention of the states would be the constitutional interposition Madison supported. In a lengthy letter published in the literary magazine *North American Review*, the seventy-nine-year-old Framer wrote: "Should the provisions of the Constitution . . . be found not to secure the Government and rights of the States, against usurpations and abuses on the part of the United States, the final resort within the purview of the Constitution, lies in an amendment of the Constitution, according to a process applicable by the states."[10]

Madison's position may have softened South Carolina's nullification campaign, and in 1832 the state applied to Congress for an amendments convention to consider "questions of disputed power" between the states and the national government. The first application for an Article V convention since New York's in 1789, South Carolina's petition was limited in subject matter and without a recommendation for specific wording for a potential amendment. Two more Southern states opposed to the "tariff of abominations," Georgia and Alabama, followed with applications to Congress for an amendments convention. Like South

Carolina's application, these two states attached no specific language for potential amendments in their petitions.[11]

Yet no other states joined in the campaign for an amendments convention, and the nullification crisis passed. The crisis and the approach taken by the three Southern states provide lessons. These states resisted federal authority with their convention applications yet backed away when they saw little support from surrounding states. Their applications focused on particular subject matter, but none offered specific language for an amendment proposal. And finally, Madison had performed a public service by his drawing attention to use of the Article V convention to aid in the settlement of disputes between states and the federal government.

Tragically for the nation, Madison's suggested uses for an amendments convention never came to fruition as the nation's civil strife grew. The sectional dispute between the North and the South over slavery and states' rights escalated through the middle of the nineteenth century, but the states could never muster the commitment to an Article V convention of states to resolve this crisis. Years after the nation's greatest crisis had passed, former president of the Confederate States of America Jefferson Davis would lament in his memoirs that "in earlier and better times, when the prospect of serious difficulties first arose, a convention of the States was not assembled to consider the relations of the various States and the Government of the Union."[12]

CONVENTIONS AND THE CIVIL WAR CRISIS

If the nation as a whole was reluctant to address the gathering storm of sectional divide with a convention, the Southern states were not. As a show of unity against perceived federal encroachment, nine slave states sent delegates in June 1850 to a regional convention in Nashville, Tennessee. Despite calls from "fire-eaters" threatening secession to protect slavery, most Southerners at the time disdained calls for disunion. The assembly adopted several resolutions asserting Southern rights. The Nashville Convention soon disbanded in the face of Kentucky senator Henry Clay's proposed Compromise of 1850, which temporarily defused the conflict over slavery.[13]

As the North–South sectional divide intensified with Abraham Lincoln's election in 1860, political leaders crafted compromise solutions, many of which included amendments to the Constitution. Kentucky senator John Crittenden proffered a plan with several constitutional amendments to ensure Southern states' rights while limiting the spread of slavery to areas of the Southwest. As these arid areas were not conducive to slave labor, the Crittenden plan likely would have doomed slavery's future. More important, the plan might have avoided the bloodiest conflict in U.S. history. Yet Congress was too deadlocked to agree on this compromise.[14]

To break the political logjam in Washington, an Article V convention drew support from several directions. Delaware, Arkansas, and Tennessee proposed a national convention to resolve the sectional differences, but none formally applied to Congress. In November 1860 President James Buchanan expressed support for an Article V convention to propose an "explanatory amendment" on slavery. Over the following months, a number of frustrated congressmen offered resolutions urging the states to apply for an amendments convention. In March, President Lincoln, who had no specific amendment in mind to address the crisis, stated he had no objections to an amendment and preferred it come from a convention of the states, as this assembly could propose changes that "originate with the people themselves" rather than indirectly through Congress.[15]

Despite support by many leaders for an Article V amendments convention, few states applied. The only gathering to attempt a compromise solution for the crisis was the Washington Peace Convention (or Peace Conference), called by Virginia as a general convention in January 1861 but outside Article V of the Constitution. With six Southern states already seceded from the Union, the Peace Convention was to act as a kind of emergency session of and substitute for an amendments convention. Twenty-one of the thirty-four states sent a total of 131 delegates, and the conclave met for three weeks in February in Washington.

Former president John Tyler presided. The convention sent a formal recommendation to Congress to pass an amendment proposal similar to the Crittenden plan. Heavily politicized, Congress rejected the conference's work, and the nation edged closer to war.[16]

Kentucky's response to Virginia's call to the Washington Peace Convention had been both to send delegates to the assembly and to apply to Congress for an Article V convention. The Kentucky application's subject matter was adoption of the Crittenden plan to ease the crisis. This first application in decades was followed by applications from New Jersey, Indiana, Illinois, and Ohio. The subject of these applications varied, but all were related to the North–South crisis. An Arkansas state convention recommended an application in March, but the state seceded before it was transmitted. More states may have submitted applications that went undocumented as Congress haphazardly recorded these petitions. Applications by more states may have been precluded by the outbreak of hostilities in April 1861.[17]

Congress's feeble reaction to the impending firestorm included passage in March of the ill-conceived Corwin amendment, which was an attempt to prohibit future amendments to the Constitution that would ban or interfere with slavery. This proposed thirteenth amendment to secure slavery was submitted to the states for ratification, but received negligible support. Ironically, it would be shelved by the successful Thirteenth Amendment that banned slavery in 1865. Three other states applied for an Article V convention during the war. Surprisingly, one of these was rebellious but apparently war-weary North Carolina, which applied in 1864 hoping for a resolution to the war.[18]

The short-lived constitution framed by the seceding states of the Confederacy provides insight into the original understanding of Article V in the nation's first century. The Confederate constitution adopted by the Montgomery Convention in March 1861 closely modeled on the U.S. Constitution, but the Confederate Article V provision reflected the South's emphasis on states' rights. Upon application by only three states, the provision required the Confederate Congress to "summon a convention of all the States, to take into consideration such amendments to the Constitution as the said States shall concur in suggesting at the time when the said demand is made." Amendment ratification required only a two-thirds-majority of the states.[19]

Requiring only three states' "demands" (applications) to trigger a convention and lowering the ratification requirement from three-fourths of the states to two-thirds reflected the South's contention that a majority of U.S. states had threatened the rights of the minority Southern states. More important to the historical context of the U.S. Constitution's Article V is the wording in the Confederate provision limiting consideration of amendments at the convention to those suggested "at the time when the said demand is made." This phrasing reflects the common understanding of the era that the subject matter considered at a convention was expressed in the states' applications. And finally, the convention was to consider amendments on which "the said [applying] States shall concur." This expressed a required concurrence, or similarity, in the subject matter of the states' applications.

In an article for a Harvard law journal, legal historian Robert Natelson pointed out several other lessons from the Civil War crisis related to an Article V convention. With repeated references to "a convention of the states" and variants of this wording, numerous state applications in this period confirm that the convention was seen as a creature of the states, and not of Congress. Also, most states used the constitutional wording of "a convention for proposing amendments." Almost none of the states' applications mistook the assembly to be a "constitutional convention."[20] Respecting the established legal tradition, the procedures and protocols for conventions from the founding era were followed to the letter at the Washington Peace Convention in 1861—the largest convention of states in U.S. history.[21]

Moreover, Natelson infers another key lesson from this crisis that should inform thoughts on our current plight of national debt and dysfunction in Washington. "No one can say definitively that a convention for proposing amendments could have averted Civil War," he contends. "Certainly some of the most respected political leaders of the day—including Presidents Buchanan and Lincoln, and a number of U.S. senators—thought that it might. *If their assessment was correct, then the events of the time show us that there can be far greater risks in failing to call a convention than in calling one.*"[22]

Through the remainder of the nineteenth century, a number of national leaders promoted an amendments convention to address various concerns, but little interest was shown by the states until the turn of the century. An oft-forgotten, national election crisis in 1876–1877 prompted Kansas senator John Ingalls to recommend an amendments convention to resolve the issue. The disputed presidential election of 1876 had left the nation without a president-elect for several months. To break the stalemate, Ingalls offered a resolution urging the states to apply for a convention to meet in May 1877 in Columbus, Ohio. Little support was shown for this action, and an electoral commission soon settled the issue with the Compromise of 1877, a party-line decision that Republican Rutherford B. Hayes had won the election.[23]

Prompted by beliefs that the U.S. Constitution was not keeping pace with massive economic and social changes from industrialization, prominent national figures urged an amendments convention in the last decades of the nineteenth century. Recent amendments to state constitutions were offered as good examples of these needed changes. Some in Congress believed an Article V convention to consider a range of amendments would be better than a fragmentary approach.

In 1897 American Historical Association president James Schouler lectured that the states were getting ahead of the national government with their constitutional innovations and urged a national amendments process that could "frame concrete propositions of amendment carefully in advance." He praised the clear wording for the process of amendment in the defunct constitution of the Confederate States of America. Presaging future efforts to control national spending, Schouler advocated a constitutional amendment limiting the federal government's ability to borrow money.[24]

Although the nineteenth century saw only two dozen or so state applications for an amendments convention, ad hoc conventions of state delegates were seen as useful during times of crisis. The Hartford Convention of 1815, the Nashville Convention of 1850, and the Washington Peace Convention of 1861 assembled numerous state representatives at critical periods. As important, several U.S. presidents—including James Madison—recommended Article V conventions to resolve important national issues. Conventions of states outside Article V faded from national consciousness in the twentieth century, but applications for an Article V convention became commonplace. Nearly seven hundred applications deluged Congress between 1900 and 1999.[25] Three campaigns in the twentieth century would fall just shy of their goal of an Article V convention.

THE ROLE OF STATE LEGISLATURES IN THE SEVENTEENTH AMENDMENT

With state legislatures selecting U.S. senators before 1913, corruption and absenteeism in the Senate prompted calls for the direct election of these officials by the end of the nineteenth century. Much of America at the time believed many Senate seats were bought by business interests, and party strife often deadlocked legislatures' selection of these officials. A prime example, Delaware had no representation in the Senate from 1898 to 1902. In 1893, Nebraska submitted the first application for an amendments convention to address this issue, probably the first state petition since the Civil War.[26]

The circumstances were ideal for one of the most successful campaigns for an amendments convention in U.S. history. First, Americans were disgusted with the Gilded Age government corruption, so support for an amendment to allow direct election of senators by the people was extremely high in the first decade of the twentieth century. Also, those directly empowered to apply for an Article V convention, the state legislatures, were personally affected by this issue and thus motivated to remedy it. Finally, the legislatures largely understood at the time that the subject matter of a convention was limited by the state applications and that the wording of the proposed amendment would be at the discretion of the convention.[27]

Still, with a century between the nation's founding and the push for direct election of senators, some constitutional memory had faded. For the first time, widespread warnings of a "runaway constitutional convention" were propagated by opponents. Many of those opposed suffered less from constitutional amnesia than from fear of a more direct hand of the people in the political process. Adding to these fears, some of those supporting the amendment hoped to frighten the Senate into action by cynically referring to the assembly as a "constitutional convention."[28]

Texas followed Nebraska with an application in June 1899, requesting a gathering "for proposing amendments" but silent on the subject matter. Texas did, however, send a copy of their application to the governor of each state with a request for concurrence. Despite the lack of specificity in the application, Texas seemed to imply a common plan with the petition's circulation to the other states.[29]

After reviewing the Lone Star State's application, the Pennsylvania Legislature appointed a five-man committee to confer with other state legislatures on the issue of direct election. The committee reported to the next legislative session a belief that the U.S. Senate would never approve this proposed amendment (the U.S. House already had) unless prodded into action by an imminent convention of states. The Pennsylvania Legislature applied for a convention and charged the committee with coordinating a campaign with the other states. In December 1900, the Georgia Legislature formed a similar committee, followed by Arkansas in 1901 and Oklahoma in 1907. Robert Natelson sees a parallel in the efforts of these legislatures. "It was, in other words," he contends, "organized in the tradition of the Revolutionary-era 'committees of correspondence' set up in the American colonies, and contemplated by James Madison as a future remedy for federal abuse."[30]

The Pennsylvania committee mailed to the other states a standardized application form modeled after their application to Congress. The model was concise and direct. It requested that "a convention be called for the purpose of proposing an amendment to the Constitution of the United States, as provided for in Article V of the said Constitution, which amendment shall provide for a change in the present method of electing United States Senators, so that they can be chosen in each state by a direct vote of the people."[31]

The wording of the model application confined the subject matter of the convention to the single issue and avoided language suggesting an unlimited convention or a constitutional convention. The standardized form also avoided any suggested wording for a proposed amendment, as the Pennsylvania legislators seemed to understand this to be the purview of a convention. Subsequent state filings generally followed this form, but several states strayed. Washington (1903), Oklahoma (1907), and Louisiana (1908) applied for unlimited conventions, but two of these applications also included language related to the direct-election issue.[32]

This model convention application was also used by a number of states in this same period to address the issue of de facto polygamy in Utah. Most of the applications, however, were confined to the direct-election issue. By 1912 thirty-one states had applied with at least a part of their respective applications related to the campaign for direct election. This was just one shy of the thirty-two needed at the time.[33]

Alarm bells rang, followed by warnings of impending doom. A promoter of stronger federal authority and big government, national commentator Henry Litchfield West, warned, "Very few persons realize how close the nation is to a constitutional convention," which he predicted would "open Pandora's box." Idaho senator Weldon Heyburn said he strongly opposed a convention. "When the constitutional convention meets it is the people," Heyburn admonished, "and it is the same people who made the original Constitution, and no limitation in the original Constitution controls the people when they meet again to consider the Constitution." Other reactionaries in the Senate argued that the existing system had produced numerous great senators in the past and needed no changes.[34]

Despite reluctance to change their mode of election, many in the Senate worried about a defeat at the hands of the citizenry—evidence of the so-called prodding effect of an Article V convention. Also at this time, many states had started a de facto popular election of their U.S. senators by pressuring their candidates for the state legislatures to honor unofficial senate elections in the states. The writing was clearly on the wall. In February 1911, the Senate held a vote for the first time on an amendment proposal allowing for their direct election by the people. It failed by only five votes, so the campaign by the states obviously had the solons' attention. Success came by spring 1912 when Congress sent the proposed amendment to the states for ratification by the state legislatures. The states acted quickly on the popular proposal, and the Seventeenth Amendment was officially adopted in May 1913, just two months after the presidential inauguration of noted progressive Woodrow Wilson.[35]

Although the Seventeenth Amendment is considered a Progressive Era amendment for its increase in democratization, Framers might have been wary of this change. States' rights proponents past and present have rightly pointed out that the Seventeenth Amendment shifted power from the state legislatures—one more body blow to federalism. Indeed, some scholars aver that with the Seventeenth Amendment progressives at the time had more on their agenda than increasing the sovereignty of the people. These big-government proponents may have seen direct election of senators as a way to augment federal power by curtailing state legislatures' participation in Congress.[36]

Nonetheless, good lessons can be learned from this amendments campaign. First, the states' working in concert with model applications played a role in getting the nearly two-thirds of the required applications to Congress efficiently. Also, the states understood that they needed to clearly specify the subject matter in their applications but not to attempt to provide wording for the amendment proposal. Last, opponents of an amendments convention had found their hobgoblin—the "runaway constitutional convention"—to generate anxiety about the states meeting in an Article V convention. Ironically, this scare tactic may have prodded the Senate into action on the direct-election amendment.

It would be a half-century before another nearly successful amendments campaign would be mounted. Still, several issues provoked a surge in state applications over the first half of the twentieth century. The drive for a convention to address polygamy continued until World War I with twenty-six states sending applications between 1906 and 1916. The next mini-surge in applications was in response to the social tinkering of the Eighteenth Amendment, which banned the manufacture and sale of alcoholic beverages beginning in 1920. Before repeal of the ban with the Twenty-First Amendment in 1933, five states applied for an amendments convention to overturn the unpopular Eighteenth Amendment.

One of the national leaders working for an amendments convention to overturn the ban on alcohol was a New York assemblyman named Louis A. Cuvillier, who pressured Congress to call a convention in the early 1930s. Cuvillier asserted, quite properly, that New York governor Franklin Roosevelt had endorsed an amendments convention with his unnecessary signing of the state's application to Congress in 1931. The proposal for the Twenty-First Amendment to repeal the Eighteenth was sent to the states by Congress requiring ratification by state conventions, the only amendment ever approved by the states in this mode.[37]

Throughout the 1930s and 1940s, states regularly applied for conventions for various issues, and a concerted effort began around 1940 related to rising federal taxation. By 1950, eighteen states had applied for a convention to repeal the Sixteenth Amendment, which authorized federal income taxes beginning in 1913. Remembering the prodding effect of the direct-election campaign decades earlier, one of the campaign leaders said the real goal was "to put the fear of God" into Congress to propose the repeal amendment.[38]

Disturbed by the movement's success, Congress mounted an attack led by Texas representative Wright Patman. Patman urged states to rescind their applications and warned advocates to "stop sneaking this reactionary plot through unsuspecting State legislatures." At a congressional hearing Patman claimed that an amendments convention could be used "for any purpose on earth" and to "rewrite the whole Constitution." Colorado's application in 1963 may have brought the total of similar applications to thirty-four, but the drive lost momentum amid claims of expired and rescinded applications.[39]

Sundry issues in the 1950s and 1960s promoted a variety of applications from numerous states. An increasing proportion showed the states' concern over encroachment of federal authority, much of this new power granted by expansive reading of the Constitution by the Supreme Court. Related to this would be a major and nearly successful campaign in the 1960s over a Supreme Court ruling on reapportionment.

THE ARTICLE V CONVENTION DRIVE AGAINST REAPPORTIONMENT

In the landmark *Baker v. Carr* ruling of 1962, the Supreme Court held that courts could decide on issues related to equitable apportionment of state legislatures. Following up, the *Reynolds v. Sims* ruling in 1964 extended this "one-person, one-vote" principle to both houses of state legislatures, requiring roughly equal populations in districts. This reapportionment requirement ushered in new power at the polls for urban areas in many states. Conservatives generally viewed this as giving new strength to progressives and an unwelcome intrusion of federal power in state government.

Working with the Council of State Governments late in 1962, state legislatures promoted three constitutional amendments related to overturning federal jurisdiction on state-level apportionment issues. These amendments were also seen as a pushback to the power of the Supreme Court. The national campaign encouraged states to submit uniform applications to Congress.

Addressing the American Law Institute in May 1963, progressive chief justice Earl Warren spoke against the amendments and a convention of states. He asked members of the institute to help prevent the Constitution from being changed "unwittingly" by poorly informed state legislatures. Warren employed the familiar scare tactic of the runaway convention with an over-the-top warning that an Article V convention "used unwisely by an uninformed public . . . could soon destroy the foundation of the Constitution."[40]

Just days later, in a commencement address at Defiance College in Ohio, former president Dwight Eisenhower rebutted Warren. He urged state resistance to "a distant bureaucracy." Although Eisenhower did not specifically endorse the three proposed amendments in the campaign, he did voice support for an Article V convention. "Through their state legislatures and without regard to the Federal Government," he noted in his address, "the people can demand and participate in constitutional conventions in which they can, through their own actions, adopt such amendments as can and will reverse any trends they see as fatal to true representative government." The former president made the by-then-commonplace mistake of referring to the amendments convention as a "constitutional convention."[41]

Under sustained attack by the American Bar Association, the American Civil Liberties Union, and the Conference of Mayors, the three amendment proposals garnered only scattered support from the states. Shifting gears, the Council of State Governments focused on a new amendment proposal to allow one house of a state's bicameral legislature to be apportioned on factors other than population. An organized media campaign promoted the amendment, and early in 1965 Republican minority leader Everett Dirksen introduced the proposal in the Senate. The Illinois senator gained strong support but could not muster the two-thirds needed to pass the proposal. Accepting defeat in the Senate, he warned his colleagues the fight would continue—a veiled threat that he would lead the push for an amendments convention of the states.[42]

Sixteen states had already filed for an amendments convention regarding a one-house state apportionment exception when Dirksen began the national campaign in 1965. The senator and state proponents hoped to keep the state applications quiet to avoid opposition. The number of states reached thirty-two in March 1967 when suddenly the drive received national publicity. A front-page story in the *New York Times* mobilized opposition in Congress and in some state capitals.[43]

Maryland senator Joseph Tydings and Senator Robert Kennedy questioned the validity of the malapportioned legislatures' applications (twenty-six were under court order to reapportion) and urged Congress to set a two- or three-year expiration on the applications. Senators William Proxmire and Jacob Javits rolled out the old "runaway convention" scare. Dirksen did little to assuage the runaway convention theory, probably as a tactic to frighten Congress into proposing the amendment.[44]

North Carolina Senator Sam Ervin was a supporter of Dirksen's campaign. To counter fears of an uncontrollable convention, he proposed the Federal Constitutional Convention Act (S. 2307) in August 1967. The bill provided legislative framework for an amendments convention and prescribed limits for it. With the success of the campaign alarming many in Congress, the Senate Judiciary Committee held hearings on the Ervin bill in October. Yet Congress took no further action at the time.[45]

Early in 1969 Iowa became the thirty-third state to apply. With success so near, the campaign took a turn for the worse. Three states rescinded their applications after succumbing to fears of an uncontrollable convention. Further diminishing the campaign, reapportionment did not seem to be hurting rural conservatives at the polls, as many had worried. Even worse for the drive, in September Senator Dirksen suffered a fatal heart attack following surgery. The convention campaign died along with its strongest advocate.[46]

Several lessons emerged from the failed efforts for this convention. First, opponents of an amendments convention were increasingly coming from the ranks of progressives in Congress. Big-government proponents in Washington held little sympathy for state resistance to federal encroachment by constitutional amendment. Second, the runaway-convention theory to dissuade support for an amendments convention was firmly entrenched. Even a convention supporter such as Senator Ervin called the convention of states a "constitutional convention" and framed legislation to control it. Apparently, no one at that time researched the legal tradition of conventions in the nation's history, the writing of Article V in 1787, or what the Framers said about the provision at the writing of the Constitution and afterward. Or perhaps some did—and kept it to themselves.

THE FIRST MAJOR DRIVE FOR A BALANCED BUDGET AMENDMENT

Efforts to restrain federal spending go back to the nation's beginning, when founding era leader Roger Sherman proposed limiting the Confederation Congress's money-raising powers to no more than that needed to pay existing debt. Thomas Jefferson took this a step further in 1798 when he called for an amendment to the Constitution, eliminating Congress's power to borrow money. The first constitutional budget amendment was offered to Congress by Minnesota representative Harold Knutson in 1936. Knutson wanted to set a limit on per-capita debt during peacetime. Another budget amendment was introduced in Congress in the 1950s by senators Harry F. Byrd of Virginia and Styles Bridges of New Hampshire.[47]

After the failed efforts against reapportionment in the late 1960s, the states' resistance to an expansive federal government continued into the 1970s with interest in a federal balanced budget amendment. Expecting little help from Congress, state representative David Halbrook of Mississippi and state senator James Clark of Maryland began lobbying in 1975 for an amendments convention to control federal spending. With the aid of the National Taxpayers Union, a serious campaign was launched. The drive included a coordinator, a model amendments resolution for the states, and informal networks of state legislators. In 1975 North Dakota became the first state to apply for a balanced budget amendments convention.[48]

Campaign efforts were boosted in June 1978 by national publicity from California's Proposition 13, a state constitutional amendment limiting local property taxes. The day after the California proposition passed, Kansas senator Robert Dole sent a letter to all fifty state governors, urging them "to consider requesting and working with your state legislature to petition Congress" for a balanced budget amendments convention.[49] By December 1978 sixteen states had applied for a convention to balance the budget. The next month the National Tax Limitation Committee presented a draft antispending amendment to Congress. The proposal was written by a panel that included Nobel Prize–winning economist Milton Friedman and future Supreme Court nominee Robert Bork. Bork wanted Congress to propose the amendment because a *constitutional convention* ought to be the last resort of a foundering nation."[50]

Suddenly the low-key convention drive vaulted into national news when California governor Edmund "Jerry" Brown voiced support in his inaugural address early in 1979. With many predicting thirty-four states on board by the end of the year, the California Assembly Ways and Means Committee began hearings in February. Testimony from renowned law professors Laurence Tribe and Charles Black provided the dire warnings the Democratic panel needed to oppose an amendments convention. Resurrecting Senator Weldon Heyburn's alarms from 1912, Tribe raised concerns about the process. "Was Senator Heyburn right or wrong?" the professor asked. "If right, then a constitutional convention could propose any imaginable amendments, no matter how limited the official scope of the convention. . . . [T]he undeniable fact is that no definitive answer exists."[51]

The national balanced budget drive soon mired in partisan politics, with mostly Republicans promoting a convention and Democrats generally opposed. Chairman of the Senate Budget Committee Edmund Muskie threatened states with cuts in federal aid if a balanced budget amendment were enacted. Duped by the "constitutional convention" scaremongers, conservative Senator Barry Goldwater hurt the drive when he came out against it: "If we hold a constitutional convention . . . we are going to wind up with a Constitution that will be so far different from the one we have lived under for 200 years that I doubt that the Republic could continue."[52]

After a surge of applications early in 1979, by April New Hampshire had become the twenty-ninth state to apply for the balanced budget convention. Publicly opposed to the drive, the Carter administration began to view these efforts as a repudiation of the president's economic policies. A nine-member White House task force was assembled to defeat the proposed convention. Complementing White House efforts, Democratic leaders organized an anti-amendment lobbying group, ironically named Citizens for the Constitution. The group conducted a legal review of the twenty-nine applications and declared invalid about half due to technical violations. To clear up some of the legal issues regarding an Article V convention, Utah senator Orrin Hatch built on Senator Ervin's earlier legislative efforts. Hatch's Constitutional Convention Implementation Act (S. 40) cleared the Judiciary Committee several years later but failed in the Senate.[53]

Polls showed three-fourths of Americans supported a balanced budget amendment in 1979, but the counterattack by the Washington political establishment was effective. Nevada was the only state to apply for a convention in 1980. Ronald Reagan's presidential campaign provided support for a budget amendment, and several states came close to a petition in 1981. Alaska became the thirty-first applicant in 1982. In August the Republican Senate passed a balanced budget amendment, but it died in the Democrat-controlled House. Congressional recalcitrance was answered by Missouri's application in 1983. With the reapplication by several of the early states, Missouri brought the total to thirty-two states with petitions for a balanced budget amendment dated within the previous seven years. Only two more states were needed to compel a convention call by Congress.[54]

In 1984 the convention drive again entered presidential politics. The platform adopted at the Democratic National Convention in July opposed "a federal constitutional convention" for the "artificial and rigid Constitutional restraint of a balanced budget amendment." The conservative Republican platform at their nominating convention in August rebutted the Democrats: "If Congress fails to act on this issue, a constitutional convention should be convened to address only this issue in order to bring deficit spending under control."[55]

Heretical to the position of his party's leaders, former Democratic attorney general Griffin Bell addressed the issue of an amendments convention as the drive continued for two more state applications. "Those who wring their hands over the prospects of a convention," the Carter-era Justice Department leader wrote, "run the risk of exposing their elitism, implying that the average citizen cannot be trusted." Appearing to have actually researched Article V and its legal background, the former attorney general contended that an amendments convention could be limited. "Congress would not be compelled, nor would it have any incentive" to submit proposals that went beyond the original call for the convention, he opined.[56]

Still, Missouri's application in 1983 would prove the high-water mark for the balanced budget convention drive. The failure of Michigan to pass a resolution in September 1984 (reviewed earlier) began a retreat by the states. The "runaway" scare tactics mounted with Yale University professors James Tobin and Thomas Emerson, respectively, calling an amendments convention "a parliamentary morass" and "a constitutional crisis that could tear the country apart." Perhaps more damaging to the campaign was Congress's passage of the Gramm–Rudman–Hollings Balanced Budget Act late in 1985. The legislation mandated automatic spending cuts if deficits exceeded predetermined levels. The failure of the Republican Senate to pass a balanced budget amendment by one vote in March 1986 was also attributed to the Gramm–Rudman–Hollings legislation.[57]

As Democratic senator Paul Simon warned the states that a convention could "modify the Bill of Rights . . . and raise all kinds of havoc," President Reagan signaled that he might personally get behind the campaign. He did just that in one of his weekly radio addresses in May 1986, predicting that the convention campaign would pick up steam again if Congress failed to enact a balanced budget amendment.

But the tide began to turn against the campaign in 1988. An

unusual coalition of liberal and conservative groups formed an unlikely alliance against an amendments convention. In a June letter solicited by Phyllis Schlafly, president of the conservative interest group Eagle Forum, retired chief justice Warren Burger warned that a convention of states could not be limited and might challenge the Constitution's "very existence." Using this letter to spread alarm, the Eagle Forum and the John Birch Society began working to prevent—and eventually to reverse—state petitions.[58]

No more states applied for a balanced budget convention as Reagan's second term expired. Even with some polls showing 85 percent of the nation favoring a balanced budget amendment in the 1980s, the orchestrated fears of a runaway convention and reliance on the ultimately ineffectual Gramm–Rudman–Hollings Act are credited with ending the convention campaign in the Carter and Reagan years.[59]

LESSONS FROM PAST CONVENTIONS AND FAILED DRIVES

From the previous review of the states' nearly two centuries of conventions and attempts to mandate an Article V convention, this well-established process can be clearly seen as a part of our constitutional, republican heritage. Indeed, conventions of the states should be considered a key aspect of federalism—the vertical division of power between the state and national governments. To our nation's detriment, we have seen a steady erosion of federalism over the last century and an accompanying loss in our heritage of conventions. We must regain both to rebalance our government institutions and end dysfunction in Washington.

We also have seen how Founding Era convention protocols and procedures were still remembered and carefully followed in our nation's first century. The Article V applications by the states reflected an understanding that the subject matter of the convention was to be fairly specific and that the wording for an amendment proposal would be defined by the convention.

During the first century after the Constitution was adopted, the nation's leaders showed little or no concern for a runaway convention from an Article V amendments convention. Washington, Madison, Jefferson, Lincoln, and other prominent officials actually spoke of an amendments convention as a useful tool of the republic. It was not until after Founding Era memory began to fade in the early twentieth century that fears of a "runaway constitutional convention" were raised. Unleashing this hobgoblin seems to have started as a new and useful tactic of both proponents and opponents of an Article V convention. The "prodding effect" of convention applications certainly played a role in the adoption of the Seventeenth Amendment. Whatever the origins of the "runaway" scare tactic, it was skillfully employed by big-government supporters (and even by conservatives in Eagle Forum and John Birch Society) to thwart states' attempts to limit federal authority in the last half of the twentieth century.

Another lesson from the last century was the remarkable—though ultimately unsuccessful—achievements of the convention campaigns when focused on a well-defined issue and with the states working in concert. Even before the communication advantages of the Internet and e-mail, the balanced budget amendment drive from 1975 to 1983 garnered thirty-two initial state applications and four reapplications. More than half of these applications came in the single year of 1979. It should also be noted that this deluge of applications came after respected and nationally recognized U.S. Senator Bob Dole wrote a letter to all fifty of the state governors, asking them to work with the legislators to apply for a balanced budget amendments convention.

The most important lesson from our nation's past conventions may be the Article V convention that never met just before the Civil War. With Congress in a political knot as the country moved closer to war, delegates from the twenty-one states at the Washington Peace Convention agreed early in 1861 on a proposed amendment that might have averted our nation's greatest tragedy. Yet when this convention met, six Southern states had already seceded and events were hurtling out of control. The hastily planned assembly had no time to apply through the legislatures under the provisions of Article V; thus, Congress was not required to send their compromise amendment proposal to the states for ratification. Significantly, Congress was too dysfunctional to approve this amendment. "And the war came," as Lincoln sadly recalled the failed compromise attempts at his second inaugural four years later—and after the death of nearly six hundred thousand Americans.

Another failure to compromise more than a century after the Civil War has led to another national tragedy. The states' campaign for an Article V balanced budget amendment foundered in the late 1980s when big-government advocates fought off these reform efforts and Congress was too dysfunctional to provide a solution. The campaign's failure ended hopes to stem the tide of debt that now engulfs the nation and threatens our future. Fiscal conservative Ronald Reagan campaigned for the presidency in 1980 on a theme to stop the burgeoning deficit spending. The national debt stood at $59.6 billion when he took office. When he left early in 1989, this debt had ballooned to nearly $3 trillion. This 1989 debt burden looks wholesome compared to our present $20 trillion accrued from continued deficit spending.

President Reagan's failure was not from a lack of effort. He did as much as any president since the 1930s to roll back the tide of big government. Reagan labored mightily to stop the profligacy, but the problem was bigger than his office. It is bigger than any president's office. *A president can only stop our nation's spending addiction if Congress is willing and determined to find fiscal restraint. Congress has failed dismally and continuously to find this restraint.* A review of chapter 1 should dispel hopes that officials in Washington can or will do any better.

The people of this nation must solve this fiscal knot through their representatives at the state level—the representatives in our constitutional republic closest to the people. These state legislators must do what past efforts by the states have failed to do, and that is to assemble an Article V amendments convention to propose a solution to our nation's spending and debt crisis—and to limit a ruinous, overreaching federal government.

Our review in this and previous chapters establishes the safety and procedures of this endowment from the Framers. The delegates at an amendments convention can legally propose no more than authorized by their state legislatures—and no more than a politicized, unprincipled Congress can propose on any day in session. As Lincoln counseled, Americans should put faith more in their state delegates in convention than in the careerists in Congress. The nation relied on Congress early in 1861—they got four years of civil war. Will our reliance on Congress now lead to a debt crisis and economic chaos? Speaking to us from the past, our founders implore us to save ourselves with an Article V convention.

FROM THEORY TO PRACTICE

Much of this book has provided theoretical information about an Article V convention of states, but the real value of this work will ultimately hinge on whether the reader is motivated to support an amendments convention. Without this support, I am convinced that the nation will see only more of the same—increasing deficits, bureaucratic growth and overreach, and a factionalized, irrational citizenry—until our current form of government completely fails.

But with constitutional change by and in the interest of *We the People*, our republican system can continue to provide the American dream to citizens within our borders and to those who lawfully come to assimilate. Studying the "experience of the ages," the Founders certainly understood how tenuous self-governance could be. The Constitution's separation of powers and system of checks and balances in government were intended to limit the central state's growth and power and to maximize the governing role and liberties of the states and the people. And, of course, they included the constitutional safety valve of an Article V amendments convention if needed.

A more recent writing by a concerned American shares the same concerns about an overreaching central government and America's future as those expressed by the Founders:

Paradoxically enough, the release of initiative and enterprise made possible by popular self-government ultimately generates disintegrating forces from within. Again and again after freedom has brought opportunity and some degree of plenty, the competent become selfish, luxury-loving and complacent, the incompetent and the unfortunate grow envious and covetous, and all three groups turn aside from the hard road of freedom to worship the Golden Calf of economic security. The historical cycle seems to be: From bondage to spiritual faith; from spiritual faith to courage; from courage to liberty; from liberty to abundance; from abundance to selfishness; from selfishness to apathy; from apathy to dependency; and from dependency back to bondage once more.[60]

This incisive observation, often titled "Why Democracies Fail," has been incorrectly attributed over the years to a number of noted historians and leaders, including Alexander Tytler, Arnold Toynbee, and British prime minister Benjamin Disraeli. The source of this wisdom was not a great historian, author, or political leader. Careful research attributes these words to a little-known businessman named Henning Prentis, a "normal" American, who included his observations in an address to the National Conference Board on March 18, 1943, in New York City.[61]

Henning attempted in his address to discourage the idea of "compulsory planned economy" as a remedy in democratic, free-market countries like the United States. "Its proponents confidently assert that government can successfully plan and control all major business activity in the nation, and still not interfere with our political freedom and our hard-won civil and religious liberties," he warned. "The lessons of history all point in exactly the reverse direction."[62]

This ordinary American—but uncommon thinker—uncannily described in 1943 the ultimate fate of the United States brought on by a mistaken reliance on big government. How instructive that this wisdom came not from a great intellectual or political leader, but from an everyday American who operated a business, met a payroll, and probably lived well within his means.

It is everyday Americans like Prentis who better understand the nation's problems and can take the necessary steps to prevent this failure of democracy through the siren song of big government. Many of these Americans have already joined the fight to save the nation from the historical scrap heap of failed democracies. They are the men and women, many in state legislatures, ardently working for an Article V amendments convention.

Can American democracy escape the seemingly inexorable march to decline? Of course it can. And it starts with you and me—*We the People*—exercising our constitutional right to bring vital and necessary change to our national government.

APPENDIX 1

COMPLETE TEXT FOR ARTICLE V OF THE U.S. CONSTITUTION

THE CONGRESS, whenever two thirds of both Houses shall deem it necessary, shall propose Amendments to this Constitution, or, on the Application of the Legislatures of two thirds of the several States, shall call a Convention for proposing Amendments, which, in either Case, shall be valid to all Intents and Purposes, as Part of this Constitution, when ratified by the Legislatures of three fourths of the several States, or by Conventions in three fourths thereof, as the one or the other Mode of Ratification may be proposed by the Congress; Provided that no Amendment which may be made prior to the Year One thousand eight hundred and eight shall in any Manner affect the first and fourth Clauses in the Ninth Section of the first Article; and that no State, without its Consent, shall be deprived of its equal Suffrage in the Senate.

APPENDIX 2

MOST SUCCESSFUL ARTICLE V CONVENTION ADVOCACY GROUPS (AS OF MAY 2016)

BALANCED BUDGET AMENDMENT TASK FORCE (BBAT)
Year established: 2008
Organizational goal: To help facilitate the ratification of a balanced budget amendment.
State applications with this goal: 28[1] (AL, AK, AR, CO, FL, GA, IN, IA, KS, LA, MD, MS, MI, MO, NE, NV, NH, NM, NC, ND, OH, OK, PA, SD, TN, TX, UT, WV)
Website address: http://bba4usa.org

CONVENTION OF STATES PROJECT (COS)
Year established: 2013
Organizational goal: To impose fiscal restraints on the federal government, limit the power and jurisdiction of the federal government, and limit the terms of office for its officials.
State applications with these goals: 8 (AK, AL, FL, GA, IN, LA, OK, TN)
Website address: http://www.conventionofstates.com

WOLF-PAC

Year established: 2011

Organizational goal: To overturn the part of the U.S. Supreme Court's campaign finance decision in *Citizens United v. FEC* protecting corporate contributions.

State applications with these goals: 4 (CA, IL, NJ, VT)

Website address: http://www.wolf-pac.com/the_plan

COMPACT FOR AMERICA (CFA)

Year established: 2014

Organizational goal: To combine four state legislative acts into one, producing a simultaneous application for a balanced budget convention and ratification of the amendment.[2]

State applications with this goal: 4 (AK, GA, MS, ND)

Website address: http://www.compactforamerica.org

APPENDIX 3

INFORMATION SOURCES ABOUT AN ARTICLE V CONVENTION

FRIENDS OF THE ARTICLE V CONVENTION (FOAVC)
Description: A nonpartisan repository of documents, articles, and other resources related to an Article V convention.
Website address: http://foavc.org

THE ARTICLE V LIBRARY
Description: A nonpartisan, public resource for Article V researchers, with copies of original source materials, accurate citations, and research notes searchable by full text; a complete and public index of state Article V applications, and related documents.
Website address: http://article5library.org

U.S. HOUSE CLERK'S MEMORIALS OF APPLICATIONS FOR AN ARTICLE V CONVENTION

Description: Each memorial purports to be an application of the legislature of a state calling for a convention under Article V, or a rescission of a prior application.

Website address: http://clerk.house.gov/legislative/memorials.aspx

ARTICLE V INFORMATION CENTER

Description: A nonpartisan collection of articles, online research, and legal analysis by Robert Natelson, the preeminent Article V legal researcher, and others at the center; a project of the Independence Institute.

Website address: http://www.articlevinfocenter.com

APPENDIX 4

ARTICLE V CONVENTION LEGISLATIVE PROGRESS REPORT
(AS OF JULY 4, 2016)

ACTIVE AVC GROUPS	STATES PASSED	STATES INTRODUCED (underscore = 2015 carryover) (dual underscore carries to 2017)
BALANCED BUDGET AMENDMENT TASK FORCE	28: OK WV (2016); AL AK AR CO FL GA IN IA KS LA MD MS MI MO NE NV NH NM NC ND OH PA SD TN TX UT	2 acive: MA VA DNP: AZ KY ME MN SC WY
CONVENTION OF STATES PROJECT	8: IN LA OK TN (2016); AL AK GA FL	6 active: MI NC NJ OH PA VA DNP: AZ CA-CT DE HI IL IA-KA KY ME MD MN MS MO NE NH-NM SC SD UT VT WA WV
WOLFPAC FREE & FAIR ELECTIONS	5: RI (2016); CA IL NJ VT	6 active: MA NC PA DNP: CT DE HI IA KA LA ME MD MN MS MO NH NM NY OK OR WA WV WI
COMPACT FOR AMERICA	4: AK GA MS ND	3 active: MI NC OH DNP: AL AZ FL LA MO OK SD TN WV WY
CITIZENS INTIATIVE (COUNTERMAND AM.)	1: AK (2016)	2 active: NC PA
US TERM LIMITS	1: FL (2016)	0 active: DNP: AL AK GA MS MO SC TN UT
SINGLE SUBJECT AMENDMENT PAC	1: FL	0 active:
DELEGATE SELECTION/ LIMITATION BILLS	8: AK* GA FL IN ND SD TN UT * countermand	6 general: VA DNP: ID KA NH OK WV WY 2 countermand: NC PA
RESCISSION EFFORTS	1: DE 2016	2 active: MA NC DNP: AL FL MD UT

•Each group receives 1 point for each state into which an Article V resolution is introduced; 1 point in each chamber if it passes all committees (2 pts in unicameral NE); 1 point in each chamber when it passes the floor (2 pts - NE); and 1 point when application is final. Thus, 6 total points can be earned in each state. The completion goal is 204 points (34 states x 6 pts./state). If an application dies during a non-carryover legislative session, then points generated for that cycle are not counted.

HOUSE COMMITTEES	HOUSE CHAMBER	SENATE COMMITTEES	SENATE CHAMBER	TOTAL SCORE*	PERCENTAGE COMPLETION*
Passed: VA; AZ WY DNP:	Passed: VA; AZ DNP: WY	Passed: SC DNP: ME	Passed: DNP:	172	84%
Passed: VA; AZ IA-KA MO NH-NM SD UT DNP: CA-ME WV	Passed: VA; AZ IA-MO NM SD UT DNP: KA	Passed: MO NH-SC WV DNP: ME SD UT	Passed: NH-WV DNP:	56	28%
Passed: DE NH NM WA DNP: ME	Passed: WA DNP: NM	Passed: CT DE IA MN MO NH DNP: ME	Passed: DE NH DNP: CT	34	17%
Passed: AL AZ DNP: SD	Passed: AZ DNP:	Passed: MI, AL MO DNP: TN WY	Passed: MI, DNP:	29	14%
Passed: DNP:	Passed: DNP:	Passed: DNP:	Passed: DNP:	8	4%
Passed: UT DNP:	Passed: UT DNP:	Passed: AK MO DNP:	Passed: AK MO DNP:	6	3%
Passed: DNP:	Passed: DNP:	Passed: DNP:	Passed: DNP:	6	3%
Passed: VA DNP: WV	Passed: VA DNP: WY	Passed: WV DNP:	Passed: WV DNP:		
Passed: DNP:	Passed: DNP:	Passed: AL DNP:	Passed: AL DNP:		

DNP = voted down, tabled, died on calendar, or otherwise did not progress. Scoring is based on available public information and may have some inaccuracies. Open convention calls are not aggregated in this report. copyright 2016 David F. Guldenschuh, Attorney-at-Law, 512 E. 1st St., Rome GA, 30161; (706} 346-3693. To join mailing list, contact: dfg@guldenschuhlaw.com. Used by permission.

APPENDIX 5

LEGISLATURE GROUPS
PLANNING FOR AN ARTICLE V CONVENTION

AMERICAN LEGISLATIVE EXCHANGE COUNCIL (ALEC)
Year Established: 1973
Description: Nonprofit organization that supports federalism, limited government, and free-market enterprise; provides a forum for legislators to discuss and plan model legislation to support conservative principles.
Website address: https://www.alec.org

STATE LEGISLATORS ARTICLE V CAUCUS
Year established: 2013
Description: State legislators promoting an Article V convention to reestablish federalism and a more limited federal government.
Website address: http://articlevcaucus.com

ASSEMBLY OF STATE LEGISLATORS (ASL)
Year established: 2013
Description: Bipartisan group of state legislators that promotes cooperation among the states to solve national problems.
Website address: http://www.assemblystatelegislatures.com

FEDERAL ASSEMBLY OF STATE PRESIDING OFFICERS
Year established: 2015
Description: Forum for state legislative leadership to meet and discuss their responsibilities under Article V of the Constitution.
Website address: None in January 2017

CONVENTION OF STATES CAUCUS
Year established: 2015
Description: Established under sponsorship of the Convention of State Project, COS Caucus intends to unite state legislators committed to limiting the federal government and to review a proposed set of convention rules to be drafted by Professor Robert Natelson.
Website address: http://coscaucus.com

NOTES

PREFACE

1. Jeb Bush, "Where Republicans Go from Here," *Wall Street Journal*, November 25, 2016, A15.
2. Arthur Brooks, *The Conservative Heart: How to Build a Fairer, Happier and More Prosperous America* (New York: HarperCollins, 2015).

INTRODUCTION

1. "U.S. Senator Tom Coburn's Farewell Address," NewsOn6.com, December 11, 2014, http://www. newson6.com/story/27608757/us-senator-tom-coburns-farewell-address.
2. Alexander Hamilton, *Federalist* No. 85, in *The Federalist*, ed. George Stade (New York: Barnes and Noble Classics, 2006) 485–86.

CHAPTER 1: A CAPITOL EDUCATION

1. Alexander Hamilton, "The Farmer Refuted," February 23, 1775, TeachingAmericanHistory.org, http://teachingamericanhistory.org/library/document/the-farmer-refuted/; emphasis added.
2. George F. Will, *Restoration: Congress, Term Limits and the Recovery of Deliberative Democracy* (New York: Free Press, 1993), 9.
3. I will, however, defend many of the lobbyists in Washington, who are a valuable source of information and often necessary to defend their clients against government overreach and injustice.
4. Tom A. Coburn, *Breach of Trust* (Nashville: Thomas Nelson, 2003), 46.
5. Ibid., 52.
6. George Stephanopoulos, *All Too Human: A Political Education* (New York: Little, Brown, 1999), 401–5.
7. "Analysis: Lott's Plan Looks to 2000," *Washington Post*, January 1, 1999, A20.
8. Coburn, *Breach of Trust*, 107.
9. Ibid., 149–51.
10. Ibid., 172.
11. Coburn 2004 Senate race campaign materials, Tom Coburn personal files.

12. Sheryl Gay Stolbert, "A Senate Race in Oklahoma Lifts the Right," *New York Times*, September 19, 2004, 1, 26, http://www.nytimes.com/2004/09/19/politics/campaign/a-senate-race-in-oklahoma-lifts-the-right.html?_r=0.

13. Senator Tom Coburn (R-OK) during debate on the Transportation, Treasury, the Judiciary, Housing and Urban Development and Related Agencies Appropriations Act (2006, H.R. 3058, Cong. Rec. S11,606–7 (daily ed. Oct. 20, 2005).

14. Senator Ted Stevens (R-AK) during debate on the Transportation, Treasury, the Judiciary, Housing and Urban Development and Related Agencies Appropriations Act (2006, H.R. 3058, Cong. Rec. S11,628–30 (daily ed. Oct. 20, 2005).

15. "The U.S. Congress Votes Database," *Washington Post*, October 20, 2005, accessed Oct. 30, 2015, http://projects.washingtonpost.com/congress/109/senate/1/votes/262/

16. Lauren Cohen, et al, "Do Powerful Politicians Cause Corporate Downsizing?" Harvard Business School, 2009, accessed November 14, 2015, http://www.people.hbs.edu/cmalloy/pdffiles/envaloy.pdf.

17. Tom Coburn, *The Debt Bomb* (Nashville: Thomas Nelson, 2012), 119.

18. Senator Harry Reid (D-NV) during debate on the "Coburn Omnibus" Advancing America's Priorities Act, S3297, Cong. Rec. S7552 (daily ed. Jul. 28, 2008).

19. Coburn, *The Debt Bomb*, 125.

20. See pages 47-49 for economist Milton Friedman's analysis of the inherent inefficiencies of government expenditures.

21. Michael Grabell et al, "The Stimulus Plan: A Detailed List of Spending," Propublica website, accessed November 14, 2015, http://www.propublica.org/special/the-stimulus-plan-a-detailed-list-of-spending.

22. Congressional Budget Office, "Estimated Impact of the American Recovery and Reinvestment Act on Employment and Economic Output from July 2011 through September 2011," Pub. No. 4454, November 2011, p. 8.

23. Coburn, *The Debt Bomb*, 144.

24. "Pelosi Floor Speech on Short-Term Continuing Resolution," press release, March 15, 2011, http://pelosi.house.gov/news/press-releases/pelosi-floor-speech-on-short-term-continuing-resolution.

CHAPTER 2: THE FAILURE OF BIG GOVERNMENT

1. Some argue that only "public debt"-to-GDP matters. This stood at about 75 percent early in 2016 but will rise dramatically without changes.

2. Madison, *Federalist* No. 10, 53.

3. Jay Cost, *A Republic No More: Big Government and the Rise of American Political Corruption* (New York: Encounter Books, 2015), 172–73.

4. "Notable and Quotable: Ben Sasse on the Senate," *Wall Street Journal*, November 6, 2015, A-13.

5. Thomas Jefferson to Samuel Kercheval, June 12, 1816, TeachingAmericanHistory.org website, http://teachingamericanhistory.org/library/document/letter-to-samuel-kercheval/

6. Adam Freedman, *The Naked Constitution: What the Founders Said and Why It Still Matters* (New York: HarperCollins, 2012), 45.

7. Peter Kasperowicz, Washington Examiner, http://www.washingtonexaminer.com/national-debt-up-1.42-trillion-in-fy-2016/article/2603499; Monthly Budget Review: Summary for Fiscal Year 2016, Congressional Budget Office, https://www.cbo.gov/sites/default/files/114th-congress-2015-2016/reports/52152-mbr.pdf

8. Thomas Woods Jr., *Rollback: Repealing Big Government Before the Coming Fiscal Collapse* (Washington, D.C.: Regnery, 2011), 8.

9. CNN Wire Staff, "Mullen: Debt Is Top National Security Threat," August 27, 2010, CNN, http://www.cnn.com/2010/US/08/27/debt.security.mullen/.

10. Opinion Editorial, "Too Much Debt Means the Economy Can't Grow: Reinhart and Rogoff," Bloomberg View, July 14, 2011, http://www.bloombergview.com/articles/2011-07-14/too-much-debt-means-economy-can-t-grow-commentary-by-reinhart-and-rogoff.

11. Christina Romer and Jared Bernstein, "The Job Impact of the American Recovery and Reinvestment Plan," January 9, 2009, http://otrans.3cdn.net/ee40602f9a7d8172b8_ozm6bt5oi.pdf.

12. William Galston, "Hillary's Chance to Hijack the Populist Surge," *Wall Street Journal*, January 6, 2016, A9.

13. Congressional Budget Office, *The Budget and Economic Outlook: 2016 to 2026* (January 2016), 15–16, https://www.cbo.gov/sites/default/files/114th-congress-2015-2016/reports/51129-2016Outlook_OneCol-2.pdf.

14. Jon Ward, "Bernanke Headlines a Day of Grim Warnings about the Nation's Fiscal Standing," *Daily Caller*, February 4, 2011, http://dailycaller.com/2011/02/04/bernanke-headlines-day-grim-warnings-nations-fiscal-standing/.

15. Nick Timiraos and Christina Petersen, "Massive Bill Leaves Deficit Fears Behind," *Wall Street Journal*, December 19–20, 2015, A6.

16. Mike Patton, "National Debt Tops $18 Trillion: Guess How Much You Owe?" Forbes Advisor Network website, April 24, 2015, http://www.forbes.com/sites/mikepatton/2015/04/24/national-debt-tops-18-trillion-guess-how-much-you-owe/#1494c1275ebd.

17. Mitch Daniels, *Keeping the Republic: Saving America by Trusting Americans* (New York: Penguin, 2012) 106–7.

18. Ibid., 108–10, 125.

19. Ibid., 3.

20. Robert Rector and Rachel Sheffield, "The War on Poverty after 50 Years," Backgrounder #2955 on Poverty and Injustice, the Heritage Foundation website, accessed November 23, 2016, http://www.heritage.org/research/reports/2014/09/the-war-on-poverty-after-50-years.

21. House Budget Committee Chairman Paul Ryan, "The Choice of Two Futures," March 2011, http://budget.house.gov/uploadedfiles/marchlisteningsessions.pdf.

22. Coburn, *The Debt Bomb*, 191.

23. Nicholas Eberstadt, *A Nation of Takers: America's Entitlement Epidemic* (West Conshohocken, PA: Templeton, 2012), 8–11.

24. Ibid., 19.

25. Brooks, *The Conservative Heart*, 63.

26. Ibid., 31, 45, 49.

27. Ibid., 61.

28. Stephen Ohlemacher, "Report: Social Security Overpaid Disability Benefits by $17 Billion," *Business Insider*, accessed December 24, 2015, http://www.businessinsider.com/social-security-17-billion-in-overpayments-2015-6.

29. Eberstadt, *A Nation of Takers*, 67–9.

30. Marvin Olasky, *The Tragedy of American Compassion* (Washington, D.C.: Regnery Gateway, 1992), 21.

31. Ibid., 98–101.

32. Ibid., 223.

33. Milton and Rose Friedman, *Free to Choose* (New York: Harvest, 1990), 96–97.
34. Friedman, *Free to Choose*, 116–17.
35. Ibid., 117.
36. Ibid., 127.
37. Brooks, *The Conservative Heart*, 79.
38. Ibid., 215.
39. James Gwartney, et al, *Economic Freedom of the World: 2015 Annual Report* (Vancouver: Fraser Institute, 2015), http://www.freetheworld.com/2015/economic-freedom-of-the-world-2015.pdf.
40. "Happy New Regulatory Year," *Wall Street Journal*, January 2, 2016, A10.
41. F. A. Hayek, *The Road To Serfdom* (Chicago: University of Chicago Press, 2007), 163.
42. Daniel Henninger, "Revolt of the Politically Incorrect," *Wall Street Journal*, January 7, 2016, A11.
43. Hayek, *The Road to Serfdom,* 219.
44. Ibid., 238; emphasis added.

CHAPTER 3: CONSTITUTIONAL AMENDMENT BY *WE THE PEOPLE*

1. Norris Hundley, *Water and the West: The Colorado River Compact and the Politics of Water in the American West* (Berkeley: University of California Press, 1975), 3, 107.
2. Robert Natelson, "The Santa Fe Convention: A Twentieth-Century Convention of States," Independent Institute, accessed April 25, 2016, https://www.i2i.org/the-santa-fe-convention-a-20th-century-convention-of-states/.
3. *Minutes and Record of the First Eighteen Sessions of the Colorado River Commission Negotiating the Colorado River Compact of 1922,* foreword, 2–4, accessed online April 25, 2016, https://www.i2i.org/files/2014/01/Minutes-CORiver-Commn.pdf.
4. Ibid., 5.
5. Natelson, "The Santa Fe Convention."
6. Bernadette D. Proctor, Jessica L. Semega, and Melissa A. Kollarm, U.S. Census Bureau, Current Population Reports, P60-256(RV), *Income and Poverty in the United States: 2015* (Washington, DC: U.S. Government Printing Office, 2016), 5, 7, 23 (table A-1), https://www.census.gov/content/dam/Census/library/publications/2016/demo/p60-256.pdf.
7. Robert Natelson, *State Initiation of Constitutional Amendments: A Guide for Lawyers and Legislative Drafters* (Denver: Independence Institute, 2014), 46–47, 57.
8. Ibid., 48–49.
9. Ibid., 67–68.
10. Alexander Hamilton, *Federalist* No. 78, in *The Federalist*, ed. George Stade (New York: Barnes and Noble Classics, 2006), 430.
11. Natelson, *State Initiation of Constitutional Amendments,"* 68–69.
12. Ibid., 77–80.
13. Ibid., 59, 70.
14. Ibid., 70–71.
15. Ibid., 82.
16. Ibid., 83–84.
17. Ibid., 85.
18. Ibid., 86.
19. Russell Caplan, *Constitutional Brinksmanship* (New York: Oxford University Press, 1988), 147–48.
20. Ibid., 148.

21. The Twenty-Seventh Amendment was proposed in 1789 with the group of amendments that became the Bill of Rights. It failed to attain approval by three-fourths of the states until 1992. As no deadline had been set by Congress on the ratification of these first amendments, the proposed amendment remained active for more than two centuries. By this precedent, some legal scholars maintain that state applications for convention also remain active indefinitely unless rescinded.

22. "The Constitutional Amendment Process," Federal Register, National Archives, accessed May 6, 2016, https://www.archives.gov/federal-register/constitution/.

23. Aaron J. Ley, "Constitutional Choices: The Ratification of the Twenty-First Amendment through State Conventions" (October 23, 2014), 31–32, available at SSRN, http://papers.ssrn.com/sol3/papers.cfm?abstract_id=2513920 or or http://dx.doi.org/10.2139/ssrn.2513920.

24. Ibid., 32–33.

25. Ibid., 33.

26. "The Constitutional Amendment Process," Federal Register website.

27. Ibid.

28. Larry J. Sabato, *A More Perfect Constitution: Why the Constitution Must Be Revised: Ideas to Inspire a New Generation* (New York: Bloomsbury USA, 2007).

29. Ibid., 9.

30. Ibid., 69.

31. George Will, *Restoration: Congress, Term Limits and the Recovery of Deliberative Democracy* (New York: Free Press, 1992–93), xiv.

32. Ibid., 59.

33. Ibid., 59–60.

34. Ibid., 72.

35. Matthew Eric Glassman and Amber Hope Wilhelm, "Congressional Careers: Service Tenure and Patterns of Member Service, 1789–2015" (January 2015), Congressional Research Service, R41545.

36. Colleen McCain Nelson and Laura Meckler, "Criticism of Democratic Party's Chairwoman Builds," *Wall Street Journal*, January 27, 2016, A4.

37. Sabato, *A More Perfect Constitution,* 110.

38. Ibid., 112.

39. Federal Register website, accessed November 26, 2017, https://www.federalregister.gov/agencies; Stephen Dinan, "Federal Workers Hit Record Number but Growth Slows under Obama, *Washington Times*, February 9, 2016, http://www.washingtontimes.com/news/2016/feb/9/federal-workers-hit-record-number-but-growth-slows/.

40. Philip K. Howard, "The Crippling Hold of Old Law," *Wall Street Journal*, April 2–3, 2016, C3.

41. Mark Levin, *The Liberty Amendments: Restoring the American Republic* (New York: Threshold Editions, 2014), 99. (Author's note: It would be better to see the whole Congress voting on this rather than allowing a callow official to blame a joint committee. Member of Congress should be on record for their vote on tough choices. That is the only way to hold them accountable.)

42. From Thomas Paine's *The American Crisis*, published during the American Revolution.

CHAPTER 4: THE CURRENT QUEST FOR AN ARTICLE V CONVENTION

1. "Rick Santelli: Tea Party," *Freedom Eden* (blog), accessed March 15, 2016, http://freedomeden.blogspot.com/2009/02/rick-santelli-tea-party.

2. Lesley Stahl, "Sen. Tom Coburn: A Proud Contrarian," CBS News, December 21, 2014, http://www.cbsnews.com/news/senator-tom-coburn-60-minutes/.

3. Robert Natelson, *State Initiation of Constitutional Amendments: A Guide for Lawyers and Legislative*

Drafters (Denver: Independence Institute, 2014), 43–45.

4. Exceptions to this are applications with "severability-aggregation provisions." This is explained later in this chapter.

5. Some question whether the new balanced budget convention applications will aggregate with the original sixteen and count toward the thirty-four required. At least initially, Congress will have the duty to make this determination.

6. David Guldenschuh, "The Article V Movement: A Comprehensive Assessment to Date and Suggested Approach for State Legislators and Advocacy Groups Moving Forward," November 2015, http://www.foavc.org/reference/Guldenschuh_Article_9_6_15.pdf.

7. "A Historical Account of the Campaign for a Balanced-Budget Amendments Convention to the U.S. Constitution," website for the Balanced Budget Amendment Task Force, accessed March 18, 2016, http://bba4usa.org/campaign/.

8. "Without these organizations, the campaign for a Balanced Budget Amendment wouldn't be possible," website for the Balanced Budget Amendment Task Force, accessed March 22, 2016, http://bba4usa.org/partnering-organizations/.

9. Office of the Clerk, U.S. House of Representatives, "Selected Memorials," accessed March 21, 2016, http://clerk.house.gov/legislative/memorials.aspx.

10. The Article V Convention Legislative Progress Report is maintained and updated frequently by Georgia attorney David Guldenschuh. The most recent report is available upon request by e-mailing Guldenschuh at dfg@guldenschuhlaw.com.

11. Guldenschuh, "The Article Five Movement," 5.

12. Ibid., 6.

13. Ibid., 13, 21.

14. Ibid., 21.

15. Ibid., 21; The Article V Convention Legislative Progress Report (May 15, 2016).

16. See Wolf Pac, http://www.wolf-pac.com/.

17. Guldenschuh, "The Article Five Movement," 6.

18. "Wolf-Pac website, The Plan, http://www.wolf-pac.com/the_plan

19. Guldenschuh, "The Article Five Movement," 22.

20. The Article V Convention Legislative Progress Report (May 15, 2016).

21. Guldenschuh, "The Article Five Movement," 7, 22.

22. Ibid.

23. Ibid., 23; The Article V Convention Legislative Progress Report (May 15, 2016).

24. Guldenschuh, "The Article Five Movement," 14.

25. Robert Natelson, "A New Theory Supporting the Use of the Tenth Amendment to Control the Article V Process—and Why the Theory Doesn't Work," Article V Information Center: A Project of the Independence Institute, March 6, 2016, http://articlevinfocenter.com/a-new-theory-supporting-the-use-of-the-tenth-amendment-to-control-the-article-v-process-and-why-the-theory-doesnt-work/.

26. Robert Natelson, "The Constitution's Article V, Not the 10th Amendment, Gives State Legislatures Their Power in the Amendment Process," Article V Information Center, February 7, 2016, http://articlevinfocenter.com/the-constitutions-article-v-not-the-10th-amendment-gives-state-legislatures-their-power-in-the-amendment-process/.

27. Guldenschuh, "The Article Five Movement," 14–15.

28. Office of the Clerk, U.S. House of Representatives, "Selected Memorials."

29. About, Article V Information Center website, accessed March 27, 2016, http://www.

articlevinfocenter.com/about/.

30. Guldenschuh, "The Article Five Movement," 17.

31. Ibid., 18–19.

32. Ibid., 19.

33. "Michael Farris Debates Andy Schlafly in New Jersey," YouTube video, 1:24:26, on the efficacy of using a Convention of States to limit the power and jurisdiction of the federal government, posted by the Convention of States Project, June 9, 2014, http://www.youtube.com/watch?v=xHd1xUo-_XE.

34. Guldenschuh, "The Article V Movement," 34.

35. Rob Standridge interview by Larry Floyd, summer 2016.

36. Ibid.

37. Thomas E. Brennan, "Return to Philadelphia: A Case for Calling of an Amendatory Convention under Article 5 of the Federal Constitution," *Cooley Law Review* 1 (1982).

38. Ballotpedia's Election Analysis in 2016, Ballotpedia: The Encyclopedia of American Politics website, accessed November 25, 2016, https://ballotpedia.org/State_legislative_elections,_2016.

39. Thomas Brennan, *The Article V Amendatory Convention: Keeping the Republic in the Twenty-First Century* (Lanham, MD: Lexington Books, 2014), 19.

CHAPTER 5: ARTICLE V: THE FOUNDERS' GIFT TO THE PEOPLE

1. Forrest McDonald, *We the People: The Economic Origin of the Constitution* (New Brunswick, NJ: Transaction, 2008), 323–24.

2. Robert C. Cotner, ed., *Theodore Fosters' Minutes of the Convention Held at South Kingston, Rhode Island, in March, 1790* (Providence: Rhode-Island Historical Society, 1929), 57; emphasis added.

3. McDonald, *We the People*, 323.

4. "Ratification of the Constitution by the State of Rhode Island," The Avalon Project: Lillian Goldman Law Library, Yale Law School, accessed November 11, 2015, http://avalon.law.yale.edu/18th_century/ratri.asp.

5. Former professor of law at the University of Montana, Natelson is a senior fellow in constitutional jurisprudence at the Independence Institute in Denver, Colorado.

6. Russell Caplan, *Constitutional Brinksmanship: Amending the Constitution by National Convention* (New York: Oxford University Press, 1988), 5–7.

7. Robert Natelson, "Founding-Era Conventions and the Meaning of the Constitution's 'Convention for Proposing Amendments'," *Florida Law Review* 65 (May 2013): 620.

8. Ibid., 629.

9. Ibid., 629–30.

10. Ibid., 630.

11. Ibid., 630–31.

12. Ibid., 632–33.

13. Ibid., 635–36.

14. Ibid., 636–37.

15. Ibid., 637–38.

16. Ibid., 638–65.

17. John R. Vile, *The Constitutional Amending Process in American Political Thought* (New York: Praeger, 1992), 1, 26.

18. Natelson, "Founding-Era Conventions," 665–66.

19. Ibid., 666–68.

20. Ibid., 671–73.
21. "Proceeding of Commissioners to Remedy Defects in the Federal Government," September 11, 1786, in Annapolis, Maryland, the Avalon Project website, accessed January 27, 2016, http://avalon. law.yale.edu/18th_century/annapoli.asp.
22. Natelson, "Founding-Era Conventions," 677.
23. Ibid., 674–77.
24. Caplan, *Constitutional Brinksmanship*, 26.
25. Natelson, "Founding-Era Conventions," 630–31.
26. Ibid., 673.
27. Ibid., 675–76.
28. Ibid., 676 (emphasis in original).
29. Ibid., 678.
30. "Resolution of the Federal Convention Submitting the Constitution to Congress, September 17, 1787," the Avalon Project, accessed February 1, 2016, http://avalon.law.yale.edu/18th_century/ressub01.asp.
31. Richard Beeman, *Plain Honest Men: The Making of the American Constitution* (New York: Random House, 2009), 371–72.
32. Ibid., 86–91.
33. Max Farrand, ed., *The Records of the Federal Convention of 1787* (New Haven, CT: Yale University Press, 1911), 1:22.
34. Vile, *The Constitutional Amending Process*, 11, 24–25.
35. Ibid., 25.
36. Farrand, *Records of the Federal Convention*, 1:121.
37. Ibid., 202.
38. Farrand, *Records of the Federal Convention*, 2:159, 188, 461.
39. Ibid., 2:557.
40. Ibid., 2:558–59.
41. Ibid., 2:629.
42. Ibid., 2:630.
43. David O. Stewart, *Madison's Gift* (New York: Simon & Schuster, 2015), 59.
44. Ibid., 63.
45. James Madison, *Federalist* No. 43, in *The Federalist*, ed. George Stade (New York: Barnes and Noble Classics, 2006), 246; emphasis added.
46. Ibid., 485–86.
47. Stewart, *Madison's Gift*, 63.
48. Ibid., 63–68.
49. Bremen, *Plain, Honest Men*, 400.
50. John Kaminski, et al., eds. *The Documentary History of the Ratification of the Constitution* (Charlottesville, VA: University of Virginia Press, 2012), 2520–22.
51. Caplan, *Constitutional Brinksmanship*, 37–38.
52. Stewart, *Madison's Gift*, 97–101.
53. Natelson, "Founding-Era Conventions," 689.
54. James Madison to George Lee Turberville, letter, November 2, 1788, Founders Online at National Archives website, accessed February 17, 2016, http://founders.archives.gov/documents/Madison/01-11-02-0243.
55. Caplan, *Constitutional Brinksmanship*, 97.
56. Ibid.

57. Alexander Hamilton, *Federalist* No. 85, 486.

58. Robert Natelson, "Proposing Constitutional Amendments by Convention: Rules Governing the Process," *Tennessee Law Review* 78 Tenn. L. Rev 693 (2011): 697.

CHAPTER 6: LIMITED GOVERNMENT FOR A SELF-RULING PEOPLE

1. Mellen Chamberlain, *John Adams the Statesman of the American Revolution: With Other Essays and Addresses Historical and Literary* (Boston and New York: Houghton, Mifflin, 1898), 249.

2. "Gen. George Washington: Farewell Letter, Circular Letter Addressed to the Governors of All the States on Disbanding the Army, June 8, 1783," reprinted on the America in Class website, accessed December 26, 2015, http://americainclass.org/sources/makingrevolution/independence/text1/washingtoncircularstates.pdf.

3. Robert Natelson, "Founding-Era Conventions and the Meaning of the Constitution's 'Convention for Proposing Amendments'," *Florida Law Review* 65 (May 2013): 674.

4. Richard B. Morris, *Witnesses at the Creation: Hamilton, Madison, Jay and the Constitution* (New York: Holt, Rinehart and Winston, 1985), 187.

5. David O. Stewart, *Madison's Gift* (New York: Simon & Schuster, 2015), 29.

6. Morris, *Witness at the Creation*, 188, 195.

7. Michael S. Paulsen and Luke Paulsen, *The Constitution: An Introduction* (New York: Basic Books, 2015), 16.

8. "Resolution of the Federal Convention Submitting the Constitution to Congress, September 17, 1787," The Avalon Project, Lillian Goldman Library, Yale Law School, accessed February 1, 2016, http://avalon.law.yale.edu/18th_century/ressub01.asp.

9. Paulsen and Paulsen, *The Constitution*, 17.

10. Ten were soon ratified by the states; one was ratified as the Twenty-Seventh Amendment in 1992; and another has yet to receive the necessary ratification by three-fourths of the states.

11. Paulsen and Paulsen, *The Constitution*, 19–21.

12. Ibid., 21.

13. Gordon S. Wood, *Empire of Liberty: A History of the Early Republic* (Oxford, UK: Oxford University Press, 2009), 31.

14. Paulsen and Paulsen, *The Constitution*, 25–26.

15. Paulsen and Paulsen, *The Constitution*, 26.

16. James Madison, *Federalist* No. 10, in *The Federalist*, ed. George Stade (New York: Barnes and Noble Classics, 2006), 52–53, 55.

17. Ibid., 53.

18. Jennifer Hickey, "Harry Reid Relishes Romney Tax Lie: 'He Didn't Win, Did He?'" Newsmax, April 1, 2015, http://www.newsmax.com/Politics/Harry-Reid-Mitt-Romney-2012-election-taxes/2015/04/01/id/635842/.

19. Madison, *Federalist* No. 51, 288; emphasis added.

20. Paulsen and Paulsen, *The Constitution*, 35–36.

21. Madison, *Federalist* No. 51, 288.

22. Ibid.

23. "OpenTheBooks Oversight Report—The Militarization of America," Open the Books, July 5, 2016, http://www.openthebooks.com/openthebooks_oversight_report_-_the_militarization_of_america/.

CHAPTER 7: A JUDICIAL FOUNDATION FOR BIG GOVERNMENT

1. Tom Coburn, *The Debt Bomb* (Nashville: Thomas Nelson, 2012), 69.
2. Ibid., 72.
3. Gordon S. Wood, *Empire of Liberty: A History of the Early Republic, 1789–1815*, Oxford History of the United States, repr. ed. (Oxford: Oxford University Press, 2011), 144.
4. Ibid., 144–45.
5. Jay Cost, *A Republic No More: Big Government and the Rise of American Political Corruption* (New York: Encounter Books, 2015), 36.
6. Ibid., 39–40.
7. Daniel Howe, *What Hath God Wrought* (Oxford, UK: Oxford University Press, 2007), 144–45; Wood, *Empire of Liberty*, 455. (A court reporter's error resulted in the misspelling of M'Culloh's name as McCulloch in the transcript.)
8. Randy E. Barnett, *Restoring the Lost Constitution: The Presumption of Liberty* (Princeton, NJ: Princeton University Press, 2005), 169, 171; emphasis added.
9. Howe, *What Hath God Wrought*, 235.
10. Adam Freedman, *The Naked Constitution: What the Founders Said and Why It Still Matters* (New York: HarperCollins, 2012), 51–52; emphasis added.
11. Barnett, *Restoring the Lost Constitution*, 301–2.
12. Freedman, *The Naked Constitution*, 57.
13. "A Tea Party That Changed History," official Social Security website, accessed January 10, 2017, https://www.socialsecurity.gov/history/tea.htm.
14. Freedman, *The Naked Constitution*, 59.
15. Ibid., 54.
16. Ibid., 54–55.
17. Cost, *A Republic No More*, 169–71.
18. Ibid., 172, 252.
19. Coburn, *The Debt Bomb*, 234.
20. Michael McConnell, "Democracy's Legal Champion," *Wall Street Journal*, February 16, 2016, A13.
21. Freedman, *The Naked Constitution*, 113.

CHAPTER 8: LESSONS FROM PAST CONVENTIONS AND APPLICATIONS

1. Russell Caplan, *Constitutional Brinksmanship: Amending the Constitution by National Convention* (New York: Oxford University Press, 1988), 79–84. Montana's attempt to use a referendum to prompt an application was found unconstitutional.
2. Kevin Klose, "Michigan Lawmaker Stalls Budget-Amendment Drive," *Washington Post*, September 14, 1984, A-7; emphasis added.
3. Caplan, *Constitutional Brinksmanship*, 81.
4. Neil H. Cogan, ed., *Union and States' Rights: A History of Interpretation of Interposition, Nullification, and Secession 150 Years After Sumter* (Akron, OH: University of Akron Press, 2014), 37.
5. Ibid., 37.
6. Ibid.
7. Gordon Wood, *Empire of Liberty* (New York: Oxford University Press, 2009), 693.
8. "Amendments to the Constitution as Proposed by the Hartford Convention: 1814," the Avalon Project website, accessed January 10, 2017, http://avalon.law.yale.edu/19th_century/hartconv.asp;

Wood, *Empire of Liberty*, 694.

9. Caplan, *Constitutional Brinksmanship*, 46–47.

10. Ibid., 48.

11. Robert Natelson, "Learning from Experience: How the States Used Article V Applications in America's First Century," Goldwater Institute Policy Brief no. 10-06, November 4, 2010, 8–9.

12. Caplan, *Constitutional Brinksmanship*, 52.

13. David Potter, *The Impeding Crisis: America Before the Civil War*, ed. Don Fehrenbacker (New York: HarperCollins, 1976), 104–5.

14. Natelson, "Learning from Experience," 11.

15. Caplan, *Constitutional Brinksmanship*, 52, 55; Natelson, "Learning from Experience," 11.

16. Caplan, *Constitutional Brinksmanship*, 52–54. Contemporary accounts referred to the assembly more as a "convention," but modern accounts lean toward "conference."

17. Ibid., 53.

18. Ibid., 55; Robert Natelson, "Learning from Experience," 13.

19. Caplan, *Constitutional Brinksmanship*, 57–58.

20. Natelson, "Learning from Experience," 14.

21. Robert Natelson, "The Article V Convention Process and the Restoration of Federalism," *Harvard Journal of Law and Public Policy* 36, no. 3 (Summer 2013): 959.

22. Natelson, "Learning from Experience," 14; emphasis added.

23. Caplan, *Constitutional Brinksmanship*, 59.

24. Caplan, *Constitutional Brinksmanship*, 59–60.

25. Thomas H. Neale, "The Article V Convention for Proposing Constitutional Amendments: Historical Perspectives for Congress," July 10, 2012, Congressional Research Service, 8.

26. Caplan, *Constitutional Brinksmanship*, 62–63.

27. Natelson, "Learning from Experience," 16–17.

28. Ibid., 17.

29. Ibid., 18.

30. Ibid.

31. Ibid., 19.

32. Ibid., 20–21.

33. Ibid., 21.

34. Caplan, *Constitutional Brinksmanship*, 64.

35. Ibid., 62, 65.

36. Robert Natelson, *Amending the Constitution by Convention: Lessons for Today from the Constitution's First Century* (IP-5-2011) (Denver: Independence Institute, July 2011), 9.

37. Caplan, *Constitutional Brinksmanship*, 66.

38. Ibid., 68–69.

39. Ibid., 69.

40. Ibid., 74.

41. Ibid., 74.

42. Ibid., 74–75.

43. Ibid., 75.

44. Ibid., 75–76.

45. Ibid., 76–77.

46. Ibid., 76.

47. Ibid., 78–79.

48. Ibid., 79. Counter to Caplan's claim, Friends of the Article V records list Oklahoma in 1955 as the first applicant for a balanced budget convention. See "Table 03: 171 Balanced Budget/General Applications by 39 Different States," accessed April 13, 2016, http://foa5c.org/file.php/1/Articles/AmendmentsTables.htm#Table03.

49. The Office of Senator Bob Dole, "Dole Issues Proposals Aimed at Easing Tax, Inflation Burdens," press release, June 7, 1978, http://dolearchivecollections.ku.edu/collections/press_releases/780607iss.pdf.

50. Caplan, *Constitutional Brinksmanship*, 80; Paul Weber and Barbara Perry, *Unfounded Fears: Myths and Realities of a Constitutional Convention* (New York: Greenwood Press, 1989), 70.

51. Weber, *Unfounded Fears*, 117.

52. Caplan, *Constitutional Brinksmanship*, 81.

53. Ibid., 82.

54. Ibid., 83; Weber, *Unfounded Fears*, 70–71.

55. Caplan, *Constitutional Brinksmanship*, 83.

56. Ibid.

57. Ibid., 84–85.

58. Ibid, 87; Warren Burger, letter to Phyllis Schafly, June 22, 1988, Independent Institute files, https://www.i2i.org/files/2013/11/Burger-letter2.pdf.

59. Neale, "The Article V Convention for Proposing Constitutional Amendments," 13.

60. Loren Collins, "The Truth about Tytler," Loren Collins website, accessed July 6, 2016, http://www.lorencollins.net/tytler.html.

61. Ibid.

62. Ibid.

APPENDIX 2

1. This includes the fifteen unrescinded states that applied for a balanced budget amendment in 1983 or before. Congress will assess whether these count toward the thirty-four required.

2. Professor Rob Natelson, a leading authority on the Article V amendment convention, contends that this approach may face legal issues, as it overstates state powers to control the process of an amendment proposal through a convention.

INDEX

A

Adams, John, 138, 141–42, 175

administrative state, the need to rebalance the, 78–79

Advancing America's Priorities Act, 21

advocacy groups, most successful Article V convention, 203–4

Affordable Care Act, 26, 44, 155, 170

Agricultural Adjustment Act of 1938, 167

Agricultural Appropriations Bill, 13

Alabama, 88, 91, 177

Albany Congress, 114

Alien and Sedition Acts, 175–76

All Too Human (Stephanopoulos), 10

amendments (constitutional). *See individual amendments by name (e.g., Twenty-Seventh)*
how amendments become part of the Constitution, 68. *See also ratification*

American Bar Association, 189

American Civil Liberties Union, 189

American Legislative Exchange Council (ALEC), 88, 98, 99, 208

American Revolution (aka Revolutionary War), 113, 114, 116, 129, 158, 124, 137, 138, 214n42

Anti-Federalists, 108, 127, 129, 143, 144

Appropriations Committee, 26, 32

archivist of the United States, role of 66, 68

Arizona, 89, 93

Arkansas, 93, 179, 180, 184

Armey, Dick, 9

Article I (of the Constitution), 147, 151, 152, 158, 160, 162, 166, 167

Article IV, 147

Article V. *See especially* chapter 5 (107–35)
complete text of, 202
during the ratification debate, 127–30
how the Framers may have viewed uses for, 129–30

Article V Amendatory Constitutional Convention, The (Brennan), 96, 105

Article V convention. *See also* convention of states
advocacy groups, most successful as of 2016, 203–4
the current quest for a. *See* chapter 4 (83–105)
information sources about an, 95–97
lessons from past conventions and failed drives, 195–97
the key to an, 100–2
legislature groups planning for an, 208–9
the process for an, 60–61
state legislatures' preparations for an, 98–100
why a convention appears imminent, 102–5

Article V Information Center, 96–97, 206

Article V Library, 96, 204

Article XIX, 125

Articles of Confederation, 34, 107, 112, 116, 117, 118, 120–21, 123–24, 141–45

Assembly of State Legislatures (ASL), 64, 97, 99, 208
"auxiliary precautions," 149–50

B

Back in Black report, 24–25
Baker v. Carr, 188
Balanced Budget Act of 1997, 11, 12, 13
balanced budget amendment (BBA), x, xiii, 69, 71–73, 83, 85, 86, 87–93, 95–96, 101, 103, 191–97, 203, 221n1
   the first major drive for a, 191–95
Balanced Budget Amendment Task Force (BBATF), 87–90, 97, 99, 101, 102, 203
Banz, Gary, 99, 101, 102
Barnett, Randy, 160, 162
Barton, William, 108, 110, 111
Bell, Griffin, 194
Bernanke, Ben, 40
Berra, Yogi, 171
Biddulph, David, 87
Biggerstaff, Robert, 96
big government, xi, 4, 76, 78, 103, 111, 139, 175, 185, 186, 190, 196, 197, 199, 200
   breaking the cycle of reactionary, 54
   the failure of. *See* chapter 2 (29–55)
   a judicial foundation for. See chapter 7 (155–72)
Bill of Rights, 7, 110, 129, 131, 144, 151, 175, 194, 214n21
Black, Charles, 192
Boehner, John, 25
Bork, Robert, 192
Bowles, Erskine, 23, 38
Breach of Trust (Coburn), 9, 17
Brecheen, Josh, ix, 101
Brennan, Thomas E., 95, 103, 105
"Bridge to Nowhere," 19
Bridges, Styles, 191
Brooks, Arthur, xvi, 47, 49
Brown, Edmund "Jerry," 192
Buchanan, James, 179, 182
budget, balancing the federal, 71–73
budget resolution, 13, 40
bureaucracy, the bloated, 77–79

Burger, Warren, 195
Bush, George W., 16, 18
Bush, Jeb, xiii–xiv
Byrd, Harry F., 191

C

Calhoun, John C., 177
California, 22, 92, 191, 192
California Assembly Ways and Means Committee, 192
California Legislature, 92–93
Caller, Emmanuel, 67
Canada, 50, 114
Caplan, Russell, 112–13, 132, 133, 221n48
careerism, 3, 8, 9, 30, 32, 75, 103
Carpenter, Delph E., 58
Carson, Brad, 16
Carter, Jimmy, 174
Carter administration, 193
Chamberlain, Mellen, 137–38
Chambliss, Saxby, 24
checks and balances, 7, 81, 154, 198
Citizen Legislature Act, 9
Citizens for the Constitution, 193
Citizens for Self-Governance, x, 3, 89, 90
Citizens United v. FEC, 91, 92, 204
Civil War, 153, 163, 181, 183, 196, 197, 198
   Civil War crisis, conventions and the, 178–82
Clark, James, 191
Clay, Henry, 178
Clinton, Bill, 10, 12, 13, 23
CNBC, 83, 84
Coburn, Carolyn, 5
Colorado, 188
Colorado River Commission, 57–58
Colorado River Compact, 57–58
commerce clause, xiii–xiv, 155, 156, 162–63, 167, 168, 170
Committee on Finance, 27
Compact for America, 93–95, 97, 204
Compromise of 1850, 178
Confederation Congress, 116, 117, 120, 121, 122, 191
Conference of Mayors, 189

Congress, ix, xii–xiv, 2–8, 11–12, 14–20, 22–23, 25–27, 31–33, 37, 40, 48, 58, 60–61, 63–80, 82, 83, 85–87, 89–91, 93–96, 99, 100, 104, 107–12, 117–118, 121–28, 130–34, 139, 142–44, 146, 154–60, 162, 165–70, 172, 174–77, 179–84, 186–88, 190–94, 196–97, 202, 214n21, 214n41, 215n5, 221n1
    initiates the state ratification process of a proposed amendment, 65–66
    term limits on, 73–75
Congressional Budget Office, 22, 30, 40
Connecticut, 43, 121, 176
Conservative Heart, The (Brooks), xvi, 49–50
conservatives, x, 9, 10, 22, 46, 84, 87, 188, 190, 196
Constitution (of the United States of America), ix, xiv, 3–4, 6–7, 9, 15–17, 31, 34, 37, 45–46, 51, 58, 60, 64, 67–68, 70, 72–73, 76–77, 80–81, 83, 86–87, 94, 102–3, 107, 108–12, 118, 120–25, 127–35, 137, 139–54, 156–60, 165–67, 171, 174, 176–77, 179–82, 185, 188–89, 191–92, 195, 202
    amendments to the. *See individual amendments; see also* chapter 3 (57–82)
    articles of the. *See individual articles*
    constitutional amendment. *See* chapter 3 (57–82)
    constitutional convention, xi, xiii–xiv, 70, 132, 174, 181, 184–86, 189, 192–94, 196
    does not allow a compact without congressional approval, 94
    how an amendment becomes part of the, 68
    two most important foundational supports of the, 149
Constitutional Brinkmanship (Caplan), 112
constitutional convention. *See under* Constitution
Constitutional Convention. *See* Federal Convention of 1787
Constitutional Convention Implementation Act, 193
Constitution: An Introduction, The (Paulsen and Paulsen), 146
Contract with America, 6, 9
convention of states
    delegation selection for the, 61–62
    rules and procedures, 62–65

Convention of States Caucus, 97, 209
Convention of States Project (COS), x, 64, 85, 89–91, 95, 97, 101, 102, 203
Convention USA, 103
corruption, xiv, 27, 31, 34–35, 49, 103, 133, 135, 140, 153, 154, 157, 158–59, 163–64, 165, 168, 169, 172, 183
Corwin amendment, 180
COS (Convention of States Project), x, 64, 85, 89–91, 95, 97, 101, 102, 203
COS Caucus, 97, 209
Cost, Jay, 34–35, 159, 168, 169
Council of State Governments, 188, 189
Credit Mobilier of America, 163
Crittenden, John, 179
Crittenden plan, 179, 180
Cromwell, Oliver, 113
cronyism, 103, 164
Cuvillier, Louis A., 187

D
Daniels, Mitch, 41–42
Davis, Jefferson, 178
Debt Bomb, The (Coburn), 21, 37, 39
debt ceiling, 24–25
Declaration of Independence, 124, 141, 153
deficit, 10, 22, 23, 24–26, 40, 156, 194, 198
deficit spending, 11, 16, 17, 22, 26, 72, 194, 197
DeLancey, James, 114
Delaware, 89, 120, 179, 183
democracy, 100, 147, 200
Democratic National Convention, 193
Democratic Party, 21, 33, 104
Democrats, 12, 20, 22, 24, 74, 104, 192, 193
Department of Defense, 23
Dirksen, Everett, 189–90
Disraeli, Benjamin, 199
Dole, Bob, 10, 191–92, 196
Dranias, Nick, 93
Duke University lacrosse team allegations, 53
duplication (in federal spending), 23, 25–26, 140, 154, 165

E

Eagle Forum, x, 100, 101, 102, 195, 196
earmarks, 18, 19–20, 22, 25, 85
Eberstadt, Nicholas, 44
Economic Freedom of the World (Canadian), 51
Eighteenth Amendment, 66, 187
Eisenhower, Dwight, 45, 189
elitism, 32, 194
Emerson, Thomas, 194
English Bill of Rights, 113
entitlements, 43–44, 45, 48, 165
enumerated powers, 7, 37, 146, 151, 154, 160
Era of Good Feelings, 177
Ervin, Sam, 190–91, 193

F

factionalism, 34, 35, 140, 147–49, 152, 153, 157, 172
factions, 34–36, 59, 145, 148, 169
Farris, Michael, x, 3, 90, 100–1, 102
federal agencies, 78
Federal Assembly of State Presiding Officers, 99, 209
federal budget, balancing the, 71–73
Federal Constitutional Convention Act (S. 2307), 190
Federal Convention of 1787 (*aka* Constitutional Convention; Great Convention; Philadelphia Convention *in text*), 63, 64, 112, 113, 114, 119–22, 132, 142–44, 152, 153
    the forging of Article V at the, 123–27
federal income tax, 164, 187
federalism, xiv, 59, 60, 64, 81, 98, 100, 145, 149, 150, 151–52, 157, 165, 186, 195, 208
    three key features of, 151–52
Federalist, 144
    No. 10, 147–48
    No. 39, 147
    No. 43, 127
    No. 45, 151
    No. 78, 76
    No. 85, 3–4
Federalists, 143, 144
federal judiciary, restraints on the, 76–77
federal overreach. *See* overreach

Federal Register, 51, 68
federal workers, 78
Feingold, Russ, 33
Filburn, Roscoe, 167–68
fire-eaters, 178
First Bank of the United States, 158–59
First Continental Congress, 115–16
Florida, 85, 87, 88, 90
Floyd, Larry, xi
food stamp program, 48
Fox News Sunday, 12
Frame of Government of Pennsylvania, 123
Franklin, Benjamin, 142–43, 144
Frankfurter, Felix, 58
fraud, 8, 19, 26, 27, 45, 140, 154, 163, 165
Free to Choose (Friedman), 47
Freedman, Adam, 162, 167, 171
Free and Fair Elections amendment, 92
free markets, xvii, 50, 59, 79
Friedman, Milton, 47–48, 49, 192, 211n20
Friends of the Article V Convention (FOAVC), 95–96, 103, 205
Fruth, Bill, 87

G

Gang of Six, 24–25
GDP (*aka* gross domestic product), ratio of debt to, 29–30, 37, 39, 45, 211n1
general welfare clause, 166, 167
Georgia, 88, 90, 93, 101, 120, 177
Georgia Legislature, 184
Gerry, Elbridge, 124, 125
Gibbons, Thomas, 161
Gibbons v. Ogden, 161–63, 167, 168
Gillette, L. A., 57
Gingrich, Newt, 6, 9, 10, 12–13
Glorious Revolution, 113
Goldman Sachs, 40
Goldwater, Barry, 192
Government Accounting Office (GAO), 25–26
government overreach. *See* overreach
government shutdown, 10, 40
government of the United States, four pillars of the superstructure of the, 145
Grace Report, 26

Graham, Lindsey, 12
Gramm–Rudman–Hollings Balanced Budget Act, 104, 194, 195
Gramm–Rudman–Hollings Deficit Reduction Act, 25
Grant, Ulysses S., 163
Great Britain, 53, 138, 146
Great Depression, 44, 50, 165
Great Seal (of the United States), 36, 139
Great Society programs, 43, 44, 169
gross domestic product. *See* GDP
Guldenschuh, David, 97, 98, 215n10

H

Halbrook, David, 191
Hamilton, Alexander, 3–4, 5, 7, 62, 76, 121, 125, 128, 130, 134, 142, 143, 157, 158, 167
Harding, Warren G., 58
Harkin, Tom, 32–33
Hartford Convention, 176, 183
Hastert, Denny, 13, 14–15
Hatch, Orrin, 193
Hayek, F. A., 51–54
health care, 5, 39, 155, 156, 169, 170
    percent of federal spending for, 39
Helvering v. Davis, 166–67
Henninger, Daniel, 53
Henry, Patrick, 129, 131
Heyburn, Weldon, 185, 192
Highway Bill, 12
Hoover, Herbert, 58
Howard, Philip K., 78
human nature, 3, 15, 34, 80, 148, 149, 150
Hurricane Katrina, 18, 19, 33

I

income maintenance, 42, 44
Illinois, 22, 92, 180
implied power(s), 158, 167
Independence Institute, 96, 206
Indiana, 41–42, 62, 91, 180
individual liberties, xvii, 7, 52, 79
Ingalls, John, 182
inner cities, 46
interest groups, 32, 34–36, 79, 154

J

Javits, Jacob, 190
Jay, John, 143
Jefferson, Thomas, ix, xv, 36–37, 46, 124, 141–42, 153, 158, 175, 177, 191, 196
jobs, xvi, 22, 39, 51, 59
John Birch Society, x, 88, 101, 102, 195, 196
Johnson, Lyndon, 43, 68, 169
Jones, Samuel, 129–30
judicial activism, progressivism and, 164

K

Kagan, Elena, 155–56, 163, 170
Kasich, John, 11–12
Keeping the Republic: Saving America by Trusting Americans (Daniels), 42
Kennedy, Robert, 190
Kennedy, Ted, 33
Kentucky, 89, 180
Kentucky Resolution, 175, 177
Kernen, Joe, 84
King v. Burwell, 170
Knutson, Harold, 191

L

Levin, Mark, 78, 79, 80, 90
Liberty Amendments, The (Levin), 79, 90
Lieberman, Joe, 43
limited government. *See* chapter 6 (137–54); also ix, xi, xvi, xvii, 8, 23, 31, 33, 34, 37, 50, 68, 79, 98, 155, 157, 161, 171, 172, 208
Lincoln, Abraham, 9, 147, 173, 179, 182, 196, 197, 198
Locke, John, 6
Lott, Trent, 11
Louisiana, 88, 91, 185

M

Madison, James, ix, xv, 34, 52, 81, 119, 123, 125–26, 128, 129, 131, 132, 140, 142, 143, 145, 147, 148, 149–51, 152, 155, 158–60, 167, 175–78, 183, 184, 196
Marshall, John, 146, 160, 161–63, 168
Marshall Court, 160, 161–62

Maryland, 121
Maryland Legislature, 159
Mary II of England (queen), 113
Mason, George, 119, 124–25, 126
Mason's Manual of Legislative Procedure, 63
Massachusetts, 89, 114, 116, 117, 121, 122, 137, 176
Massachusetts Legislature, 117, 137, 175
McConnell, Mitch, 2, 20, 23
McCulloch v. Maryland, 160
McNamee, Ruth, 174
M'Culloh, James, 159
Meckler, Mark, x, 3, 90
median household income, 59
Medicaid, 24, 39, 3, 44, 169
Medicare, 17, 18, 24, 39, 42–45, 169–70
Michigan, 22, 88, 173–74, 194
Mississippi, 94
Missouri, 193, 194
Montana, 173, 219ch8n1
Montesquieu, Baron de, 6, 150
Montgomery Convention (the Provisional Congress of the Confederate States), 180
More Perfect Constitution, A (Sabato), 69–70, 72–73, 76
Morgan, John Pierpont, 164
Mullen, Michael, 38
Muskie, Edmund, 192

N

Napolitano, Andrew, 94
Nashville Convention, 178, 183
Natelson, Robert, 63–64, 86, 87, 94, 97, 100, 105, 113, 114, 121, 132, 133, 134, 181, 184, 206, 209, 216n5, 221n2
national authority, xv, 4, 107, 127, 128, 134
national debt, xiii, 10, 17, 30, 32, 36, 37, 38, 40, 42, 74, 80, 84, 104, 111, 140, 157, 161, 169, 174, 181, 197
current, 59
National Federation of Independent Business (NFIB), 88
National Tax Limitation Committee, 192
National Taxpayers Union, 87, 103, 173, 191

Nation of Takers: America's Entitlement Epidemic, A (Eberstadt), 44
Nebraska, 66, 183, 184
"necessary and proper" clause, 158. 160–61, 167, 168
Nevada, 22, 193
New Deal, 50, 78, 165, 167–69
New Hampshire, 88, 120, 129, 144, 193
New Jersey, 92, 119, 120, 161, 180
New York, 108, 109, 114, 115, 177, 121–22, 129, 131, 132, 144, 161, 164, 177
New York Legislature, 117, 161
New York Times, 17–18, 190
NFIB v. Sebelius, 170
Nickles, Don, 16
Nixon, Richard, 68
North American Review, 177
North Dakota, 88, 94, 191
nullification, ix, 175, 176, 177–78

O

Obama, Barack, 18–19, 22, 24, 25, 26, 33,40, 51, 53, 83, 84, 155, 170
Obamacare, 26. *See* Affordable Care Act
O'Connor, John, 67, 68
Office of the Federal Register (OFR), 68
Ogden, Aaron, 161
Ohio, 88, 167, 180
Oklahoma, ix, 4, 5, 15, 16, 21, 27, 54, 89, 91, 99, 101–2, 184, 185, 221n48
Oklahoma Legislature, x, 101
Oklahoma Legislature, x, 101
Olasky, Marvin, 46–47
O'Neill, Tip, 88
Opportunities to Reduce Potential Duplication in Government Programs, Save Tax Dollars, and Enhance Revenues, 25–26
overreach (government), xiv, xv, 7, 15, 16, 31, 33–34, 76, 77, 78, 89, 95, 98, 100, 102, 103, 104, 111, 128, 144, 150, 152, 156, 156, 158–59, 163, 170, 171, 172, 176, 177, 197, 198, 210n3

P-Q

pandering, xiv, xvi, 36, 53, 59, 78, 148

partisanship, 3, 11, 24, 30, 34, 74, 80, 152, 153

"Party of Yes," 20

Patman, Wright, 187–88

Paulsen, Luke, 144, 146, 150, 151

Paulsen, Michael S., 144, 146, 150, 151

Peace Convention of 1861, 62, 63, 179–80, 181, 183, 196

Penn, William, 123

Pennsylvania, 120, 123, 141, 184–85

Pennsylvania Legislature, 184

percent

of annual growth of individual taxpayer's share of the federal debt, 40

of annual federal spending made up of entitlement spending (1960–2010), 43

average of economic growth since 2005, 39

decline in work participation by men, 44

of federal spending for health care, 39

gross national debt-to-GDP radio, 30, 37

overall poverty rate in the United States, 44

public debt–to-GDP ratio, 211n1

of senators having currently served in the House, 75

Perkins, Frances, 166 , 170

Philadelphia Convention (*aka* Constitutional Convention; Federal Convention of 1787; Great Convention *in text*), 63, 64, 112, 113, 114, 119–22, 132, 142–44, 152, 153

the forging of Article V at the, 123–27

political correctness, 35, 53

political process, 32, 74, 77, 92, 156, 164, 184

Poulson, Barry W., 87

poverty rate, 44

Prentis, Henning, 199–200

Preston, Levi, 55, 137–38, 139, 152

Progressive Era, 186

progressivism and judicial activism, 164

Prohibition, 66

Protecting Social Security Disability Act, 27

Proxmire, William, 190

public good, 3, 10, 35, 139, 148, 150, 153, 154, 157, 159, 163, 165, 167, 169

Publius, 143. *See* Hamilton, Alexander; Jay, John; Madison, James

R

Randolph, Edmund, 123, 124, 125, 158

ratification (of a proposed amendment)

debate, Article V during the, 127–30

by legislature or state convention, 66–68

process, Congress initiates the state, 65–66

Reagan, Ronald, 15, 83, 193, 194, 195, 197

reapportionment, the Article V convention drive against, 188–91

Reid, Harry, 1–2, 21, 26, 27, 149

Reinhart, Carmen, 29–30, 38–39

republicanism, 81, 134, 147, 152

Republican Party, 5, 13, 14, 15, 27, 105

Republican Revolution, 5, 10, 15

Republicans, xiii, 5, 6, 10, 11, 13, 18, 20, 40, 74, 84, 99, 104–5, 192

Restoration (Will), 74

Revolutionary War. *See* American Revolution

Reynolds v. Sims, 188

Rhode Island, 107–11, 115–16, 144

Road to Serfdom, The (Hayek), 52

Roberts, John, 77

Rogers, Scott, 87

Rogoff, Kenneth, 29, 30, 37, 38–39

Roosevelt, Franklin, 50, 164, 165–66, 187

Rubio, Marco, 85

Rule of Nobody, The (Howard), 78

"rumble speech" (Coburn), 19, 85

"runaway" constitutional convention, 70, 88, 93, 97, 100, 105, 119, 122, 184, 186, 189, 190, 194–96

Rutledge, John, 126

S

Sabato, Larry, 69–70, 72–73, 76, 80

"Santa Fe Convention" (of 1922), 58–59, 60, 61, 63

Santelli, Rick, 83–84

Sasse, Ben, 36

Scalia, Antonin, 171

Schlafly, Andy, 100

Schlafly, Phyllis, x, 195

Schouler, James, 182

Second Continental Congress, 116

Senate Appropriations Committee, 26

Senate Judiciary Committee, 190

Senator Paul Simon Study Abroad Foundation Act, 20

separation of powers, 79, 145, 149, 150, 152, 154, 198

Sepp, Pete, 87

serfdom, America's road to, 50–54

Seventeenth Amendment, 165, 183–86, 196

Sherman, Roger, 126, 191

Simon, Paul, 194

Simpson, Alan, 23

Simpson-Bowles Commission, 23–24, 38

Sixteenth Amendment, 164, 187

slavery, 108, 126, 142, 153, 163, 177, 178–80

Smith, Adam, 153

Social Security, 14, 17, 24, 38, 39, 42, 44, 45, 167, 168, 169

Social Security Act, 166, 169

Social Security Administration, 45

Social Security Disability Insurance Program, 27

South Carolina, 89, 121, 177

South Dakota, 88

Specter, Arlen, 33

spending, xiii, 6–20, 22–27, 29–31, 33, 36–37, 39–43, 45, 46, 47, 48–49, 50, 69, 72, 73, 74, 84, 85, 89, 90, 92, 141, 153, 169, 182, 191, 194, 197

four categories of, 48–49

"spending power," 166–67

Squawk Box, 83, 84

Stamp Act Congress, 114–15, 116

Standard & Poor's, the U.S. credit downgrade from, 25

Standridge, Rob, ix–xi (foreword by), 99, 101, 102

stare decisis, 171

State Legislators Article V Caucus, 97, 98, 208

state legislatures' role in the Seventeenth Amendment, 183–87

Stein, Ben, 40

Stephanopoulos, George, 10

Stevens, Ted, 19, 20–21

stimulus, 22–23, 29, 84

Stivers, Steve, 96

Stone, Harlan, 166, 170

Supreme Court, 26, 58, 76, 77, 91, 94, 155–56, 159–60, 161, 166, 168, 170, 171, 188, 192

Synar, Mike, 5

T

Taft, William Howard, 164

Tea Party, 3, 20, 24, 84–85, 90

10 Amendments for Freedom (Fruth), 87

Tennessee, 88, 91, 178, 179

Tenth Amendment, 94, 110, 151, 158

term limits, xiii, 9, 69, 73–77, 103

on Congress, 73–75

Texas, 184

Thirteenth Amendment, 153, 180

Tobin, James, 194

Tocqueville, Alexis de, 29

Toynbee, Arnold, 199

Tragedy of American Compassion, The (Olasky), 46

Treaty of Ghent, 176

Tribe, Laurence, 192

Trump, Donald, xiii, xiv, xv, xvii, 36, 85

Turberville, George Lee, 132

Twenty-First Amendment, 66, 67, 187

Twenty-Seventh Amendment, 66, 68, 214n21, 218n10

Tydings, Joseph, 190

Tyler, John, 180

Tytler, Alexander, 199

U

Union Pacific Railroad Company, 163

United Kingdom, 50

United States government, four pillars of the superstructure of the, 145

U.S. Constitution. *See* Constitution (of the United States of America)

U.S. Department of Defense, 23

U.S. House Clerk's Memorials of Applications for an Article V Convention, 206

U.S. Marine Corps, armed federal workers outnumber members of the, 151

U.S. Term Limits v. Thornton, 94

Utah, 88–89, 185

Uygur, Cenk, 91

V

Vermont, 92, 175

victimhood, pretensions of, 35

Vietnam War, 34
Virginia, 89, 92, 99, 117, 119, 120, 129, 131, 132,
    144, 175–76, 179, 180
Virginia Legislature, 175
Virginia Plan, 123, 145
Virginia Resolution, 175, 177
virtue (as defined by the Founders), 3

W–X

Walker, Bill, 95–96
Walker, David, 37
Wall Street Journal, 40, 51, 78
War of 1812, 176
Warner, Mark, 24, 26
War on Poverty, 42, 44, 49
Warren, Earl, 188–89
"war on women," 53
Washington, George, xv, 57, 107, 119, 121, 129,
    139, 142, 143, 157, 158, 196
Washington Peace Conference (or, Convention),
    62, 63, 179–80, 181, 183, 196
Washington Post, 11
Washington (state), 185
Wasserman Schultz, Debbie, 75
waste (federal), 6, 8, 12, 14, 15, 16, 18, 19, 21–27,
    45, 47, 49, 140, 154, 165, 169
Waxman, Henry, 33
Wealth of Nations, The (Smith), 153
Webster, Daniel, 137
Welch, Robert, x
welfare programs, 43, 47, 49
West, Henry Litchfield, 185
West Virginia, 89
Wickard v. Filburn, 168
Will, George, 7, 74–75, 94
William II (prince of Orange), 113
Wilson, James, 125
Wilson, Woodrow, 164, 186
Wolf-PAC, 91–92, 204
Wood, Gordon, 145
World War I, 187
World War II, 38, 47
Wyoming, 89

Y–X

Year of the Commission, 23, 25, 30
Young Turks, The (online talk show), 91

CONVENTION *of* STATES
ACTION

If you were inspired by this book and would like
to learn more or become part of the solution,
go to COSAction.com.

Then:

1. Sign the petition. We need YOUR support.
   When you sign the COS petition it gets delivered
   automatically to your state representatives urging
   them to support the COS resolution.

2. Get our Newsletter and stay informed.

3. Volunteer to help.

Convention of States is the ONLY solution as big as the problem in Washington D.C.

You can also visit us on Facebook:
facebook.com/conventionofstates

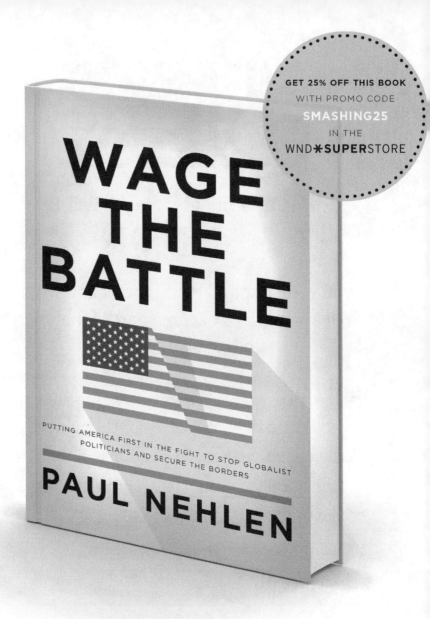

WAGE THE BATTLE is a call to action. It is the amazing story of how self-described "manufacturing guy" Paul Nehlen took on Speaker of the House Paul Ryan in one of the most closely followed congressional races in the nation. Nehlen's run presaged the international movement against globalism which reached its climax with the election of President Donald Trump. It's a firsthand look at the development of one of the original "Trump Republicans" and the populist message which is sending shockwaves through the Beltway Right.

🏴 WND Books • WASHINGTON DC • WNDBOOKS.COM

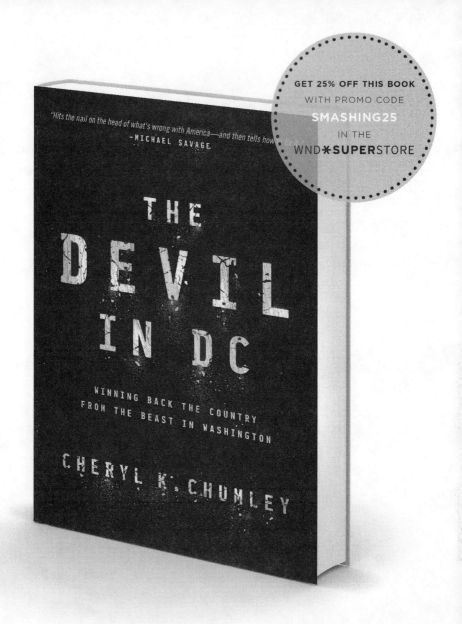

"Hits the nail on the head of what's wrong with America—and then tells how
—MICHAEL SAVAGE

THE DEVIL IN DC

WINNING BACK THE COUNTRY
FROM THE BEAST IN WASHINGTON

CHERYL K. CHUMLEY

THE DEVIL IN DC is such an important book to read," explains former governor Mike Huckabee.
[It] takes the fight of patriotic Americans to an even higher level, appealing to Christians and those
of faith to get in the ring, jump in the fight. And what I really like about this book is it then shows
them just how to do it." THE DEVIL IN DC gives more than a dozen different ideas on how to turn
back Big Government and in the spirit of what Founding Fathers envisioned reestablish that our
rights our God granted, not government given.

WND Books • WASHINGTON DC • WNDBOOKS.COM

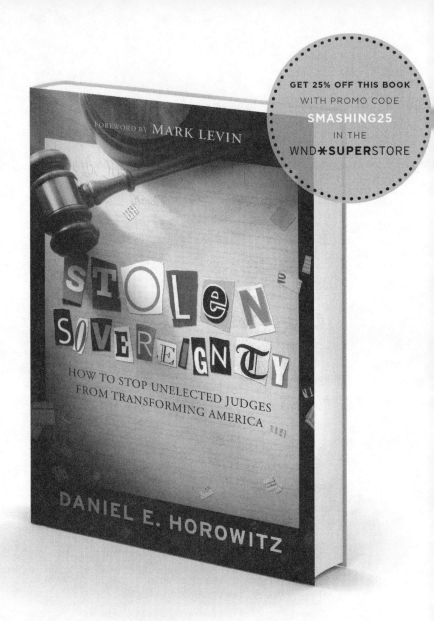

In STOLEN SOVEREIGNTY, Daniel Horowitz reveals just how disenfranchised voters have become. On issue after issue we are witnessing a transformation of our society before our very eyes, all without the ability to stop it through the political process. We are becoming a government not of the people, by the people, for the people, but of the elites by the justices and for the few. First the courts went after your income. Then they went after the right to abortion. Then the right for men to marry men and women to marry women. Next they will go after the right to our sovereign borders. Where will it end?

WND Books • WASHINGTON DC • WNDBOOKS.COM